The Duke of Alba

The Duke of Alba

Henry Kamen

Yale University Press
New Haven and London

For information about this and other Yale University Press publications, please contact:
U.S. Office: sales.press@yale.edu   yalebooks.com
Europe Office: sales@yaleup.co.uk   www.yalebooks.co.uk

Set in Adobe Garamond by Northern Phototypesetting Co. Ltd, Bolton, Lancs
Printed in the USA

Library of Congress Cataloging-in-Publication Data

Kamen, Henry Arthur Francis.
   The Duke of Alba/Henry Kamen.
      p. cm.
   Includes bibliographical references and index.
   ISBN 0–300–10283–6 (cl: alk. paper)
   1. Alba, Fernando Alvarez de Toledo, duque de, 1507–1582. 2. Spain—History—Philip
II, 1556–1598. 3. Statesmen—Spain—Biography. 4. Nobility—Spain—Biography. I.
Title.
   DP191.A6K36 2004   949.2'03'092—dc22   2004001543

A catalogue record for this book is available from the British Library

10 9 8 7 6 5 4 3 2 1

Published with assistance from the foundation established in memory of Oliver Baty
Cunningham of the Class of 1917, Yale College.

Contents

Illustrations

Preface

The third duke of Alba was the most famous Spanish soldier of Spain's great epoch of empire, but his historical reputation has been uniformly unfavourable. Almost forgotten in his own country, outside it he became notorious as the bloodthirsty 'butcher of Flanders', responsible for the massacre of thousands of innocent men, women and children, a man who considered it better (in his own words) to lay waste a country than leave it in the hands of heretics. His menacing figure, glowering out of the portraits, came to form an integral part of the widely held image of Spanish cruelty. Historians have fought shy of him and not until the twentieth century, when the Alba family began to publish the rich documentation in their archive, did it become possible to obtain a fuller image of his role. And not until 1983, with the publication of the excellent biography by Professor William Maltby, was a reliable and authoritative life of the duke written. The present short study accepts the main thrust of Maltby's book but pursues slightly different lines of enquiry in a story whose broad outlines are familiar to historians. Because my account is directed principally to the general reader, it avoids entering into scholarly detail over the many matters in which the duke was involved and the many personages who affected his life. That would have been another book; this one is quite simply an attempt to understand what the duke did and why he did it, set against the background of his life, travels and military and political career, and related where possible in the words of his own correspondence. Only the two kings he served, Charles V and Philip II, are given a generous part of the space in a study that attempts to consider motives and to explain rather than simply to condemn. The short bibliography serves as a guide to further reading.

The modern spelling of the duke's title, Alba, is the one adopted in this book, though it should be mentioned that the duke himself normally used the form Alva when signing his name.

The First Dukes of Alba

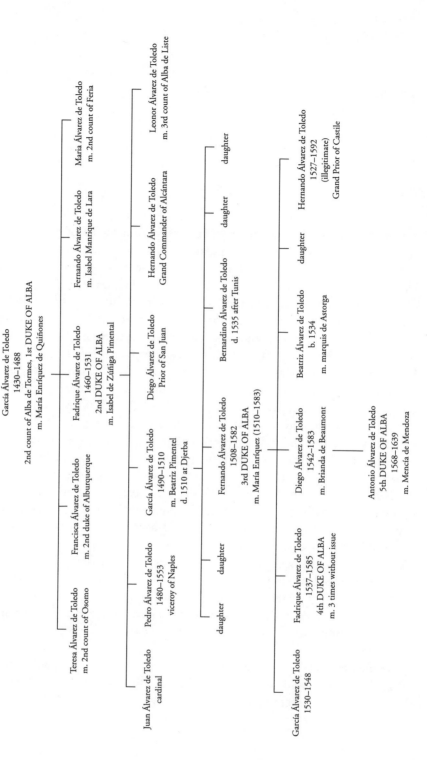

García Álvarez de Toledo
1430–1488
2nd count of Alba de Tormes, 1st DUKE OF ALBA
m. María Enríquez de Quiñones

Teresa Álvarez de Toledo
m. 2nd count of Osorno

Francisca Álvarez de Toledo
m. 2nd duke of Alburquerque

Fadrique Álvarez de Toledo
1460–1531
2nd DUKE OF ALBA
m. Isabel de Zúñiga Pimental

Fernando Álvarez de Toledo
m. Isabel Manrique de Lara

María Álvarez de Toledo
m. 2nd count of Feria

Juan Álvarez de Toledo
cardinal

Pedro Álvarez de Toledo
1480–1553
viceroy of Naples

García Álvarez de Toledo
1490–1510
m. Beatriz Pimentel
d. 1510 at Djerba

Fernando Álvarez de Toledo
1508–1582
3rd DUKE OF ALBA
m. María Enríquez (1510–1583)

Diego Álvarez de Toledo
Prior of San Juan

Hernando Álvarez de Toledo
Grand Commander of Alcántara

Leonor Álvarez de Toledo
m. 3rd count of Alba de Liste

daughter

daughter

daughter

García Álvarez de Toledo
1530–1548

Fadrique Álvarez de Toledo
1537–1585
4th DUKE OF ALBA
m. 3 times without issue

Diego Álvarez de Toledo
1542–1583
m. Brianda de Beaumont

Bernardino Álvarez de Toledo
d. 1535 after Tunis

daughter

Beatriz Álvarez de Toledo
b. 1534
m. marquis of Astorga

daughter

Hernando Álvarez de Toledo
1527–1592
(illegitimate)
Grand Prior of Castile

Antonio Álvarez de Toledo
5th DUKE OF ALBA
1568–1639
m. Mencia de Mendoza

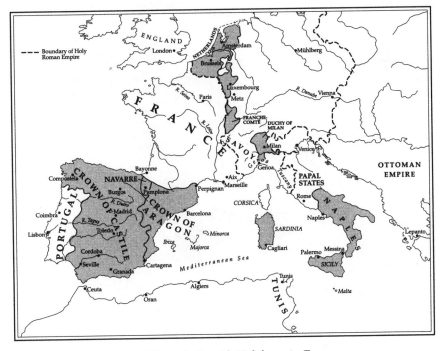

The early Spanish Habsburgs in Europe

The Netherlands in 1555 (above) *and 1609*

1   Family Beginnings, 1507–1533

... Ferdinand, aflame with ardour
to bathe his lance in Turkish blood.

Garcilaso de la Vega, 'To the Duke of Alva'

In the realms of the Iberian peninsula, the middle years of the fifteenth century would long be remembered as an epoch of never-ending troubles. A courtier who lived through those days recorded 'the times of darkness and distress that came to pass in Castile'.[1] Chroniclers could find little to praise in the kings who reigned or the nobles who profited from the prevailing anarchy. The lands of Castile, covering two-thirds of Spain, were particularly prey to conflicts over the succession to the throne. Their king, Henry IV, who reigned from 1454 to his death in 1474, was a modest and cultured man but completely unable to control the ambitions of his nobles or the plotting of his half-sister, Isabella, who eventually succeeded him as ruler. In Henry's last years, the struggle for power intensified. The crown of neighbouring Portugal sent in small armies to press its own claims, and in the principality of Catalonia there was a rebellion against the king. For many Spanish noble families the best protection was to stay armed and ally themselves opportunely with the strongest magnates. A chronicler of the time compared the troubles to a many-headed Hydra that could not be subdued: 'as soon as one problem was pacified and settled, immediately another arose and then others, in very great number'.[2]

Peace came eventually in 1476, with the general acceptance of Isabella as queen in Castile. In 1469 as a princess, she had married the young prince of Aragon, Ferdinand, at a key moment during the civil wars. In the same months peace also came to Catalonia, where Ferdinand was now ruler. The couple began to govern their realms and set their affairs in order, but they maintained the complete independence from each other of the crowns of Castile and Aragon. Some years later they received from the pope the title which they thereafter used with pride, that of 'Catholic Monarchs'. The real power in their realms was the nobility, whose support for Isabella had decided the outcome of the conflict. Shortly after Henry IV's death a greater part of the chief nobles of Castile decided that it was in their interest to support her rather than Henry's heir, his young daughter Juana. Among those who took this option was the count of Alba de Tormes.

Alba was a quiet, unprepossessing little town on the banks of the river Tormes, fifteen kilometres from the city of Salamanca. There are no reliable figures for its size around the year 1500, but two centuries later it was the third largest town in the province, with a population one-eighth that of Salamanca. In the sixteenth century the lands that formed part of the estate of Alba de Tormes consisted of around sixty small villages. From 1369 they were owned by the Álvarez de Toledo family, whose small medieval castle in Alba was, much later in the 1500s, improved and transformed into an Italian-style Renaissance palace. From 1439 the head of the family enjoyed the title of 'count'. In 1470 the second count, García, was rewarded for his services to king Henry IV with the title of 'duke' of Alba. The estates belonging to the title were at the same period formed into an 'entail', a legal arrangement that fixed the rules of succession to the property. After Henry's death García broke his ties with the group supporting the succession of Juana and instead allied himself to the cause of the princess Isabella. Apart from political motives he had a good family reason for doing so, since his wife was María Enríquez, daughter of the hereditary admiral of Castile and sister to the mother of Ferdinand of Aragon. In this way he became directly linked to the royal family that created the destinies of early modern Spain. He took part in the battles of the civil war in Castile, particularly in the decisive victory at Toro (March 1476), which was always thereafter celebrated in the Alba estates as a day of special rejoicing.

The Álvarez de Toledos of Castile had their origins in a single family name, but by the fifteenth century were already divided into a number of different lineages that acquired distinct titles – Alba, Oropesa, Villafranca – and strengthened their considerable power by intermarriage. García's son Fadrique, the second duke, who succeeded his father in 1488, also enjoyed the titles of marquis of Coria, count of Salvatierra and Piedrahita, and lord of Valdecorneja; the names were those of the principal landed possessions of the family. His faithful service to king Ferdinand the Catholic brought substantial new benefits to the Toledos. He commanded the army that fought the French on the Catalan border in 1503, and directed the forces that invaded and conquered Navarre in 1512. He was prominent as the king's 'captain general' in Andalucia, a territory in which he was granted possession of the town of

Huéscar in 1513 as a reward for his services in Navarre. By the time of Ferdinand's death he had extended the family's estates up the valley of the Tormes towards Salamanca, and owned large tracts of land in the north of Extremadura. His marriage in 1480 to Isabel de Zúñiga blessed him with five sons: García, his eldest and heir; Pedro, who later became marquis of Villafranca and viceroy of Naples in 1532; Diego, who acquired the title of prior of Castile in the order of St John; Juan, who became a cardinal in the service of the papacy; and Hernando, who became grand commander of the order of Alcántara. His daughter Leonor married the count of Alba de Liste. In every sector of noble activity, the family of Alba occupied some of the highest positions of power and influence in Castile. Like many other noble families in Europe they had a single obsession, which they pursued with passion: that of maintaining the honour of their house through service to the crown.[3]

The single-minded dedication of the Toledo family to public service paid off. Well before the end of the reign of the Catholic Monarchs, the duke of Alba enjoyed a privileged position among the advisers of the crown, as grand chamberlain of the king's household. Queen Isabella had died in 1504 and been succeeded as ruler of Castile by her (and Ferdinand's) daughter Juana. The king was subsequently obliged to assume the office of regent of Castile because of Juana's mental instability. Ferdinand hoped that the duke would succeed him as regent, but the man who in fact came to fill the post was cardinal Cisneros of Toledo, then at the height of his career. The rivalry between Cisneros and Alba did not diminish the latter's influence. When Ferdinand drew up his last testament in Aranda de Duero in 1515, the duke was among the seven nobles chosen to witness it. Alba was also at the bedside of the dying king in the village of Madrigalejo in 1516.

The Alba family's power was not limited to Castile. As a result of their service to their king and queen, they also became well ensconced in the Mediterranean lands of the crown. The influence of the Toledos in Italy, for example, derived entirely from their support of the king of Aragon's highly successful efforts to establish his power firmly in that peninsula. Ferdinand's family, the Trastámaras, had once ruled over the kingdom of Naples, and Ferdinand still retained the title and possession of the kingdom of Sicily. In the wars that his military commander the great captain, Gonzalo Fernández de Córdoba, waged on his behalf in Naples, Ferdinand succeeded in obtaining control over the whole of that kingdom. The wily monarch was determined to build a strong chain of alliances, and in the process allied himself with the greatest families of central and southern Italy, creating 'a dense network of political interests, feudal rights and possibilities for extending family influence'.[4]

Ferdinand of Aragon's heir was his grandson, the young duke of Burgundy, Charles of Habsburg, who succeeded simultaneously to the throne of Castile (where his mother Queen Juana 'the Mad' continued to be recognised as co-ruler until her death). When Charles travelled to Spain in 1516 to take over his dominions, the duke of Alba was among those waiting to receive him in Valladolid. The latter rapidly rose in the king's employ to become as trusted an adviser as he had been to the previous king. Charles held the first peninsular chapter of the Burgundian order of the knights of the Golden Fleece in Barcelona in March 1519, and Fadrique was among the few Castilian nobles honoured with investiture. The Alba family was now committed to participating in a destiny that was not simply Mediterranean in scope but embraced all Europe, for the new king was elected Holy Roman Emperor in 1520 and had to go to Germany to claim his crown.

It is one of Fadrique's grandsons, the eldest, Ferdinand, who is the subject of our story. Fadrique's son García rose to become commander of the king's Mediterranean fleet, which was normally based in Sicily and Naples. He married Beatriz de Pimentel, daughter of the count of Benavente, and had four children by her: Catalina, María, Ferdinand and Bernardino. Ferdinand was born on 29 October 1507 in the convent of the family village of Piedrahita. As the eldest son, he was heir to his father in the dukedom. García never lived to take up the title. He died inopportunely during a military campaign in 1510. In an attempt by the Spaniards to strengthen their hold on the North African coast, forces of up to 15,000 men under the command of Pedro Navarro, count of Oliveto, and García de Toledo, sailed in August that year from their rendezvous in Tripoli. The objective, apparently a simple one, was the island of Djerba, which had only one inhabited town. It was the month of August, and the army made the mistake of carrying too little water. The inhabitants of the island killed those who did not perish of thirst in the African sun. Over three thousand men died, including Don García, and five hundred were captured. A thousand more men died when some of the escaping galleys capsized.[5]

García's eldest son was wholly deprived of any memory of a father. In a society subject to persistent violence and epidemics, with low life expectancy, the loss of a father was a frequent enough occurrence. But in the case of Ferdinand it came to play a fundamental role in the formation of his character. He clung closely to what remained of his family – his mother and his brother – but also learned to make his own decisions, guided by his own judgment. He grew up (we may conclude from the way he developed later) as an introspective young man with a fierce loyalty to his own kin but also with an absolute confidence in the correctness of his own resolutions. There are, unfortunately, no documents to guide us about his early years,[6] and he comes to our attention only through incidents that his biographers chose to highlight.

Duke Fadrique stepped in to preside over the education of his fatherless grandson. Ferdinand went everywhere with the duke. He was aged only six when he accompanied his grandfather in the army that accomplished the conquest of Navarre. From his infancy, war and the clash of arms was the environment marked out for him. Though brought up as a soldier, he was not, however, deprived of other elements of life. His early years were spent mostly with his family in the three residences they possessed in Alba, Piedrahita and Coria. When Charles V left Spain in 1520 to go to northern Europe for his coronation as emperor, the duke, his sons and grandsons (in reality, a whole household group, for a chronicler refers to the duke's 'sons and grandsons and relatives and servants'⁷) accompanied him in the flotilla of ships that sailed out from La Coruña two hours before dawn on 20 May. There is no direct account of the family's part in the emperor's activity, but we know that they went with him everywhere as part of his retinue. Ferdinand was old enough to appreciate the wonders of a continent he had never seen and in which he would spend the greater part of his long career.

His first contact with northern Europe turned out to be England. The emperor-elect's ships went into harbour at Dover in the afternoon of 25 May, to wait for the rest of the flotilla to catch up with them.⁸ When the English learnt of Charles' arrival they hastened to greet him and persuaded him to go ashore. He rode with the English nobles to Canterbury, where for two days he was the guest of King Henry VIII, husband of his aunt Catherine of Aragon.⁹ Henry then escorted Charles and his group back to Dover, where they resumed the voyage to the Netherlands. (Henry himself crossed the Channel immediately afterwards and headed for France, where he held his famous rendezvous with King Francis I at the Field of the Cloth of Gold.)

The young heir to the dukedom of Alba found himself in the centre of a flurry of royal diplomacy and entertainment. No sooner had the two kings terminated their respective affairs in the Netherlands and in France, than they met again in July at the frontier of the Netherlands. 'The emperor took the king by his right hand and both princes went off jointly to Gravelines, where His Majesty treated the king of England to an elaborate supper which together with the music that was played went on until the break of day.'¹⁰ Another big supper was held a couple of days later, with Henry as host, at the English port of Calais. A few days afterwards Charles was back in Bruges, and in the autumn the entire Imperial party headed south to Aachen, where at the end of October the emperor in a magnificent ceremony (which for the young Ferdinand would have been unforgettable) was crowned Holy Roman emperor. It was a lengthy stay in Germany, almost certainly the period when Ferdinand began to pick up enough German to converse in it. He was in Worms when the Imperial Diet (the parliament of German princes and cities) began its meetings in January 1522, but there is no evidence that he was present in the famous session when a confrontation took place between the emperor and the defiant friar Martin Luther, instigator of the protest movement that became known as the Reformation.

The Toledo family were with the emperor when the decision was made to go back to Spain by the same route that they had come, through England. In the third week of May 1522 the whole Imperial company took ship from Calais and landed in Dover, where they were met and entertained by the English king. In London a week later they were entertained to dinners and medieval tournaments, and spent the feast of Corpus Christi at Windsor, where the two monarchs issued a joint declaration of war against Francis I of France. The Spaniards also went farther afield, visiting Winchester in order to get a glimpse of the Round Table said to have been used by the knights of king Arthur. When Charles eventually sailed from the port of Southampton on 6 July, it was in a large fleet of 'eighty sail, and in the ships went six thousand Germans and many Spaniards and Italians'.[11] They reached the port of Santander ten days later.

Much had changed in the country since their departure. Throughout his absence the emperor had been in touch with events in Castile, where even before he left in 1520 the revolt of the Comuneros had broken out. It was an uprising of the major cities of northern Castile that left its mark on the country for decades, but neither the duke of Alba nor his grandson experienced the stirring events of those years at first hand. By 1522 the upheavals had been suppressed, and Charles began to put his government in order. In 1526 Fadrique was made a member of the Council of State, and the next year assisted at the baptism of the emeror's son, Prince Philip. From this time onwards the duke's life was irreparably dominated by his illness, and he remained secluded almost continuously at Alba de Tormes until his death in 1531. He had the satisfaction of knowing that he had contributed decisively to the influence and wealth of his family, which a contemporary estimated to be among the six richest in the kingdom of Castile.

During these years Fadrique took great care with the education of his heir. Italy and the Netherlands were seen at the time as the source of all knowledge. During his trip abroad with the emperor, Fadrique took the opportunity to look for a tutor for Ferdinand. While he was in Bruges he came into contact with the Valencian humanist Juan Luis Vives, who had been resident in northern Europe for over a decade, and seized on the idea of inviting him to Alba de Tormes to instruct his family. Vives wrote to his friend, the famous humanist Erasmus, that 'the duke of Alba made me an offer that I could not have refused had I known about it in time. He was very eager that I should take charge of the education of his grandchildren in Spain.' Fadrique had just left the Netherlands but set down his offer in a letter which he entrusted to an Italian Dominican friar, Severo Marini, to carry to Vives. At the same time he explained the details to a friend who was going to the Netherlands. What transpired next can best be described in Vives' own words. Severo arrived in Louvain, where Vives then was. 'He had more than ten meetings with me,' Vives explained to Erasmus, 'but never spoke a word about the duke nor handed me the letter. When the duke saw that I had not accepted, he entrusted the education of his grandchildren to Severo.' Vives eventually learned of the offer when Alba's noble friend arrived in the country, spoke to him and expressed surprise that he had not accepted. Severo's despicable conduct was probably never brought to the attention of the duke, but Vives was bitterly disappointed by the whole affair. He had been seeking an opportunity to return to his homeland. 'How could I have disdained what the duke was offering me, when I was so anxious to find a way to demonstrate to him the very great willingness I had to serve him?'[12]

As tutor in letters the duke chose the Catalan poet Joan Boscà, who was contracted and in residence shortly before 1520. It was the beginning of a good relationship between Ferdinand and Boscà; they maintained a friendship that lasted for over twenty years, until the death of the latter on the Catalan frontier in 1542. Ferdinand informed Charles V at the time – it was mid-September – that 'Boscà came with me to Perpignan and on the way back he fell ill and died three days ago'. It has been the custom among some scholars to exaggerate the spread of the new Italianate culture (the 'Renaissance') among the nobility of Castile. Ferdinand was among the few who absorbed some of it. He was fairly exceptional in his command of the Latin language, and though his life was devoted to arms he was always actively interested in learning. His subsequent travels enabled him to pick up a good command of French and Italian, and he had some knowledge of German. With the years his dedication to the arts increased, as he came into touch with European culture and purchased works of art abroad.

The court of the Toledos at Alba was similar to other noble courts of the late Renaissance in its active dedication to culture.[13] With the wealth available to them and the contacts they enjoyed through their political influence, the dukes were able to recruit artists, scholars and musicians to provide some brilliance to what would otherwise have been a mediocre provincial society. The first duke employed a Flemish composer to set to music the songs he himself had written, and for a while enjoyed the services of the chronicler Alonso de Palencia. He was instrumental in inviting to Castile the Sicilian scholar Peter Martyr d'Anghiera, who accepted among his pupils Fadrique's son García.

Fadrique in turn patronised the work of the Castilian poet Juan del Encina. He had an active interest in medicine, employing Jewish doctors and pharmacists in the two decades before the 1492 decree which expelled Jews from the Spanish mainland. He acquired the medical services of the most famous doctor of the time, the *converso* (that is, of Jewish origin) Francisco López de Villalobos, physician to both Ferdinand the Catholic and Charles V.

In the multi-cultural society of that time, the dukes could not fail to participate in the civilisation of both Jews and Muslims. At Huéscar they were lords over an overwhelmingly Muslim population (the Muslims throughout Castile were after about 1500 obliged to convert to Christianity and became known as 'Moriscos') which resented the Toledos and sometimes revolted against them. It was certainly an active interest in Islam that persuaded Fadrique in 1496 to borrow a copy of the Koran from the nearby University of Salamanca to investigate its contents. Latin literature was represented in the 150 books that made up the duke's library. Preference for Flemish art was patent in the inventory drawn up at his death, showing that he possessed some thirty works of religious art, mostly from Flanders, as well as a number of Flemish tapestries. Above all, the family was noted for its part in the fiestas, bullfights, jousts and other noble entertainments that complemented the popular celebrations of the region. It was an age of chivalry, and the Toledos had every reason to be proud of their part in the military triumph of Toro. As good Catholics, they patronised and embellished local churches, and were firm in the support they extended to the local nun María de Santo Domingo, known as the 'Beata [Holy Woman] of Piedrahita', who became famous for her alleged visions and, despite criticisms from many people, was (thanks to the help of the Albas and of Cardinal Cisneros) given a clean bill of health by the Inquisition in 1510.

War remained the primary concern of the Toledos and therefore of Ferdinand. It was typical of the young Ferdinand's impetuosity that he chose to go on his first military campaign, in 1524, without asking permission of anyone. The frontier fortress of Fuenterrabía was in the hands of the French and of Navarrese rebels. The sixteen year old went off to join the siege being conducted by Spanish forces under the command of the constable of Castile, Iñigo de Velasco. After the fortress was recovered late in February 1524, Ferdinand returned home briefly but was sternly reprimanded by duke Fadrique for his initiative. All the same the incident served to enhance the young soldier's reputation. A chronicler reports that 'the Constable ordered Don Ferdinand of Toledo, grandson of the duke of Alba, to take charge of the town and its fortress, and though he was still young he began to do so with every evidence of being a worthy and brave soldier'.[14] The post of governor of Fuenterrabía was the first official appointment of his career. He may well have received the personal congratulations of the emperor, for Charles passed through Alba de Tormes in November that year during one of his periodic journeys through his kingdoms.

In the Fuenterrabía campaign Ferdinand also struck up a friendship with the soldier-poet Garcilaso de la Vega which became firm and close, lasting until the latter's death in 1536. Ferdinand had few literary aspirations, but it may have been as a result of his friendship with the poet that he penned his only known verse, a six-line piece on a theme about dancing.[15] Garcilaso, for his part, offers us in his *Eclogues* fascinating information about aspects of Ferdinand's early career. He pays tribute in particular to the contribution made to Ferdinand's cultural formation by Boscà, who had given the young nobleman

> good bearing, breeding and manners,
> maturity and fitting simplicity,
> noble and detached virtue.

It is a memorable judgment, light years away from the image that Ferdinand was to project forty years later when political and military events imparted a quite different aspect to his character.

The only evidence of Ferdinand's sexual adventures dates from 1527, when a brief liaison with a miller's daughter on his lands in Piedrahita bore fruit with the birth of a son, Hernando, whom he readily accepted as part of his family. The boy was brought up with the other children and enjoyed all the privileges of being a Toledo. The most important step forward in the life of any great noble was marriage, a ritual that established links of power with other families and produced heirs to the estate. Ferdinand's wedding, celebrated at Alba on 27 April 1529, was part of an agreement between the Albas and the neighbouring family of Alba de Liste. His bride was his first cousin María Enríquez, daughter of Diego Enríquez de Guzmán, third count of Alba de Liste, and his first wife, duke Fadrique's daughter Leonor. The marriage was clearly within the forbidden degrees of consanguinity laid down by canon law, but rules on the matter were at that time frequently disregarded. The Toledo family continued to create such links because they reaffirmed existing alliances of blood and property. María's brother was Antonio de Toledo, grand prior of the military order of St John in the kingdom of León, who was destined to play an important role in Castilian politics. There were eventually four children from the union between Ferdinand and María: García, who died in 1548 aged only eighteen; Beatriz, born in 1534; Fadrique, born in 1537; and Diego, born in 1542. María fulfilled to perfection the role of a traditional wife: she ran the family household in all the years that she could not accompany her husband when he was away on business; she kept alive the political links that her husband could not maintain because of his absences;

she served roles at court when required; and at home she looked after the religious interests of the Toledos. Her whole life was spent in patient service to her husband, and she died one year after him, in 1583.

With his return in 1522 the emperor initiated the longest and most fruitful of all his sojourns in the peninsula, seven years during which he devoted his attention assiduously to Spanish affairs. It was a period of important developments, not only in Spain but also in the New World, where Hernan Cortés had just overthrown the empire of the Aztecs, and in Europe itself, where the conflict between France and the Habsburgs seemed to have no end. In October 1524 the king of France, Francis I, personally led his forces across the Alps and into the duchy of Milan. Charles' commanders, at the head of an international force of Italians, Spaniards and Germans, prepared to defend the city of Pavia.[16] An attack on the French positions began in the evening of 23 February 1525, and by dawn next day the Imperial victory was assured. On the field of battle a group of Castilian soldiers from the regiment ('tercio') of Naples captured the king.[17]

The battle of Pavia was won for the absent Charles on his twenty-fifth birthday, 24 February, and had profound consequences for Spain's emerging role in European politics. The public in Spain seems at first to have had little interest in the campaign, for the only Spaniards participating were those serving with the 'tercios' in Italy. It was not every day, however, that the most powerful king in Europe was taken prisoner in battle. Francis I was brought to Madrid, where he arrived in August 1525 and was treated with full honours but kept under guard. He was not released until January 1526, when he immediately engineered an alliance with the pope to 'put an end to the wars devastating Christendom', in other words, to curtail Charles' successes in Italy. The new coalition failed to achieve anything in the shape of military action, and early in 1527 the Imperial detachments joined forces at Piacenza and began to move south towards France's ally Rome.

Meanwhile in 1526 the emperor had chosen the end of the war against Francis I to make arrangements for his marriage to the beautiful princess of Portugal, Isabella. The wedding was celebrated in Seville in April, then from May until the late autumn Charles spent his honeymoon in Granada, amid the delights of the Alhambra. The whole court, including Duke Fadrique and young Ferdinand, accompanied him. In January 1527 the court moved back to Valladolid, where in May Isabella gave birth to the future Philip II. The happy events in Castile, however, were interrupted by sombre news from Italy. In May 1527 the Imperial army burst into Rome, looting, killing and burning.[18] Spaniards took part equally with Germans and Italians in the destruction. When Charles received the news he was horrified, but the rest of Christian Europe laid the blame squarely on him. His adherents, and in particular the Spaniards, were quick to blame the French and German generals who had led the Imperial troops. In private there was considerable satisfaction in many quarters at the outrage perpetrated on the papacy. Political opponents felt that the pope deserved to reap the fruits of his policies, while religious reformers and humanists felt that corruption in the Church was at last being punished. Duke Fadrique was among those who could not accept what had happened. He protested strongly to the emperor over the outrage to the papacy.

Events in Italy soon reached a satisfactory conclusion, however, thanks in part to the defection of the great Genoese admiral Andrea Doria to Charles V, whose warships were the key to naval power in the Mediterranean. The Peace of Cambrai in 1529 confirmed the emperor's supremacy in Italy. That summer an immense gathering of the Imperial court, notable for the very many members of the Castilian aristocracy present, filled the city of Barcelona where Charles V was preparing to leave for Italy. Fadrique was already ill and unable to accompany the emperor whose steps he had followed faithfully for thirteen years. He went to Barcelona to take his leave of Charles, then withdrew to his estates, where he had the company of his recently married grandson Ferdinand. Ferdinand's uncle Pedro de Toledo the marquis of Villafranca was the only leading member of the Toledos to join the Imperial party. It was a historic journey to Italy, for during it the emperor achieved his wish to be crowned personally by the pope, an event that took place with unprecedented ceremony in the cathedral at Bologna in 1530.

In October 1531 the second duke of Alba, Fadrique, died of his illness in Alba de Tormes. He was succeeded in the title by his grandson Ferdinand, now twenty-four years old, who was serving at the time in the governorship of Fuenterrabía and who hurried home when informed of the duke's condition but arrived too late to be present at his last moments. From this period the new head of the house of Alba signed himself 'the duke marquis', the marquisate being that of Coria. These were decisive months in the history of the family, not only because of the succession to the dukedom but also because of the decision of the emperor, one year later, to appoint Ferdinand's uncle Pedro de Toledo as his viceroy in Naples. It was an appointment that dictated a good part of the new duke's future career.

The third duke of Alba very quickly became immersed in the duties that went with his title. As one of the great nobles of Castile, he was obliged to respond to an appeal from the emperor, who in the spring of 1530 had gone from Italy to Germany, for help against the Turks. It was the high tide of the Ottoman Empire, which under Suleiman the Magnificent had advanced

Turkish power through the Balkans up to the limits of the Holy Roman Empire, and through the Mediterranean up to the shores of Italy and Spain. In north Africa, Suleiman's agent Khayr al-Din, known to the Christians as Barbarossa, had established a base for attacks against the Christian powers of the West. In 1529 the Turkish forces assembled a great army that threatened to overwhelm the Imperial capital of Vienna and continued in the region for the next three years. Charles V's appeal for help echoed throughout Europe, and from all parts of Christendom hundreds of knights and nobles rallied to the cause. Castilians had already given their full backing to Charles in his Italian enterprise, and were committed by their own traditions to warfare against the Muslims of the Mediterranean. They now took on the wholly new challenge of a conflict against Muslims in central Europe.

Ferdinand left Piedrahita for Vienna at the end of January 1532, accompanied by his friend Garcilaso. They crossed the Pyrenees through snow and ice, and Garcilaso noted down their wonderment at the majesty of winter in the mountains:

> In midwinter he crossed over
> the Pyrenees that gave the appearance
> from below of their peaks touching the sky
> and from above of their foothills in a bottomless pit.
> The snow whitened all, and the streams
> ran soundlessly under bridges of glass
> and through frozen channels underground . . .
> Through this landscape the daring duke made his way . . .[19]

The pair travelled north overland through Toulouse towards Flanders with the intention of joining Charles V and his nobles in Brussels. Alba was unfortunately taken ill in Paris and had to delay his journey. When he finally arrived in Brussels the emperor and his group had already left. Ferdinand and Garcilaso followed them, travelled across to Cologne, sailed up the Rhine and then cut across towards the Imperial city of Regensburg, where they arrived in March 1532. Hundreds of noble adventurers from all over the continent also made their way to Vienna that spring to serve against the Turks. Among them were a good number of Castilian grandees who wished to demonstrate their loyalty to the emperor. Alba was anxious to come to grips at last with the Muslim enemy. The duke of Béjar, the marquises of Villafranca and Cogolludo, the counts of Monterrey and Fuentes, and scions of the great noble families – the houses of Medina-Sidonia, Nájera, Alburquerque, Mondéjar – were among the many who came north from Spain and Italy. Their appearance was in the event largely symbolic, for on seeing the immense army that the emperor had managed to assemble for the defence of

Vienna – some 150,000 men and 60,000 cavalry, described admiringly by the Franche-Comtois Féry de Guyon as 'the biggest and most beautiful army that anyone had seen in half a century' – the Turks decided to strike camp. Some Spanish tercios arrived later in the year, but the Turkish withdrawal had already begun and consequently they never saw any fighting.

The Imperial court returned from Vienna to Italy with Alba and other nobles in tow. It was the young duke's first experience of the wonders of the Renaissance civilisation of northern Italy, with festivities in Mantua, Bologna and the other cities through which they passed. Charles arrived in Barcelona late in April 1533 and was met by the empress Isabella. From Catalonia, Alba and Garcilaso together made the journey back to Toledo and then home to the banks of the Tormes. The emperor had to attend to business in the Cortes of the Crown of Aragon held at Monzón in mid-June. No sooner had he reached Monzón, however, than he received news that Isabella was ill. He virtually flew back, in what has been reckoned the fastest journey he ever made, covering nearly 150 miles in twenty-four hours, and returned to Monzón only in early July when Isabella had recovered.

Alba was also anxious to see his wife. Garcilaso recorded how the young duke put behind him the ardour for war and dashed across the peninsula to greet the lady he had not seen for sixteen months.

> Burning with the fire of love
> the duke flew and did not stop,
> he passed Catalonia, he left it behind him,
> he has already passed Aragon, and in Castile
> he arrives without once leaving the saddle.
> His heart yearns for the happiness
> awaiting him, tranquillises
> his countenance and drives far from his vision
> death, wounds, ire, blood and war;
> love alone is now his aspiration,
> affection and burning passion
> are plain and present in his eyes.

The poet was also present to see the tears of happiness in María's face.

> And the beloved wife in haste
> doubting the happiness even though she sees it
> locks his neck in the tight embrace
> of her delicate arms;
> tears filled their eyes which shone
> brighter than the sunlight.
> With her dear and beloved lord Ferdinand at her side

the countryside, the fields, the river, the hills, the plain
all in unison were happiness.[20]

Alba's lengthy absence had not produced any military action or glory, but proved to be of crucial importance in his career. Unlike some of the Castilian grandees, Alba willingly embraced the challenges posed by Spain's commitment to the cause of Charles V. During his visit to Vienna he met and talked with the emperor's senior advisers, notably Charles's chancellor the Franche-Comtois Nicolas Perrenot. The task of promoting himself was notably helped by the presence at court of his uncle the marquis of Villafranca. Ferdinand's natural virtues must also have helped considerably. Courteous, firm and well-spoken, he combined the qualities of seriousness and authority. This encouraged others to trust both what he did and what he said. From this period he became a regular member of the Imperial entourage. Through his friendship with Perrenot, he entered into a network of influential contacts in the Empire, an entity that was not limited only to the Germanic lands but also included the Netherlands. His travels through the whole of western Europe, from the Thames to the Danube, from the Rhine and Seine to the Po, gave him a maturity and experience that confirmed his position at the right hand of the emperor.

2   The Emperor's General, 1534–1556

We have a right to defend ourselves. The purpose of war is quite simply self-defence.[1]

August 1556, Naples

During the few months of his stay at Alba de Tormes the duke was accorded an exceptional honour by the emperor. Charles spent the first half of the year 1534 in Castile, and in the course of one of his journeys came to reside at the ducal palace for a weekend, from Saturday 13 June until the following Monday. During the visit they must have devoted time to talking about the enterprise that was now uppermost in the emperor's mind: a campaign to crush the naval threat from the North African port of Tunis. At that time, Khayr al-Din Barbarossa, who commanded the Turkish fleet based at Tunis, was causing considerable damage to shipping throughout the western Mediterranean, raiding the coasts and enslaving Christian villagers. It was time for action.

The famous expedition to Tunis assembled at its rendezvous in the port of Cagliari, Sardinia, in the early days of June 1535. It was, as all operations in the western Mediterranean came to be, an international undertaking but with a predominantly Italian complexion, since the defence of the coast of Italy was principally in question. Genoa, the papacy, Naples, Sicily and the Knights of Malta sent vessels. Charles was in Barcelona, where he presided over a magnificent display of Christian power. The enormous expenditure, elaborate display of chivalry and participation of great princes, gave it less the appearance of a military operation than that of a gigantic entertainment put on for the benefit of the western European aristocracy. Virtually all the higher nobility of Castile were present (among them the Toledos), dressed in cloth of gold and silver, with all their soldiers, and with them the cream of the nobility of Italy and the Netherlands as well as prelates and ministers.[2] The emperor sailed to the rendezvous from the port of Barcelona with fifteen Spanish galleys, and vessels came from Portugal under the command of the empress Isabella's brother. Ten thousand new recruits from Spain were ferried in transport ships supplied by the authorities in Vizcaya and Málaga.

The force that assembled in Cagliari was an imposing sight, totalling over 400 vessels.[3] Of the 82 galleys equipped for war, 18 per cent were from Spain, 40 per cent from Genoa (mainly the vessels of Andrea Doria), and the remaining 42 per cent from the other Italian states (including the galleys of Naples under García de Toledo). There were over 30,000 soldiers in the fleet; they included the Spanish recruits, together with 4,000 veterans from the tercios of Italy, 7,000 Germans and 8,000 Italians, as well as several thousand European adventurers who came along at their own expense.[4] The operation was put under the direction of two Italian generals, Andrea Doria for the navy and the marquis di Vasto for the troops. The costs of the exercise were met in great measure, if involuntarily, by the Inca emperor Atahualpa, part of whose ransom, demanded by Francisco Pizarro, had now reached the peninsula.[5] It was perhaps the first significant European enterprise paid for by American money, and the Genoese bankers who advanced credit were also repaid in American gold. The Tunis expedition was the most imposing ever mounted by Christian powers in the long history of the western Mediterranean.

The military action began on 20 June 1535 with a siege of the fortress of La Goletta, at the entrance to the bay of Tunis and defended by a strong Turkish garrison. It lasted for three and a half weeks, during which a number of reinforcements from friendly local Muslim leaders arrived. The fort eventually fell on 14 July, a day of intense heat that afflicted victors and vanquished alike. Muslim losses at the fort were estimated at some two thousand men. 'We won the victory despite the terrible heat,' Féry de Guyon recalled in his memoirs, 'that day there was no water to be had in wells or rivers, and the battle began after four in the afternoon; the soldiers were so worn out that immediately after winning the battle they just sat or lay down on the ground.'[6] Charles decided to press on to the city of Tunis, which was captured on 21 July and sacked by the triumphant soldiery. Thousands of Christians were released from slavery, but at the same time thousands of defenceless Tunisians were murdered in their homes and an estimated ten thousand sold as slaves. The great moment of the campaign for the duke of Alba came when the emperor presented him with his father's suit of armour, which had been captured at Djerba and was now discovered in the armoury in Tunis.

Barbarossa escaped, and was replaced as ruler of Tunis by Muley Hassan, who swore allegiance to the emperor, while La Goletta was left with a Spanish garrison and some galleys. Charles had every reason to be content with a campaign that brought rejoicing and comfort to the Christian Mediterranean: the massive encounter had cost no more than the lives of one hundred of his soldiers. The enormous navy then made its way home to its various destinations. Off the coast of Italy one of the galleys, loaded with German soldiers, capsized and all on board – some 1,500 men – perished.[7] Ten times more soldiers died in the accident than during the entire military action at Tunis. The brief comments that Garcilaso made on the campaign were perhaps little more than a literary conceit on the evanescence of glory, but they serve also as a perspective on the whole affair:

> What was gained from all this? A bit of glory?
> A few accolades or cheers?
> Whoever reads this may perhaps know.
> As the smoke disappears into the wind
> so too our labours will come to nothing.

The emperor and his entourage made their way to the kingdom of Naples. The territory had been under Spanish rule[8] since it was formally acquired by Ferdinand the Catholic, but little had been done to extend the power of the crown. With the arrival in 1532 of the new viceroy, Alba's uncle Pedro Álvarez de Toledo, second marquis of Villafranca,[9] important changes began to take place. The Imperial party under Charles headed first for Sicily, arriving at Trapani on 22 August. Alba was accompanied by his infant son and heir, five-year-old García, and by his brother Bernardino. No sooner had they arrived than Bernardino fell seriously ill and, on 26 August, died. The cause, apparently, was a venereal infection. Ferdinand had been deeply devoted to his brother, and the loss was profound. Garcilaso penned an elegy:

> . . . you seek your beloved brother, who was
> half your soul and when he died
> it remained without a great part of itself.[10]

The Imperial party was feasted in Naples as victors, and the viceroy took care to give prominence to the role of his nephew. There were, however, a few business matters to be settled by Pedro and Ferdinand, arising out of the title recently inherited by the latter. The 'entail' on the family estates limited enjoyment of the assets of the duchy of Alba only to the heir, and left other relatives to fend for themselves. It was an issue that the uncle and nephew tried to sort out between themselves.[11]

Charles prepared to spend the winter of 1535–6 in the salubrious environment of the southern Mediterranean. He used the four months of his stay to consolidate his authority in the kingdom. During Pedro de Toledo's period as viceroy, steps were made to turn the territory into the basis of Spanish military and naval power in the Mediterranean.[12] At the same time, the young Alba came to have direct contact with a crucial aspect of his family's power: its influence in Italy and the complex network of the Alba connexion there.

Intermarriage between Italian and Spanish nobles laid the basis for cooperation between the two nations for nearly two centuries, and created in Italy a
recognisable governing elite of soldiers and administrators. In the 1530s the
daughter of viceroy Pedro de Toledo, Leonor, married the Medici duke of
Florence, Cosimo I, who later adopted the title of Grand Duke of Tuscany;
Toledo's son married the daughter of the marquis di Vasto; di Vasto's brother-
in-law Vespasiano Colonna married the sister of Ferrante Gonzaga; and
Gonzaga's son married the daughter of Doria. In these years Toledo held the
post of viceroy of Naples, di Vasto that of viceroy of Milan, and Gonzaga that
of viceroy of Sicily before he succeeded di Vasto in Milan. The closely linked
network of blood and influence served to identify the interests of the elite
with those of the ruling dynasty. In the affairs of the papacy the Toledos also
had a direct voice through Ferdinand's uncle, cardinal Juan de Toledo, who
until his death in 1557 played a vital role in papal and Spanish Church politics. With a cardinal in Rome, a viceroy in Naples and a general at court, the
Toledos were well placed to play a considerable role in Charles V's empire,
and particularly through their links with the Medici of Tuscany they extended
their influence across Italy.

The Imperial party left Naples in March 1536, heading northwards. On
5 April it entered Rome, where Charles was accorded a triumphal entry in
celebration of Tunis. The pope came out in person to meet him, and the
emperor rode into the city flanked by his chief commanders, among them
Alba. The occasion, however, was soured by international politics. Two days
earlier, French troops had crossed the frontier into Italy, and there was now
war between France and the emperor. Charles had been marshalling his land
and naval forces at Genoa, to which he proceeded as soon as he had
completed his business in Rome. With Alba and the other commanders, the
emperor spent the months of May to July at Asti, on the borders of the duchy
of Milan, where he prepared plans to invade the south of France in the hope
that this would achieve peace.

Alba, along with other young court nobles from Spain, participated fully in
the subsequent invasion of Provence. There were 2,000 Spaniards and 15,000
Landsknechte (German mercenary troops) in the army that invaded from
Milan under the command of Antonio de Leyva and the emperor in May
1536. It was at first intended to attack Turin, but Charles favoured an invasion of Provence. Some units entered the plain of Provence by land, but the
greater part were ferried along the coast by Doria and set ashore at Antibes.
Eventually all sections of the army joined together at Fréjus. The marquis di
Vasto commented that 'the emperor had never had such a large and well-
equipped army in camp for war against another Christian power'.[13] The Imperialist troops set up camp at Aix-en-Provence, which was deliberately left

undefended by the French, who knew it could not support the number of men required to garrison it. It was at this stage that the emperor and his men began to comprehend the strategy adopted by the constable of France, Anne de Montmorency. The constable fortified only cities that could be reasonably held, such as Marseille and Arles, kept his forces in camp at Avignon, and concentrated on closing down all sources of food in the region, such as the mills for grinding grain. He resolutely refused to engage in battle with the invaders. The Imperialists, deprived of the chance to use their superior power, were reduced to raiding the countryside for provisions in order to survive. Inadequate food in the army contributed to an outbreak of dysentery that quickly turned into a mortal epidemic. It was an experience that the young Alba would never forget, and certainly influenced his ideas on military strategy. Avoiding engagement, he realised, could be more fruitful than resorting to battle.

The Spanish troops were commanded by the marquis di Vasto, while Charles and Alba led the German units. After three months in Provence, they had made no headway. On the last day of August Alba's men were caught in an ambush near Marseille. 'Late that day the duke of Alba arrived with his men and camped down among the vines. Here they spent the night and the next day they began to move out,' but walked straight into a surprise attack. 'In this skirmish they had the good fortune to lose few dead and wounded.' Alba ordered a hasty retreat. 'They marched in order through a level and dangerous valley with many olive trees and various other orchards full of delicious fruits and vines, until they came to an opening which led to Marseille. The sea entered in here between the mountains, and on the beach Prince Doria was waiting with fifty galleys.'[14] Other detachments of the army had similar experiences among the hills and vineyards of southern Provence. The invasion collapsed because there was nobody to fight, and no supplies were found to support it. Leyva fell ill and died at Aix. Among the thousands of casualties who died was the poet Garcilaso, Alba's friend and companion. The emperor withdrew his forces at the end of September, 'with dishonour and loss' as the French soldier Blaise de Montluc subsequently put it,[15] and sailed from Nice back to Genoa.

The fleet of ships carrying the dispirited emperor back to Spain left from Genoa on 16 November 1536, and reached the port of Palamós on 5 December. Charles set out across the peninsula with a small group of courtiers, of whom the most prominent was Alba. After a night in Barcelona, they resumed their journey cross-country, heading for Tordesillas, where the emperor's first duty was to pay his respects to his mother, Queen Juana. For Alba, the return home was opportune for two reasons. Six months later, in July 1537 his mother died. Then shortly afterward on 21 November his second son Fadrique was born.

This was also the period when Alba made a rare but significant intervention in the politics of Castile, acting as he always did in support of the crown.
Charles V was faced with enormous debts as a result of his war campaigns and
attempted to recoup part of the expense from his subjects in Castile. He had
encountered opposition in the matter previously, and attempted to overcome
the problem by exercising pressure. In October 1538 he convened at Toledo
a plenary session of the Cortes, including the upper clergy, ninety-five
members of the aristocracy, and the representatives of the eighteen principal
cities of Castile. Each chamber met separately, and the emperor explained
that extraordinary circumstances had motivated this special meeting. In
reality he was trying to obtain a direct vote of taxes from the clergy and
nobility, who had always considered themselves exempt. Charles's move did
not succeed. In the assembly of the Castilian nobles, two-thirds opposed the
proposed taxes, and instead urged that the emperor should stay in Castile and
devote himself to its affairs. A minority, made up of Alba, the duke of Infantado, and seventeen others, who understood the importance of Charles's
international commitments, accepted the tax and what it entailed but were
unable to influence the assembly. It was evident that no progress could be
made on the matter. Dismissing the grandees curtly from the Cortes in
February, Charles's chief minister Cardinal Tavera said: 'Your lordships are
not required any longer; each of you can go home or where you will.' It was
the last time that nobles and clergy were ever summoned to a working Cortes.

The duke continued to give his faithful support to the emperor in the
crucial diplomatic meetings of these years. Various peace agreements were
made with the French king during 1537, but they failed to stop the fighting.
It seemed that only a meeting between Charles and the French king, in
person, would resolve the issues involved. Accordingly a summit was arranged
to be held in the city of Nice in June 1538. The emperor sailed from
Barcelona at the end of April, with a retinue that included Alba among the
other great lords. Nice was neutral ground, since it belonged to the republic
of Genoa, and the pope, Paul III, volunteered to mediate personally between
Charles V and Francis I. In the end it turned out to be a curious summit, for
the two kings never once met each other face-to-face, preferring to maintain
their diplomatic contacts only through the pope. A ten-year truce was agreed,
but it was obviously an unsatisfactory arrangement since many issues were left
unsettled. At the urging of the queen of France, Charles's sister Leonor, the
two kings consented to repeat the summit one month later, at Aigues-Mortes,
the Mediterranean port on the frontier between France and Spain. This time
the setting was different. Charles greeted the French king on board his galley,
then went ashore the following day to accept Francis's hospitality. The kings
embraced each other, swore friendship and even shared the same bedroom. In

all the official meetings Alba was at the emperor's side. Promises were made to concert marriage alliances, and unite in struggle against heresy and against the Ottoman fleet.

The year 1539 was particularly distressing for the emperor because of the death in childbirth of the empress Isabella on 1 May. Despite his long absences and occasional dalliances abroad, Charles had loved his wife deeply. Grief-stricken,[16] he immured himself in a convent for seven weeks. In the autumn he once again had to take leave of his family. The problem was a rebellion of the authorities of his hometown of Ghent in the Netherlands. He went accompanied by a small group of twenty nobles, among them Alba. The auxiliary staff included two secretaries, a doctor, a barber and two cooks. Thanks to the cordial relations that had now been established with France, Charles was invited to cross the kingdom and accept its hospitality. The memorable entertainments laid on for the emperor prolonged the journey, which ended up lasting two months from the end of November 1539, when the group was at Bayonne, to the end of January 1540, when they took leave of the French court at Valenciennes. The dauphin accompanied them for most of the trip, and the king was their host during the Christmas season at Blois and Paris. They spent the first week of the New Year 1540 in Paris. At a supper given by the French king, those seated at the main table were royal persons, two cardinals, the duke of Guise and only one Spaniard: the duke of Alba.[17] The emperor allowed himself to predict to a French noble that the duke of Alba had the makings of a good general. 'He has started well,' Charles said, 'and I shall promote him according to his merits, of which I have great hopes.'[18]

Alba had not been to northern Europe for nearly twenty years, and was very conscious of this. 'Since we left France,' he wrote to Francisco de los Cobos, Charles's secretary of state, from Valenciennes in the Netherlands, 'we feel like strangers. Men have come to visit the emperor whom I thought dead twenty years ago.'[19] When Charles arrived in Ghent in mid-February 1540, he used his available troops to crush all opposition ruthlessly. More than fifty city burghers were arrested, and sixteen were beheaded for treason; the privileges of the city were annulled. The measures, commented a Spaniard in Charles's entourage, 'were so severe that their like was unknown in Constantinople'.[20] It was probably an influential experience for the young duke, who a generation later would feel the need to impose similar repressive measures on the Netherlanders. He also got to know something more of the geography of the country, travelling in the late spring with the emperor to Antwerp, Brussels and the other principal cities he had visited two decades before. On

Christmas Day Charles and his retinue left for Germany, taking the route through Namur and Metz and arriving in Regensburg in the last week of February 1541 for a meeting of the Imperial Diet. A formal debate was held under the presidency of the emperor, between Catholic and Lutheran theologians. Despite all efforts, no compromise was reached, and in July the emperor decided to dissolve the Diet. Alba had spent six months in Germany, two in France, and over a year in the Netherlands, a formative period in which he had acquainted himself profoundly with all aspects of the political and religious situation in the north of Europe.

Charles and the rest of the Imperial party left Germany at the end of July and reached Innsbruck in the first week of August. From here they took the traditional route into Italy, arriving in Milan two weeks later. Alba, it appears, went on directly to Spain. The emperor, however, had other business. During the months of absence from the Mediterranean, his officials had been collecting the money, troops and ships required for another descent into North Africa. When he sailed from Genoa early in September, it was not with the intention of going to Spain. Instead, the fleet went down the coast of Italy, then across to Mallorca, the planned rendezvous for the expedition. According to the official estimates, Naples and Sicily were to meet 60 per cent of the costs, Castile 40 per cent. Similar proportions applied to the galleys, of which the Italians would supply two-thirds and Spain one-third.[21] Two-thirds of the soldiers would be Italians (commanded by Vespasiano Colonna) and Germans (commanded by Alba), one third Spanish (under Ferrante Gonzaga). Alba was unwell during the month of August and remained in Alba de Tormes, but on 1 September he arrived in Cartagena to prepare men and ships for the campaign. The emperor was due to arrive there later from Mallorca, with the bulk of the army. In Cartagena Alba stirred up much illwill because of his disciplinary demands. The Castilian nobles who presented themselves assumed that it would be, as in Tunis in 1535, another occasion for lavish display. They therefore came with their women, their servants, and their baggage. Alba had to threaten to exclude those who would not leave their impedimenta behind, and ordered some camp followers to be flogged. Several nobles left the camp in protest. The duke had never been one to seek popularity, and earned the hostility of many nobles who felt that war against the infidel should be in the nature of an enjoyable excursion.[22]

The assembled forced sailed from Mallorca in mid-October 1541, picking up on their way the duke of Alba, who was waiting at Cartagena. It was well into the season of unstable weather in the western Mediterranean, as several advisers pointed out to the emperor, and high winds impeded ship manoeuvres; but Charles decided to go ahead, rather than waste the money that had already been spent on preparations.[23] The total force was estimated at 65 galleys, 450 support vessels and transports, with 12,000 sailors and 24,000 troops. Among the captains was the conqueror of Mexico himself, Hernán Cortés. On 23 October the infantry began to go ashore six miles from the city of Algiers. In the afternoon, a sudden storm hit the coast.[24] 'That day, Tuesday,' Cardinal Tavera later reported, 'such a big storm arose that not only was it impossible to unload the supplies and guns, but many small vessels were overturned and also thirteen to fourteen galleys.' The storm continued unabated for four days, destroying a good proportion of the ships and many of the men. ('Thank God,' noted Tavera, 'no one of importance was lost, only ordinary men and servants and sailors.') It was impossible to unload the artillery. On 26 October, to the amazement of the besieged Algerians, the emperor began to withdraw his forces. The bad weather continued, hindering an orderly withdrawal; Charles had to take refuge for three weeks in the port of Bougie and did not reach Mallorca until the end of November. The total losses suffered by his forces were possibly not less than 150 vessels and 12,000 men, without counting cannon and supplies.[25] It was the emperor's first resounding defeat, an unmitigated disaster in every sense, a profound humiliation, and, for all the foregoing reasons, his last expedition against the forces of Islam. Alba's efforts during the disaster earned him Charles's gratitude, and in the middle of the retreat, before they arrived at the safety of Bougie, he was named head of the emperor's household.

Charles returned to the peninsula from Mallorca after a week's rest. Even had he wished to, he could not spend more time in the Mediterranean, for in 1542 another war broke out with France. He was urgently required in northern Europe, and took appropriate steps to leave his son and heir Philip in charge of the government in Spain. At the same time, he required money and summoned the Cortes of the Crown of Aragon to Monzón. The threat from France on the Pyrenean frontier was countered, in the meantime, by sending Alba to Navarre in January 1542.

It was the duke's first major assignment within Spain, and must have brought back memories of his youthful campaigns in the area. This time, however, there were no military adventures, only hard administrative work. 'I arrived in Logroño on the 16th this month,' he informed the emperor, 'and the morning after I left to inspect the country.'[26] He spent a few days travelling round to visit the fortifications, and found serious defence deficiencies everywhere. The most sensitive problem, however, was how to take initiatives in a country where the emperor controlled no aspect of political, economic or military administration. Navarre (like other non-Castilian provinces of the peninsula) was an autonomous kingdom that formed part of Spain but conserved its own laws and structure. Alba's comments provide fascinating insight into how his views would develop, for in later years he would be accused of attempting to destroy the autonomy of other and larger states of the Spanish monarchy.

In the capital, Pamplona, 'there are two thousand armed men from this country, but not a single soldier of Your Majesty'. The gates of the walled city were always open, and the king (or his representative the viceroy) had no power to order that they be closed. Alba advised that the king must take steps to cooperate with those who controlled Navarre: 'it is good that Your Majesty place your trust in the people here, but the trust should be the very minimum'. Over the next few days he spoke to the officials of Pamplona and managed to get them to agree to his request that royal soldiers enter the garrison, and that other aspects of defence come under royal control. At the same time he took steps to convoke a meeting of the Cortes of the realm, the only assembly that could grant money for defence. The proposal coincided perfectly with the emperor's plans, for in those weeks Charles was preparing once again to leave Spain.

Meanwhile the emperor and the prince were making a long round trip, through the north of Spain and heading towards the Mediterranean. Charles wished to make sure that his son would be received as his legal heir by taking the customary oath of office in each kingdom. The royal party accordingly went to Pamplona early in June 1542, where Philip – in the presence of Alba – accepted the allegiance of the Cortes. The duke then accompanied the party on their journey to the Crown of Aragon, where Philip was supposed to attend the meeting of the Cortes but fell ill and remained indisposed throughout July and August. The delay was highly inconvenient, for the French forces took the opportunity to lay siege to the city of Perpignan. Once again Charles had to rely on Alba, whom he sent off to the Catalan frontier to examine the state of defences. He himself went on to Barcelona at the beginning of October, leaving Philip to wind up business in Monzón and follow him later.

As in Navarre, Alba was the soul of efficiency. As in Navarre, he was dissatisfied with the way the people of Catalonia were defending their own country against the French, and recommended that royal troops be sent in. For the duration of Habsburg rule in Spain, the problem of trying to make the non-Castilian provinces provide soldiers for their own defence would remain at the top of the political agenda. 'I have had a look here at some of the soldiers recruited in Catalonia, and am so dissatisfied with them that I dare not mention it to Your Majesty. I beg you to order that the greatest urgency be given to sending men from Castile and from other areas where they are recruited.' He was tireless. 'I arrived here tonight,' he wrote from La Jonquera, 'and tomorrow I shall set out before dawn and arrive very early in Perpignan; there no time will be wasted in seeing what can and must be done.' In Navarre he had coincided with the winter snows. In Roussillon he braved the summer heat of August, but after a few days in Perpignan went down to the coast to the pleasant port of Collioure, where he could more easily maintain contact with supplies as they came in from the sea. His letters to the emperor, signed by him simply as 'the duke marquis', show him to perfection as a director of military operations, arranging to raise money, recruit troops, and import cannon and firearms. To help defend Perpignan he wanted three thousand soldiers from Castile, and eight thousand more if it was a question of defending the whole county, for 'Your Majesty should not count on the Catalan soldiers'. For defence, he wrote, it was better to have Castilians than Catalans (in practice he accepted and worked well with Catalan troops). His comprehensive reports to the emperor on how best to protect Catalonia against the French and the Turks, provide impressive evidence of his attention to detail. 'I am travelling through this country,' he wrote to Charles from Collioure in the second week of August, 'with the reins of my mule loose and my beard relaxed on my shoulder.' He was ready, he told the emperor, to go everywhere in his service.

He was, in effect, needed everywhere. Charles recognised that he could put his confidence in Alba, who was now his chief Castilian army commander. Preparations for the defence of Perpignan went ahead, with the assistance at sea of the fleets under Spanish naval commander Bernardino de Mendoza, and the Genoese commander Juan Andrea Doria. 'All is work and patching up in Perpignan, and here [in Collioure] we are busy collecting the munitions in order to store them in Perpignan,' he informed the emperor. 'There is an urgent need for money, and these Catalans are people who have no patience when waiting to be paid.' He was facing serious desertion of Catalan soldiers, who had not received their wages: 'you think you have Catalans in the evening but by the morning they are not there'. In this situation, he gave proof of one of the most revealing characteristics of a successful general: the ability to get on with his soldiers. Troubled by discontent among Catalan recruits, who in addition to problems about being paid also had little confidence in the nobles who were meant to be leading them, Alba decided to take matters in hand personally. He left Collioure and went to Perpignan.

I returned from Collioure because they told me that the Catalan soldiers were saying they would not continue there if I was not with them. I spoke to them all and told them that Your Majesty had ordered me not to confine myself to the fort, but that if they thought it would improve matters if I stayed with them then they should tell me and I would do so, because an order from Your Majesty could only be disobeyed with good reason if they so wished it. They all replied that not for all the world should I do so, and that they would sooner die than quit their places there. They are now in such good spirits and so well disposed that I am fully confident that they are trustworthy men, and if that is true then the fort is secure.

In the end, despite all the obstacles and lack of money, he was able to put the whole frontier into an impressive state of defence. In the city of Perpignan, according to an official, there were four thousand soldiers. 'The place is well provisioned,' he wrote to Charles in late August, 'and tomorrow I shall leave for Girona and Barcelona. I am ready to carry out Your Majesty's orders whenever you require it, and shall apply myself with all the effort and care of which I am capable.' The defence forces were, of course, not enough for a war situation. From Barcelona in September Alba continued to work busily to put together an army for Roussillon, with a strong detachment of Germans. In the end the preparations helped to avoid any engagement, for as Alba surmised from their movements the French were not anxious for a fight, and during August the Dauphin began withdrawing his forces from the area. 'We showed our teeth in Perpignan and they don't want to take the risk.' Nor, he informed Charles, would the French succeed if they tried to besiege it, for there were enough supplies in the city to enable it to hold out.

The two months spent by Alba on the Catalan frontier demonstrated his powers of leadership, his unerring military instinct, and his ability (which he retained all his life) to win and retain the loyalty of his men. He showed himself capable of talking to the Catalan authorities both in Perpignan and Barcelona, and of obtaining from them all he needed without problems: men, money and supplies. He also successfully coordinated the movement of naval forces off the Catalan coast. His success in dealing with the 'anxiety of this summer', as he described it to the emperor, confirmed him in his unique position as Charles's principal commander. However, those months also showed up once again the duke's greatest weakness: his inability to get on with some of his closest and most highly placed colleagues, who complained among themselves of his arrogance. Alba never tolerated contradiction, no matter from which quarter it came. He clashed repeatedly with the then viceroy of Catalonia, Francisco de Borja, duke of Gandía, over matters concerning the preparations for war. The conflict was so serious that Alba retained a personal aversion for Borja all his life. 'He could never put up with or stand the presence or the sight of the duke of Gandía, and was unable to repress his extreme dislike', a diplomat in Madrid testified several years afterwards. This hostility was only towards Borja, for even with his great rival Ruy Gómez there were acceptable social relations. Borja a few years later abandoned his career and title, and entered the recently formed Society of Jesus to become eventually its second general; after his death he was canonised as a saint. The change in the status of Borja (who as it happened was a close friend and ally of Ruy Gómez) did not affect Alba's attitude or his profound dislike. He once bitingly commented that 'the duke would have done much better to have stayed in Gandía cultivating his sugar'.[27]

The emperor had decided by the end of 1542 that his presence in Germany could not be postponed. The confrontation with France was also having serious repercussions in the north. In the first week of May 1543 he set sail from Palamós, on the Catalan coast, after naming his son regent of Spain. He also left a regency council behind in Castile to advise his son: its members were the president of the royal council, cardinal Tavera; the secretary of state Francisco de los Cobos; and Alba. Charles also left in the hands of the prince's tutor, Juan de Zúñiga, two handwritten letters of 'Instruction', one described as 'confidential', the other as 'private'.

In the second document he communicated to his son his personal advice and opinion about the members of the regency council and advised Philip not to fall into the hands of any of them. He was critical about the factions among his ministers. His advice about Alba is remarkable for its insight and frankness.

> I feel that the duke of Alba is of no faction save that which will benefit him. Since it is not good that grandees should enter into the government of the kingdom I did not let him take part, which he resented very much. In the time that he has been in my service I have discerned in him great ambition and the desire to rise as high as possible, even though he began with great humility and meekness. Take care, son, that he does not dominate you for you are much younger. Be careful not to let him or other grandees get a firm footing in government, because they will use every means they have to gain control over you, and afterwards you will regret it. Apart from that I let him participate in the councils of State and of War. Employ him and honour him and favour him, for he is the best [general] that we have at present in these realms.[28]

Before the emperor left, Alba took the precaution of handing him a request for payment of services. The standard procedure in use at the time was for the great nobility to carry out their military or diplomatic duties at their own cost, and then to be suitably rewarded by the crown. They could be compensated in the form of titles or property or income, or all three. Alba's most pressing need at the moment was cash, as he explained to the emperor: 'the constraint arises because I owe 200,000 ducats. In the twelve years that I have followed Your Majesty you have conceded me many grants of money, but they do not serve in any way to cover the expenses that I have had lately.'[29]

After taking their leave of the emperor, Alba and Cobos left Barcelona on 28 May 1543 and returned to Castile through Saragossa. By 19 July the duke was back in Alba de Tormes with his wife and family. 'I arrived here in good health,' he informed Cobos as soon as he got home, 'and found the duchess in good health as well. I would like to take a spin round some of my villages and won't be long doing so.'[30] The respite did not last long. Ten days later he received instructions from the emperor to return to work in government business at Valladolid. It was the beginning of what would become the second great phase of his career as servant to the crown. At this time he became Philip's principal adviser in both war and peace. He was brought fully into all the business dealt with by the prince regent. 'His Highness received the Instructions,' Zúñiga reported to the emperor, 'together with the powers which Your Majesty sent for governing these realms and those of Aragon. After he had read it all, he sent the special instructions to the tribunals and councils. He has begun, conscientiously and with resolution, to study what he has been ordered to do. He is in touch always with the duke of Alba and the Grand Commander of León [Cobos].'[31] Alba was destined to retain that dominant position for around a quarter of a century longer.

It was, however, no easy matter to reconcile the interests of the many proud men who ran the country in the emperor's absence. Alba very soon showed signs of the haughtiness that Charles well knew. In the summer of 1543 the emperor appointed Juan Manrique, marquis of Aguilar, as viceroy of Catalonia, with broad powers covering both political and military matters in that province. Alba immediately protested to Charles that this detracted from his position as supreme military commander. His own position in the Council of the Realm, he said, gave him 'power and authority over all viceroys and ministers', and he would not accept having to take orders from Manrique. He demanded that the viceroy's commission be modified. 'If this be done,' he wrote, 'my honour will be safeguarded; otherwise I shall tender my resignation of all charges and retire to my estates.'[32] On the emperor's instructions, Cobos made efforts to sort out the problem.

Alba's key position in matters both personal and political is illustrated by the arrangement of Philip's first marriage, to the princess Maria of Portugal. The princess of Portugal was aged just sixteen, six months younger than Philip. On 2 November the prince and his courtiers left Valladolid and passed through Tordesillas to receive the blessing of Queen Juana, Charles's mother, who had been living in the palace there since Charles's accession to the throne. They then proceeded to Alba de Tormes. The marriage was due to take place in Salamanca, and the prince wished to steal a glance at his future bride before the ceremony. The estates of Alba were conveniently placed for him to carry out this plan. One of the duke's towns, La Abadía, was on the road from Cáceres to Salamanca, and from a building there the prince and his group watched María pass. On Monday 12 November Philip made a ceremonial entry into Salamanca. The princess entered a few hours later, and the couple were married by cardinal Tavera on the same day.[33]

Two highly significant debates in the prince's council shed incomparable light on Alba's ideas at this time. The peace of Crépy in September 1544 between the emperor and France induced Charles to consider the possibility of a marriage alliance between a member of his family and Francis I's second son, the duke of Orléans. Charles thought of offering either his daughter María, with possession of the Netherlands at his own death; or his niece Anne of Hungary, with possession of Milan a year after the marriage. Which of these territories, the Netherlands or Milan, could he afford to give away as part of a marriage settlement? The emperor consulted his advisers in each realm about the matter. In Valladolid the debate in the royal council in November revealed a clear difference of opinion between councillors who saw Flanders as essential to the monarchy, and those who felt that Milan was more valuable. Of the nine councillors present in the Council of State, four felt that Flanders was vital and must never be alienated. The other five, among them Cobos and Alba, felt that Milan was the more important. Although the Netherlands 'will always be beneficial to these realms because of our trade there,' said Alba, 'the state of Milan is both important and essential not only for the defence and protection of Naples and Sicily, but also for the security of these realms of Castile and because they afford Your Majesty a clear route of access to Germany and Flanders'.[34] He seems never to have changed his perspective thereafter on the relative value of Spain's connexions in the Mediterranean and those in the north of Europe.

The second significant debate concerned America. The so-called New Laws which the crown had decreed there in 1542 provoked fierce opposition in Peru, where the new viceroy Blasco Núñez de Vela failed to stifle a rebellion by the conquistador Gonzalo Pizarro. On receiving news of the troubles, in 1545 the prince called a meeting of the council. Eight members were present including Cardinal Tavera, Cobos, and Alba. The duke was alone in suggesting that the rising should be crushed 'with great strength and force' and 'a large and powerful armada'. It was a typical soldier's solution, calling for the immediate use of brute force without any adequate consideration of the logistical obstacles involved. He seems to have given little thought to the problems of transporting an army and a navy across the Atlantic and into the Pacific. In time Alba would attain enough experience to realise that there were limits to the use of force when exercised against faraway countries. All the other councillors, wiser and more experienced than he, considered his solution wholly impractical.[35] They concluded with the remarkable decision, which in the end turned out to be wholly successful, to send one lone man out to Peru to subdue the rebellion.[36]

It is relevant to contemplate the solitary position of Alba in the debate over the Pizarro rebellion. It was typical of him to suggest and sustain an idea that appeared to him to be correct, even though everybody else objected. He was never afraid to propose solutions that might attract opposition, and his preference was always for the military option – the quick kill – rather than for the ways of diplomacy and compromise. He felt that too much talk held up solutions and made problems worse; action resolved matters quickly. He seldom got his way. Throughout his professional life, and despite his great power and influence, he was constantly condemned to carry out policies that others had decided and with which he invariably disagreed. He was a paradigm of the soldier who is lost in the world of politics.

Alba also had to come to terms with his relationship with prince Philip. A few years later (in 1548) he was appointed high steward of the prince's household when he brought the Burgundian ceremony to Castile. Twenty years the prince's senior, tall and commanding in presence, he inevitably dominated him both physically and morally. As the country's only prominent soldier, and close companion of the emperor, his judgment in military matters could not be questioned. But his lack of tact in personal relations proved to be a barrier. Philip respected what the duke said but was not always happy about the patronising way in which he said it. Cobos reported to the emperor in 1543 an incident that illustrated the issue perfectly.[37]

> It happened one day last month that His Highness asked the duke something about the war with France. The duke, with his accustomed impetuosity, replied that as long as the emperor and he were alive they would soon take care of France. The prince very quietly said to him: 'After the emperor, no one holds a place before me. I am of the opinion that anyone who does not understand that and boasts in my presence, either does not know me or is trying to displease me.' With that His Highness turned his back, and the rest of us who were there were amazed at his angry reply. We all had to intervene to restore the duke to his favour.

In 1545 the emperor summoned Alba to northern Europe to take part in the military campaign against the Lutheran princes of the Schmalkaldic League. Charles was at this time based in Brussels, but made journeys when necessary to Germany. Alba was present on 24 September at the meeting in Brussels of the emperor's council, when the military options facing them were discussed. It was a time of uneasy peace with France, and some advisers favoured preparing a campaign against that country. Alba, however, favoured a solution of Charles's problems in Germany through a war against the Schmalkaldic

League. The emperor tended to share his views. In the first week of January 1546 Charles held an investiture of the Order of the Golden Fleece in Utrecht.[38] Twenty-two new knights were named, among them four Spaniards (the dukes of Alba, Infantado, Nájera and Feria, of whom the last three were in Spain and had their nominations sent by special messenger). The new knights included Charles's other military commanders Cosimo de' Medici (the grand duke of Tuscany), Emanuele Filiberto (the duke of Savoy), and the new count of Egmont, Lamoral.[39] Charles, accompanied by Alba, then travelled to Regensburg in April 1546, to take part in the Diet and to confirm the alliances made with various princes. The problem that most blighted the emperor's health and prematurely aged him was the spread of the Protestant Reformation through the German lands. At Regensburg he debated his options again with his council, and his Spanish confessor Pedro de Soto joined in to support the voices favouring a military solution.

Preparations for the campaign were not easy to make, for there were few funds available and Charles had to take into account the very complex and varied interests of the German princes. Fortunately he was able to achieve a secret alliance with one of the members of the League, duke Maurice of Saxony, who had his eye on the title and territory of the Protestant leader elector John Frederick of Saxony. Throughout his military campaign in the year 1546 against the princes of the League, the emperor relied heavily on troops brought in from Italy, both Italian and Spanish, together with levies made in the Netherlands. Alba was continuously at his side, though it would be more exact to say that it was Alba and his household that accompanied the emperor and his household. The common practice in Europe was that nobles, from the least to the greatest, did not go on journeys without their servants. The noble soldiers in the tercios of Spain, for example, took their servants and women with them. Alba did not take his wife to Germany, though he did take her to England in 1554 and subsequently to Naples. The group he usually travelled with tended to include his sons and other close relatives, and the cost of transporting so many people was always a problem. During the campaign in 1546 the finance granted him by the emperor for his services assumed that he would have a staff of twenty-five gentlemen in attendance, a number of guards, messengers, interpreters, and three military engineers.[40] Everything else had to be financed by the duke. He obtained loans in 1546 from the Genoese financiers Spinola and Lomelini, to help him with costs in Germany. In the end, he lost money on every period of service abroad, and had to rely on grants from the crown. It was normal in these circumstances for great nobles to fall into debt, though they were also able to recoup some losses by using their influence and position to obtain various material benefits.

In the summer of 1546, the military situation appeared more favourable for the emperor. Tercios came from Lombardy and levies from Germany. In August twelve thousand Italians paid for by the papacy arrived at the emperor's base at Landshut. In total, the emperor had close on forty thousand troops, perhaps slightly less in number than those of his Schmalkaldic enemies. In the second half of 1546 the Protestant forces failed to exploit occasional successes. At his camp at Ingolstadt the emperor in the autumn had the greater number of troops, but preferred to wait and see. A major encounter between the two opposing forces was postponed for several months, with the inevitable result that many troops on both sides had to be paid off and sent home. By this time the political situation was affected by the internal conflict in Saxony, where Charles counted on the support of his newly acquired Lutheran ally, duke Maurice, against the elector John Frederick.[41] In January 1547 Charles' brother the archduke Ferdinand appealed for troops to be sent to the Saxon front. Charles responded by sending a force commanded by another Protestant ally, the margrave Albert Alcibiades of Brandenburg, which was unfortunately routed by John Frederick's army in March. The emperor was forced to take the field. In mid-April his troops joined those of Ferdinand and duke Maurice at Eger in Bohemia, then crossed into the territories of the elector.

The Imperial army was made up of men of many nations under the command of the emperor and his commanders, one of them the duke of Alba. There were some 8,000 Spaniards, most of them veteran tercios from Italy; some 16,000 *Landsknechte*; 10,000 Italians commanded by Ottavio Farnese; and 10,000 Netherlanders commanded by Maximilian of Egmont, count of Buren. This total of 44,000 infantry was supported by 7,000 cavalry, mostly Germans and Netherlanders.[42] The emperor, afflicted by gout and unable to walk, moved on horseback among his men,[43] talking to them and raising their spirits. In the morning of 24 April 1547 the army reached the left bank of the river Elbe, near the town of Mühlberg. The League forces under the elector had crossed to the right bank and had destroyed the only available bridge; they were confident that the emperor could not cross. The emperor's Hungarian cavalry, however, constructed a makeshift bridge, and a convenient ford was also discovered. The troops managed to cross over within an hour, and shortly after nightfall came upon the unprepared enemy in a wood.

The action at Mühlberg is always referred to as a battle, though in reality it never took the form of one and by its nature more resembled a rout. The Saxon forces had no opportunity to defend themselves adequately against a sudden attack from an unexpected quarter. The consequences were to be expected. It was estimated that the Imperialists lost only about fifty men, and of the enemy some 2,500 were killed and several hundreds were taken prisoner together with their artillery, standards and baggage. A Saxon nobleman, Thilo von Throta, captured the elector John, who was trying to flee after being wounded in the action.[44] When he was brought before Charles, the elector asked to be treated according to his rank. The emperor replied curtly that he would be treated as he deserved, and ordered Alba to take him away. The duke was entrusted with the custody of the prisoner, whom he placed under guard in the castle at Halle.

Among the Castilian nobles who served in the Imperial forces was Luis de Ávila y Zúñiga, a close companion of the emperor and a leading member of his royal council, who did not doubt that the strength of the emperor's army lay in the German troops.[45] He reserved his highest praise for the Hungarian cavalry, 'who with incredible rapidity began to accomplish the victory that they were particularly capable of securing'. 'There were so many weapons strewn over the ground,' reported Ávila, 'that they greatly impeded those who were achieving the victory. There were very many dead and wounded, and so many prisoners that many of our men came back with fifteen or twenty each. On all sides the bodies were piled up in heaps.' The Castilians played an important part in the combat, though not quite the dominant one presented by the official historian López de Gómara.[46] The Venetian ambassador, who was there, criticised the Spanish troops for being 'brutish, rough and inexperienced, though they are becoming good soldiers; those I have seen in Germany have all been veterans [of other wars]'.[47]

Much of the credit for the victory was given at the time to Alba, though his role in it appears to have been no greater than that of the other commanders. It was perhaps the first action in which he was able to act as a general in his own right. He dressed for the part, riding a white horse and wearing white armour and long white plumes in his helmet.[48] The theory was that it would enable his men to identify him, but Alba always knew how to put on a show for his public. Rumour had it that at Mühlberg, like Joshua, he commanded the sun to stand still for a while and was obeyed. How else could crossing the river which was only concluded at six o'clock, and the accompanying defeat of the Protestant forces, all have been achieved within the space of one evening? The reply of the duke to Henry II of France, who questioned him subsequently upon the subject, became famous. 'Your Majesty, I was much too occupied that evening with what was taking place on the earth beneath, to pay much heed to the evolutions of the heavenly bodies.'[49] The emperor's victory, certainly the most famous of his entire career, was immortalised in the superb equestrian portrait by Titian, now in the Prado.

Castilian tercios were still in Germany to help Alba in his last disastrous campaign in 1552, at the unsuccessful siege of Metz, where they made up less than a tenth of the infantry and under 4 per cent of the cavalry.[50] The Spanish presence in western Europe was still in its early days and barely perceptible outside the Italian peninsula. However, it had already begun to attract comment, both favourable and unfavourable. Whereas a Castilian poet, Hernando de Acuña, greeted the possibility of a universal dominion for Charles, with 'one monarch, one empire and one sword', non-Spaniards were distrustful of the implications.

From Germany, Charles V expressed his anxiety and impatience to see Philip. He was concerned by the instability in many of his territories, and the state of his own health. Gout was laying waste his body. He wished to make arrangements to pass on a secure succession to his son. Moreover, a whole epoch in European history ended in the year 1547. On 28 January, Henry VIII of England died. A few weeks later saw the death, on 31 March, of Charles's great antagonist Francis I of France. The previous year, 1546 (when Martin Luther died), marked the end of the career of the scourge of the Mediterranean, Khayr al-Din Barbarossa. It became urgent to prepare Philip for the new scenario in European politics. Fortunately, the west was now at peace. The victory at Mühlberg restored some tranquillity to central Europe. It was safe for the prince to travel abroad. In January 1548 Charles sent the duke of Alba to Spain with instructions to reform the ceremonial of the Spanish court and bring Philip back with him. In January in Augsburg he drew up a long set of *Instructions* which he sent to Spain with Alba, for the prince to consider before he left the country.[51]

When Alba arrived he brought the emperor's orders to introduce the ceremonial of the court of Burgundy into Spain.[52] Charles was conscious of the poverty of royal ritual in Spain and wished to prepare the prince for the more elaborate forms used in the north. The new ceremonial was officially inaugurated (despite the hostility of many Castilian nobles and of Alba himself) in the Spanish court on 15 August 1548, to coincide with the festivities of the Feast of the Assumption. The ceremonial also brought to the duke a new dignity that he retained for the rest of his life and gave him a formal precedence over all other nobles at court. He was created high steward, which made him director of Philip's household and everything pertaining to it; he had the right to accompany the prince to chapel and to all official engagements, decide rules of precedence and arrange all audiences. The post gave him substantial influence over the prince's court and the approximately 1,500 personnel employed in it.[53] With his great experience in political and military matters, he had a right to feel that he was indispensable.

On 13 September the archduke Maximilian, who was to exercise the regency during Philip's absence, arrived from Vienna with his retinue of

Austrian and Czech courtiers. A marriage had been arranged between him and Philip's sister María, and was formally celebrated two days after his arrival. Everything was now in order for the royal journey to the Netherlands. At daybreak on 2 October Philip's party set out from Valladolid for Barcelona. It was a large and distinguished group, including Alba, Ruy Gómez, and other leading nobles. There were also noted humanists, among them Gonzalo Pérez, the prince's personal secretary. Just before leaving Valladolid the duke received news of the death from an illness at Alba de Tormes of his son and heir Diego. Quite obviously he could not abandon his family at such a moment. But though it was a terrible decision to make, he very typically put duty first and decided to continue with the journey. 'The duke made his decision,' the prince's chronicler observed, 'with that firmness of spirit with which he usually undertakes great matters. His courage and consideration left everyone greatly impressed.'[54] Once in Catalonia, the prince and nobles eventually sailed from the port of Rosas in the fleet of fifty-eight galleys commanded by the great Genoese admiral, the 82-year-old prince Andrea Doria, on 2 November.[55] Alba went in the prince's ship. For Philip the journey was a new pleasure and highly educative. Alba, by contrast, knew the route very well, and was familiar with all the European leaders they would meet.

The trip was of crucial importance in the formation of Philip's political views,[56] and also reveals interesting aspects of the duke. In view of Alba's enduring reputation as a conservative, it is intriguing to see how he participated in the fundamentally moderate policies of the emperor in Germany at this time, notably his backing for religious tolerance and his alliances with Protestant princes. During the visit to Italy he also revealed his social accomplishments. At the banquet given for the prince in Milan on New Year's Day 1549 by governor Ferrante Gonzaga, Alba initiated the ball of torches by dancing with the governor's wife. 'When he danced he made a spin around with the torch as is required by that dance, then he picked out a lady and handed her the torch, bowed to her and returned to his place.'[57] The memorable journey took the royal group through Trent, Innsbruck, Munich, Augsburg and Heidelberg, to the Netherlands. From Trent to Augsburg they were accompanied by the Protestant ally of the emperor, Elector Maurice of Saxony, and just before reaching Heidelberg were escorted by the Protestant master of the Teutonic Knights. At the end of March the group finally entered the Netherlands.

Since the country played a crucial part in Alba's later career, it is timely to say a word about it here.[58] The Netherlands were (as the name implied) a small group of unspectacular, low-lying provinces whose economic sustenance came mainly from the sea. The major port, Antwerp, was a hive of trading activity. Despite its unassuming aspect, the country was as always a potential source of problems. Its seventeen provinces had no political unity beyond their allegiance to a common ruler, Charles. They technically formed part of the Holy Roman Empire ruled by Charles, but the emperor had some years before secured their effective autonomy. The Netherlands had a common constitutional assembly, the States General. But real political power rested with the great nobles and above all with those who were governors (*stadhouders*) of the leading provinces. Charles had attempted to strengthen control in the capital, Brussels, by setting up a system of three central councils. Political rivalry between the provinces was aggravated by cultural divisions. The greater part of the provinces, roughly the northern areas down to as far as Brussels, spoke Dutch. In the south, economically richer and more densely populated, the principal language was French.

The dual culture affected politics. The Netherlanders felt themselves kin to both the Germans and the French. Most greater nobles had French origins, but they frequently married into German families. The most prominent grandee was of German origin: William of Nassau, prince of Orange, six years younger than Prince Philip. Holder of extensive estates in both France and Germany, he was also *stadhouder* of the provinces of Holland, Zealand and Utrecht. Some years later he married, as his second wife, the daughter of Maurice of Saxony. Another of the magnates of the country was Lamoral, count of Egmont, four years older than Philip and stadholder of the southern provinces of Flanders and Artois.[59] The cosmopolitan links of Netherlands nobles tended to make them the focus of international interest, particularly in matters of religion. The Dutch had a well-deserved reputation as religious liberals, and had produced the humanist Erasmus. But it was also the country where the radical Anabaptists most flourished, and where, during the 1530s, they were the most bitterly persecuted. In the months that they were in the Netherlands, the Spaniards became familiar with an environment where the existence of religious dissent was accepted as almost natural.

The purpose of Philip's tour was to have him sworn in as heir to each province. The journey was undertaken in two phases. In July and August 1549 they toured the southern provinces and afterwards returned to Brussels. Then in September and October they went round the northern provinces. On this second lap they visited Antwerp, the commercial metropolis of northern Europe. They also paid attention to Rotterdam, the birthplace of Erasmus, which they visited on 27 September. The prince went to mass at the church near Erasmus's family house, and 'the leading lords and gentlemen of the court', among them Alba, went inside the house to pay their respects.[60] The duke had received a humanist education, and the gesture of homage to one of the luminaries of European humanism was a natural one.

In June 1550 the journey home began, taking the same route back. On 8 July they reached their principal objective, the Imperial city of Augsburg, to which the emperor had summoned the Diet. The prince of Spain and his retinue now spent a whole year in the Germanic lands. It was an important period when many vital decisions had to be made, including that of the succession to the lands ruled over by the Habsburg family. In several stormy sessions, the members of the family met in Augsburg and came to an agreement about who should succeed to the Imperial crown. Alba was at the side of both emperor and prince, backing up their decisions and participating in the periodic festivities. During those months he also strengthened his friendship with the emperor's chief adviser Antoine Perrenot (the future cardinal Granvelle), who had succeeded his father Nicolas as head of Charles's secretariat. At the end of May 1551 the prince's party, with Alba in it, left Bavaria and began its journey home, through the mountain valleys of the Tyrol, down to Trent and then across the north of Italy to Milan. On 6 July they set sail in a huge fleet under the command of Andrea Doria. The thirty-eight galleys included Doria's vessels as well as the galleys of Naples under Alba's cousin García de Toledo and those of Spain under Bernardino de Mendoza.[61]

When Alba eventually arrived home in the summer of 1551, there were new family and political realities he had to face. The crucial family event was the marriage, which had taken place in May 1551, of his son and heir Fadrique to Guiomar de Aragón, daughter of the duke of Cardona. The most decisive political development was the role at court of Ruy Gómez de Silva, whose rise had a crucial impact on Alba's career. Silva's grandfather, from high Portuguese nobility, came to Spain as steward of the empress Isabella, wife of Charles V, and Ruy Gómez grew up as a page in the royal household. He became a close friend of prince Philip, who was seven years younger than he, and came to occupy important posts in the prince's household. His rise was inexorable. At Philip's accession he became a councillor of State, obtained control of the king's finances, and was made chamberlain, which gave him jurisdiction over the king's private apartments. He was also created grandee and prince of Eboli. The rise of a Portuguese noble inevitably caused friction. In the days of the emperor, influence and control in Spain was exercised largely by Cobos and his associates, among them Alba. In the early 1550s, when Philip gradually took over, there was a scramble among officials to place themselves in the orbit of Gómez, who was seen as his favourite and therefore the man of the future. The Venetian ambassador reported that he was known as 'rey [king] Gómez' rather than 'Ruy Gómez'.

The birth of a Gómez 'group' of nobles, and the beginning of its differences with nobles who were friends of Alba, can probably be traced back to the year 1552. From as early as that date, the emperor's secretary Francisco de

Eraso gravitated to Gómez as political patron,[62] and was subsequently rewarded with key posts in the treasury, the Council of the Indies and the council of State. By 1563 he was the most powerful member of the state administration, virtually another Cobos.[63] Several other notables were associated with the Eboli interest at this period, notably Juan Manrique de Lara, younger son of the second duke of Nájera. The group had, it seems, formed round Philip in the three years of sojourn in the Netherlands, Italy and Germany. Logically, its supporters could also be found among nobles who came from these three areas. They were bound together by self-interest and occasionally by shared outlook. The Alba grouping, on the other hand, was principally dynastic, consisting of leading members of the Toledo clan in their various posts in the central and overseas administration. In Spain, for example, Alba leaned heavily on his brother-in-law Antonio de Toledo, who occupied high office all his life. In addition, Alba could count on the friendship of cardinal Granvelle and of Philip II's personal secretary Gonzalo Pérez. In the past, historians have sometimes tried to identify ideological differences between the Eboli and Alba groupings; the general opinion now is that there were often sharp differences based on interest, rivalry and personality, but none regarding specific political ideas.[64]

When Gómez and his friends came back to Spain in 1552, they prepared for a cleansing of the Augean stables, a radical change in the administration. 'It was utterly necessary,' confided Ruy Gómez to his friend Francisco de Eraso, 'for His Highness to return to these realms. Every day one discovers things which, had they been allowed to go on, would have occasioned great concern. Now there is profound fear among those involved, and they make great efforts to appear snowy white.'[65] Progress was slow. 'Affairs proceed in the Spanish way,' Gómez complained, 'slow and disordered. His Highness does all that he can.'[66] Major scandals were uncovered, notably in the country's principal court of justice, the Chancery of Valladolid.[67] Inevitably, the duke of Alba felt he was being edged out. In a gesture that he would repeat several times throughout his career, he went off to his estates in high dudgeon. Ruy Gómez observed to Eraso: 'The duke of Alba has gone off in a huff but he has no reason to do so, because the prince extends a great deal of favour to him and gives him a part in everything without exception. In spite of this, he is not satisfied, because he doesn't have everything. As you and I have discussed on occasion, I don't know if this conduct helps him.'[68]

The political quarrels in Castile were soon overshadowed by events in Germany. Distracted by his ill-health, too confident over his victory at Mühlberg and the secure succession agreed at Augsburg, the emperor was caught unawares by his enemies. In the summer of 1551 the Turks captured Tripoli and prepared to move in the Mediterranean, while the French prepared an alliance with the German Protestants. In 1552 the latter acted against the emperor. Maurice of Saxony, on whose friendship Charles had depended heavily, joined the other Protestant princes and came to an agreement with Charles's principal enemy, France. Henry II of France immediately laid claim to the Habsburg lands in Italy. He also sent an army into Lorraine while the German princes massed another army in Franconia. The emperor was at Innsbruck, without sufficient forces. His brother Ferdinand would not or could not help him. Accompanied only by his entourage, in late May 1552, Charles was forced to flee for safety from Innsbruck over the Brenner pass, in the midst of a raging snowstorm; riding all night and the following day, they reached the safety of Villach in Carinthia.

When news about the emperor's plight in Germany reached Spain there was indignation. The news of his father's humiliation angered Philip. Those who remembered Maurice as a friend were the most indignant. 'What Maurice did was an act of great villainy,' Ruy Gómez protested.[69] Several Castilian nobles, among them Alba, who felt he had nothing to gain by staying in Spain, set off at once to help the emperor, sailing from Barcelona in 1552 in the fleet of Andrea Doria. Charles wasted no time in preparing a counter-offensive. Alba arrived from Milan with seven thousand Spanish infantry, and other tercios were brought from Italy.[70] The reinforcements allowed Charles to begin putting together a large army from Germany. The need for military action against the Schmalkaldic League was postponed when its leaders agreed a truce, the peace of Passau, signed by both sides in the summer of 1552.

The emperor decided to use all his available forces against France. In the autumn of 1552 he could count on the alliance of one of the Schmalkaldic leaders, the margrave of Brandenburg, Albert Alcibiades. Charles's objective was to recover from the French the city of Metz, which they had captured six months previously. It was late in the season to begin a campaign, but Charles and Alba were certain that it could be done. The emperor was ill, and moved around on a litter. In the first week of November the Imperialists began a bombardment of Metz, which was invested from the south-east by the Imperial army and from the north-east by the army of Flanders under the count of Buren. Alba joined the Imperial commanders who were directing the siege, but their joint efforts did not serve to overcome the city's defences. After a week of bombardment a breach was opened in the walls, but when the smoke cleared the dismayed besiegers discovered that duke Francis of Guise and his men had constructed a new rampart behind the old wall. The emperor's soldiers also began to suffer the impact of a particularly severe winter. After two expensive months before Metz, and with no hope of success in sight, in the first week of the New Year 1553 Charles decided to abandon the campaign. It was perhaps his greatest defeat, for he had chosen the objective and had failed despite possessing a huge army. 'The emperor is thinking of abandoning everything,' wrote cardinal Granvelle, 'and going back to Spain'.[71]

Alba returned to Spain in 1553, disappointed by the turn of events in Germany and by his own uncertain future at the court of prince Philip. 'Till now I have not seen anybody,' he commented gloomily on his arrival in October 1553, 'nor do I intend to do anything more than go off tomorrow to my home, where I shall wait to see if something comes up in which I might possibly be asked to serve, God grant me strength and money to be able to do my part.'[72] He had the satisfaction, at least, of being received by the prince. 'I went to Aranjuez and met His Highness, he was very generous and treated me well, I was there only a day, His Highness told me that when the occasion to serve arose he would employ me.' He could hardly have expected much more from the prince than thanks, for his services had been principally to the emperor. And Alba did not fail to make the point clearly to Charles. 'I have served Your Majesty till the present,' he wrote a few months later, 'with my labours and my person and my patrimony, and of all these it is my patrimony that has suffered and diminished since I began to serve you. I have spent it all serving Your Majesty, and now I beg you to help me continue working as I have done for twenty years.'

The debts run up by his travels and his service to the emperor made it imperative for him to go home and see how his affairs were doing. After the interview with the prince he went off to his estates. 'I saw today that my house and patrimony are in such a state that, had I not seen it this winter with my own eyes, everything was heading for a crash from which it would have been impossible to recover either in my lifetime or that of my son. Now that I am here I have begun to meet with some of the agents and give them instructions for the future, and in view of this I have to request Your Majesty for a licence, which is the first time that I have asked for it since I entered your service. Twenty years of service to Your Majesty should count for something.' The 'licence', which began to be employed in this period by many great nobles, allowed them to pay off their debts on a long-term basis. At Alba de Tormes the duke was once more among his own. 'When I came home I found my wife and children in good health, I cannot describe to you my pleasure at seeing them again. Later I plan to go and spend the winter in Extremadura.'[73]

Alba's habit, as shown in 1552 and now in 1553, of retiring to his estates when he felt that he was not getting his own way, reveals an aspect of his character that marked him all his life. Profoundly introspective and passionately attached to his own kith and kin, he brusquely excluded from his environment anything and anyone that threatened his interests. In social terms, this attitude took on the aspect of arrogance. In personal terms it really signified a deep feeling of insecurity and loneliness that cut him off from intimate contact with others. It may have been this aspect, rather than the difference in age, that made it difficult for the prince and the duke to establish a good working relationship. By contrast, the prince continued to favour and develop his attachment to Ruy Gómez, whose position became stronger when in 1553 Philip negotiated his marriage with the young daughter of the Mendoza clan, Anna de Mendoza (who later as princess of Eboli was to play a well-known role in the political intrigues of the time through her friendship with the king's secretary Antonio Pérez).[74]

No sooner had he begun to immerse himself in the business of his estates than affairs of state called Alba out of his self-imposed retirement. In July 1553 the young Edward VI of England died. The succession to the still largely Catholic country fell to his elder sister, the unswervingly Catholic princess Mary. It was a heaven-sent opportunity to create an Anglo-Imperial alliance against France. Charles had himself been briefly betrothed many years before to Mary, and he now proposed that she marry Philip, who agreed obediently though reluctantly. Like the other great nobles, Alba was expected to accompany the prince to the wedding that would be celebrated in England. As he would do throughout his life, he put his obligations before his interests. The duchess was apparently in no condition to travel, and for himself he doubted whether he had the money to pay for the journey. But there could be no doubt of his decision. 'I shall accompany His Highness. I have now done this journey from Spain there and back eighteen times, and my profit from all this has been to have to sell 20,000 ducats from the income of my entail. I have said it so many times that I cannot any more, and I shall just have to keep quiet from now on.'[75]

The immense royal expedition sailed from La Coruña in July 1554, having left Philip's sister Juana as regent in Spain.[76] The fleet consisted of seventy large vessels and several lesser ships, bearing the leading lords and ladies of Castile, together with four thousand troops. An escort of thirty armed ships brought up the rear. It was an uncomfortable voyage in choppy seas, and when the Spaniards reached the port of Southampton seven days later they were greeted by typical English weather, wind and pouring rain that did not stop for several days. Philip thought better of disembarking his whole retinue at once, and went ashore accompanied by only nine nobles, among them Alba and the counts of Egmont and Hornes. The royal wedding took place, with appropriate splendour, in Winchester cathedral on 25 July, feast-day of St James, patron of Spain. It occasioned some bad feeling among the Spanish nobles (and their wives), most of who were not permitted to enter the cathedral because of the lack of space. Only fifteen Spanish grandees were allowed to go in, among them Alba. Decisions were also made to limit the number of Spanish who could accompany Philip, to avoid giving the impression that the king was a foreigner. The celebrations marked a high point in the relations between England and Spain, and most of the Spanish nobles took the opportunity to visit the tourist sites that Alba knew very well from thirty years before. But there were also tensions that did not serve to improve understanding between Spaniards and English.

In terms of government, the new co-ruler of England studiously avoided any interference in English affairs, in order not to stir up the delicate political and religious situation there. Alba also played an uncomfortably passive role, taking no part in English politics and, at the same time, being poorly informed about what was happening in Spain. He wrote from Richmond in August that 'I am so out of touch with everything that if matters are not placed directly in my hand I have no way of guessing what goes on'.[77] Though he was at Philip's side he had little voice in the way the prince–king chose to act in matters concerning England. Just over a year later, in August 1555 and accompanied by most of his immediate entourage, Philip crossed over the Channel to the Netherlands to have talks with the emperor and assist at Charles's planned abdication. Alba was not with him. The duke had already left on a vital mission to the Mediterranean. During his absence he was able to keep in touch with the court concerning the major events that took place in Brussels in October 1555, when the emperor divested himself of the rule of all his territories save the Empire, leaving Spain, the Netherlands and the Indies in the hands of his son. The decisions were formalised in the course of 1556. From this date Alba's master was no longer the emperor but the new king of Spain, Philip II. The change had for the moment little practical influence on Alba's duties in matters of war, but it began a new phase in his career, when he would have to struggle constantly to maintain his position in Spanish politics.

Continuing French ambitions in Italy threatened the Spanish situation there. Matters were made worse by an anti-Spanish revolt in the city of Siena that was not subdued until April 1555. The turn of events in Italy was difficult to manage from Germany, where Charles was, or from England, where Philip was trying to establish himself. The obvious solution was to send Alba. Months later, the duke was to complain that the decision to send him had been a plot contrived by his enemies, who wanted to remove him from Philip's side. At the time, however, he not only appreciated the importance of the commission – made out in April 1555 – appointing him captain general in Italy, governor of Milan and viceroy of Naples, but sought and welcomed it, for through it he could protect his family interests in Italy. The Venetian ambassador in London commented that Alba's commission gave him 'authority such as perhaps at no time was ever heard to have been vested in any minister or prince, having been given full and absolute power as if he were the king in person'. And, he added, 'he has already commenced exercising his authority, having appointed his eldest son Don Fadrique general of the Spanish troops in Lombardy, to start him with repute in the military profession'.[78] Fadrique's appointment was, however, controversial, and was to be only the beginning of the long saga that would link the destinies of father and son.

The entire Toledo family packed their bags and prepared to leave London. 'The Spaniards who accompany the duchess are about 300, on horseback', the Venetian ambassador reported. 'Two of his Excellency's sons departed subsequently, and tomorrow will be followed by García de Toledo and Juan de Figueroa, his Excellency's near relations.' From Dover on 20 April Alba informed Philip that 'I am embarking today. The duchess is with me, every day she is in worse health, I am afraid of taking her to sea but in order not to delay any more we decided to cross, because she does not wish in any circumstances to be separated from me.' Four days later he was in Brussels, from which he told the prince that 'I arrived here on Wednesday 24 at night and the morning after I went to kiss His Majesty's hand, I found him fatter than I left him two years ago ... Yesterday I was with His Majesty, in the two hours that we talked we spoke only of matters in England.'[79]

From across the Channel the duke was able to contemplate in clearer perspective the state of affairs in the country he had just left (and to which he would never return). The talks between the emperor and his general over English affairs give us our first clear insight into what Alba thought about the exercise of power. As we have seen, he had been impatient with the restrictions on royal power in Navarre and in Catalonia. In England he had for months suffered in silence the wholly passive role that Philip had chosen to accept. Now, having spoken to Charles, he felt that this would not do. 'For heaven's sake,' he now urged Philip at the end of April, 'your Majesty should aim to be lord of that kingdom, the most absolute lord that ever was, and nothing is wanting in order to achieve it except the desire to show them that you are so, and that it is inevitable, because that is what everybody wishes outside that small handful of wretches.' The words seem to suggest that he was demanding more political power for the crown in respect of state bodies such as the council or Parliament. The idea would not have been wholly alien to Philip's wishes, yet it also went clearly against the king's cautious policy in those months and there was no chance that the advice would be accepted. It is also possible that the duke, as a general, was thinking simply about the power to take more initiatives within the existing set of rules. He returned to the theme six months later, this time in a letter from Italy: 'about England, Your Majesty for the love of God should aim to be absolute lord of that kingdom and govern it at your feet'.[80] Alba had little interest in political theory nor did he ever debate it, so that it is difficult to imagine what the word 'absolute' signified for him. Judging simply from his impatience with established institutions in the provinces of Spain and his position in the Castilian Cortes of 1538, it is likely that what interested him was the capacity of the crown to decide without unnecessary concern for customary practice. Someone must command, and command firmly. He commented to Ruy Gómez at the end of 1555, referring to the duchy of Milan: 'as for the government of the duchy, a stick is enough'.[81] The tone was that of a military man who believed in a strong hand, but in political terms it was undoubtedly also authoritarian or 'absolutist'. And Alba was perfectly serious about his approach. In January 1556 he sent the king a detailed proposal for changing the constitution of Milan.[82] His view was that the nobles had usurped the powers of the prince, and the only way to eliminate corruption was by clipping their privileges.

Alba played a fundamental role both as general and as head of the group of nobles and officials who reflected his political interests. But he was also one of the great constructors of the empire inherited by Philip II. As member of the council of State, general and viceroy, he travelled to every corner of the territories ruled over by the Habsburg dynasty: he was at ease equally in Vienna, Brussels, London, Rome, Naples and Madrid, and his adequate command of French and Italian, together with an elementary knowledge of German, enabled him to speak on equal terms with leaders of every nation. Travelling between his assignments, he became the lynch pin for major decisions affecting the functioning of the monarchy, a sort of imperial executive with responsibilities in all matters concerning politics, war and finance.

On the eve of his historic mission to Italy, Alba was typically pessimistic. He wrote in May 1555 from Brussels to the financial officials in Valladolid asking them to supply money speedily 'and get me out of this devil of Italy with honour after these few days that I have to spend there, and they will be as few as I can manage'.[83] It did not prove so easy to obtain funds from Spain, for those in charge of the treasury were by no means Alba's friends, and did not intend to pave the way to his success. 'For the campaign in Milan and Piedmont,' he informed the fleet commander in the Mediterranean, Bernardino de Mendoza, 'we need to have a good supply of gunpowder, cannonballs and saltpetre; when you reach Naples in the galleys you will need to send me five hundred hundredweight of gunpowder.' In the same month, still in Brussels, he assured Charles V, who was in Vienna, that troop recruitment for Italy was going well: 'speaking of the Spanish troops, I have no doubt that Germans will be sufficient for now and will be very good. When I arrive in Italy I shall do what seems necessary, and shall try to raise troops from the appropriate nations and in the number required.'[84]

He took the route that was now familiar to him, through the south of Germany and Austria, across the mountains into Italy. There was no hurry, because the cash for the army had yet to be made available. Moreover, gout also slowed him down. From Innsbruck he informed Charles early in June that 'the pain that I had in my hip in London has struck me again, if I walk for one day it leaves me unable to walk a step for three whole days. I am pursuing my route very slowly to Milan, in so far as I can with the poor health in which the pain leaves me.' At the same time he complained bitterly to Mendoza that he had been promised that the money would reach him two days after leaving Brussels; 'seventeen days have gone by and I have not received a single word about it. I can see that I dare not arrive in Italy for fear of provoking despair in people who see me coming without money.' When he eventually reached the city of Milan on 12 June he found that everyone was waiting for him as if he were coming with bags of gold. It was during this journey that Alba first became aware of the impediments being put in his way by his former collaborator, the royal secretary Francisco de Eraso, who was now closely connected to Ruy Gómez. He warned Philip of 'those in charge of the finances who do greater harm to your cause than the king of France with all his forces can do'.[85] Once in the duchy, he tried to organise things his way. 'I have been very well received by all the authorities,' he wrote to Cardinal Granvelle in June, 'but my life here is something nobody else has ever experienced, from dawn when I get up to four in the night I move from my work only in order to eat.' Several months later the story was the same: 'out of twelve hours in the day I have just one free, for eating. I tell you that I am *muy mal, muy mal, muy mal.*'[86]

Milan was Spain's principal military base and recruitment centre, and Alba found that all the soldiers' wages were in arrears. It would have been impossible to begin a new military campaign with an unpaid army. As ever, Alba rose to the challenge. He assured the troops that he would do everything in his power to help them. The duke always spoke to his men as though they were his equals. 'Honourable sirs' was his form of address to the noble captains of the tercios, and the ordinary men were always 'noble sirs'. His discourse was directed mainly to the latter: he praised their valour and achievement and promised that they would receive their pay in full: 'I promise you this and give my word I shall carry out without fail what your good service deserves.' He hoped they would 'think of me as your friend, which I am; and since I ask this favour of you, gentlemen, and it is the first time I do so, I am confident that you will do it for me and help me in this task in which I have to care for the interests of each of you.'[87] In order to obtain the money, however, Alba had to maintain good relations with all the officials in Spain and England who ran affairs, as well as with all the Italian nobles and financiers who might make his operation possible. Never before in Spain's history had a general held so much responsibility. And the duke carried out his task remarkably well. Despite the rivalry with Ruy Gómez, he made sure to remain on good terms with him in order to obtain his help. From Brussels early in 1555 he wrote to Gómez, who was then in London, 'to you alone I wish to give satisfaction and dare to bare my wounds, to His Majesty I shall not say a word'. Later, in August, when he was already on the march, he found time to add a personal note in an official letter to Gómez, who as we have seen had recently married: 'Tell me how you are getting on at home with your father-in-law, his income and his expenses, really I don't know how you manage to live.'[88]

The immediate threat in Milan came from the French, who had seized territory on the Piedmont border. When he was general in the Holy Roman Empire, Alba had shared command with other captains, not least with the emperor. By contrast in Italy he enjoyed sole and complete power. All decisions were his, and he alone was responsible for them. It was in Italy that he earned the reputation for the ruthlessness that later struck terror in his enemies. In every case, the 'ruthlessness' seems to have been a consequence less of deliberate brutality than of a merciless observance of the rules of war. Those, for instance, who did not respond to an offer of mercy if they surrendered, could not afterwards appeal to the offer if they continued to resist and provoked more casualties. His own soldiers would have protested at such a cynical sacrifice of their lives. In one fortress, for example, he called on the French garrison to surrender with a guarantee of their lives. They refused but had to surrender anyway when captured. 'I have given orders to hang all of them,' the duke reported.[89] 'In the Siena business,' Alba wrote to Ruy Gómez, 'I feel that I have done good service to our master [Philip] in resolving for him such a ruinous matter. Thank God, for it has given me more headaches and more sleepless nights than I could make up in ten years.'[90] His report to Antonio de Toledo at the beginning of August was a little more frank about how he was dealing with the difficulties posed by the campaign. 'Now I am entering territory that it is vital for us to control; it is well fortified and of difficult access and full of the best soldiers that they [the French and their allies] have. I have begun to wage war as it should be waged, because I hang them and send the survivors to the galleys in dozens, I cannot do this with the infantry soldiers and these are executed. The army that I am leading is the same that has been in the duchy for a long time, I have augmented it with 1,500 Spaniards and with it I keep the whole country in awe.'[91]

The urgent problem at the end of 1555 and early in 1556 was money. 'It is three months since I have heard from His Majesty,' he wrote to Ruy Gómez from Portofino, 'and I go about begging for news of what is happening at His Majesty's court. The matter of money is in such straits that I do not know what can be done this summer if His Majesty does not send to Spain at once for some supply.' The soldiers were encouraged to pillage; 'if they do not do so,' Alba informed Fadrique, 'it is not possible to maintain the Spanish soldiers here, and with it they can live and keep themselves occupied while they wait for their wages'.[92] It was not simply a question of paying them, for he himself had not been paid for years. He reflected to Antonio de Toledo that 'I have served the king [Philip II] for nine years and in that time I swear to God that I have spent over 600,000 ducats. In all that time he has not given me the equivalent of ten pennies nor a plot of land, but only two horses and 25,000 crowns to face expenses in England . . . Believe me, the way I have to live here is shameful, because I eat as a borrower, drink as a borrower and I imagine that I sleep as a borrower also; this cannot go on. In thirty years he [the king] and his father have given me only two knighthoods [*encomiendas*] for my sons and 25,000 crowns in cash.'[93] This was, he felt, negligible compensation for a lifetime of service.

'When I was in Livorno,' he wrote to Philip, 'I made two contracts with Niccolò di Grimaldo for 110,000 escudos; I used 70,000 of it to pay off the wages owing to the men in the army of Tuscany and Orvieto up to the end of 1555, and sent the remaining 40,000 to Milan to pay the Germans.'[94] Between supervision of recruitment, wages and supplies, and the very many other matters requiring his attention, Alba made sure that the various realms of the monarchy contributed together to the common effort. The task had never been done adequately before, and now called for serious attention. Historians have too easily assumed that the duke had only to put himself at the head of the famous Spanish military machine for it to function smoothly. There was in reality very little machine, and it barely functioned. 'I arrived in Italy,' he wrote in 1556 to the regent of Spain, Philip's sister Juana, 'and found the army was due 1,200,000 escudos. What was supposed to come from Spain has never arrived, and I have had to wage war for a whole year with an army that is almost always mutinous and disobedient.' Nor was the shipment of troops to Italy any comfort. Vessels bringing tercios from Sardinia to Naples in February sank at sea, with the loss of one thousand men, a major disaster. At New Year in 1557 he had little reason to be satisfied with the new troops sent to him. 'The galleys have arrived with the Germans and the Spaniards, but they are all in such a condition that we cannot expect much from them. Over half the 2,300 Germans are sick, and two-thirds of the seven hundred Spaniards are moribund. I am here without men and without money.'[95]

During the year 1555, meanwhile, a further complication arose when the eighty-year-old cardinal Gian Pietro Caraffa was elected pope in May, taking the name of Paul IV. In order to strengthen the influence of his own family, the pope began a persecution of other Roman noble families, some of them – like the Colonna – allied to the emperor. His political actions and verbal outbursts were increasingly directed against the emperor and his allies. Henry II of France could not fail to be overjoyed, and in October 1555 he secured a formal alliance with the pope. Another war in Italy seemed inevitable. Alba made sure that Milan was secure before he undertook the next stage of his journey, to his viceroyalty in Naples. In advance he warned his lieutenant there, Bernardino de Mendoza, to have troops ready at the frontier with the papal states.

The journey to Naples augured well. Alba sailed with his ships from Portofino at the end of January 1556, stopping on the way at Livorno, and then at the coastal towns of Porto Ercole and Orvitello, which formed part of the coastal territory known as the Stato dei Presidii, where the garrisons were Spanish and maintained by the viceroy of Naples. He found all the troops in a mutinous state because they had not been paid. Eventually he arrived at Naples on 4 February and made a formal entry into the city five days later. The visit coincided with the carnival festivities. In good humour during the days of celebration, he dropped a cheerful comment into his letter that week to Philip: 'They tell me that Your Majesty goes to masked balls every night, it makes me laugh to think how Your Majesty will enjoy yourself and how Don Antonio [de Toledo] will restrain himself amid all the pleasures.'[96] For the next six months he was busy settling affairs in the always unsettled kingdom of Naples.

The possibility of conflict with the papacy was one of the most severe tests ever endured by Alba. It went against all his principles of unquestioning loyalty to authority and to the head of Christendom. His grandfather had been foremost among the Castilian grandees to complain to Charles V at the time of the Sack of Rome in 1527. Alba may have known of that situation; in any case, he was not anxious to become the scourge of the papacy. 'God is witness to what I feel about entering on this war.' At the same time he was heir to a long Spanish tradition that had felt it just to curtail the pretensions of the pope as secular prince. In April 1556 the pope declared the Colonna family to be rebels, and confiscated their estates. Alba felt it essential that Spain intervene to protect her friends, if not 'we shall lose respect among all our allies in Italy'.[97] In July 1556 Paul IV, whose hatred of the Habsburgs amounted to an obsession that verged on madness, went so far as to deprive Philip II of his title of king of Naples. It was a deliberate act of war, and Alba felt that he would not be the aggressor if he struck back. 'We have a right to defend ourselves. The purpose of war is quite simply self-defence, and we shall disarm as soon as His Holiness gives us assurances.'[98] The solution would be a quick, sharp campaign. In the first week of September 1556 he set out from the viceroyalty with an army of 12,000 men, among them Marcantonio Colonna (with whom, incidentally, he was never on good terms) and the princes who were in dispute with the pope. The citizens of Rome were terrified at the possibility of another sack of their city like that in 1527. Paul IV quickly suggested talks, and a truce was agreed, through the intervention of Alba's uncle Cardinal Juan de Toledo, in November.

It was only a subterfuge, for the pope very soon obtained help from France, whose troops under Duke Francis of Guise crossed into Italy in January 1557. Guise by-passed Milan, and after visiting the pope in Rome headed southwards. Paul IV's troops captured the cities of Tivoli and Ostia, and the French invaded Naples. Alba had faced Guise before, at the siege of Metz, and was clear in his mind about the strategy he would adopt. Quite simply, he intended to avoid an armed engagement, preferring to make the French troops, who were far from their supply bases, exhaust themselves. As a result of these tactics, which happened to work extremely well and were an application of the methods of the famous Roman commander Fabius Maximus, the duke earned a reputation in Italy for being a hesitant general. The French campaign quickly petered out, in part also because Henry II had problems defending the northern frontier of France as a result of the stunning disaster suffered by his army in July 1557 against Philip II's troops at St Quentin, and had to recall Guise. A year later the Flanders troops, under the command of the count of Egmont, won a further victory over the French at Gravelines.

The brief confrontation in Italy between the generals of France and Spain was opportunely noted down by Nostradamus in his famous *Centuries*, published that year. The author added a few imaginative flourishes:

Le grand Duc d'Albe se viendra rebeller,
A ses grans peres fera le tradiment:
Le grand de Guise le viendra debeller,
Captif mené & dressé monument.

(The great duke of Alba will rise in rebellion
and betray his grandfather;
the great Guise will war against him,
capture him and erect a monument.)[99]

Paul IV was left to sort out his terms with Alba's army. At the beginning of August 1557 the duke informed Princess Juana from his base in Atri that what has in substance happened in these parts since the 22 June until today, is that after occupying some territory of His Holiness near Ascoli we encountered the French cavalry and seven troops of Gascons; I had 1,000 Spanish musketeers, 1,000 Germans and 400 cavalry. We broke their ranks and pursued them two miles, they lost a banner and a great many dead and prisoners. Knowing that His Holiness had 3,000 Swiss I sent Marcantonio Colonia from this army, they arrived in such good time that three days ago they fought the 3,000 Swiss and 1,500 Italians and slaughtered or took prisoner the greater part of the soldiers, so that His Holiness is now left without any forces.[100]

Alba entered Rome at the head of his troops and immediately went to pay his respects to the pope, who formalised a peace agreement on 27 September 1557. Paul IV agreed to recognise Philip as the legitimate king of Naples; in return the duke presented the pope with the symbol of Spain's feudal obedience, a white horse from Naples. The king formally accepted the agreement five months later. It was the beginning of a long period of fairly successful collaboration between Rome and Spain. Alba had carried out all aspects of his mission with striking efficiency. The duke's campaign had been highly successful, but nevertheless some of the fruits of victory were soon snatched away.

In the months that he was toiling in Italy to protect the welfare of his royal master, historic decisions were being made in Spain, decisions not in Alba's interests. Though members of his family continued to occupy key posts in the administration of the new king, his own situation was being seriously threatened. He had suspected this would happen when he left the court in London and undertook the voyage to Italy. His position at the court in Brussels was not for the moment in doubt. But in Spain, where he had already experienced problems with the supply of money, the management of political matters was drifting out of his control. Early in 1556, the affairs of Italy that had formerly been the preserve of the council of State, were put into the hands of a separate secretary, Diego Vargas, a partisan of Francisco de Eraso and Ruy Gómez.[101] In July 1558 the business handled by Vargas was put into the care of a new council, called the council of Italy, which was to be presided over by Ruy Gómez's father-in-law, the duke of Francavilla. Meanwhile, in 1557 and 1558 as Alba withdrew from his duties in Italy the posts he had occupied were filled by nominees of Ruy Gómez. The new viceroy of Sicily was the duke of Medinaceli, who would return ten years later to play a part in another chapter of the Alba story. Alba continued to be the greatest noble of the crown, but the basis of his power in Italy was being seriously eroded by Ruy Gómez and his friends.

3   *The King's Counsellor, 1557–1566*

We have had long experience over many years of what fickle and bad friends the French are. Because of this my opinion is that in no way should Your Majesty decide to enter into any agreement with them.

To Philip II, Paris, June 1559

His work in Naples finished, Alba began the long journey back to Brussels. On 5 December 1557 he arrived in Genoa with the Mediterranean fleet, twenty-eight galleys carrying three thousand German soldiers. There were letters from king Philip awaiting him. His presence was needed at the peace negotiations with France. A fortnight later he set out for Milan, where he spent no more than one day. On 23 December he wrote to the regent, 'I am leaving tomorrow for the court to discuss with His Majesty some matters relating to his service'.[1] This time he took the quicker route to the north, through Piedmont and Franche-Comté, arriving in Brussels at the end of January 1558. His experience of the route would serve him well on the next occasion that he used it, nine years later.

When he returned to the court in Brussels late in January, Alba found a wholly new political scenario. After abdicating from all his territories save the Empire, Charles V had left for Spain in September 1556, leaving his son the new king of Spain, Philip II, in full control. There was an inevitable jostling for political power and advantage among the nobles who served the crown, though by no means the bitter struggle suggested by some writers.[2] Alba, for one, seems to have made the transition from Charles' regime to that of his son quite painlessly, since he was Spain's only general and therefore indispensable to both. Like all the others, he had been preparing for the inevitable change of regime. He was given a warm welcome by most of the courtiers, even those who did not agree with him. Only Ruy Gómez, who made the excuse of being indisposed, refused to move from his apartments to receive him. In the field in Italy Alba had enjoyed the liberty of being able to make his own decisions; back at the court he entered once again into the struggle for power.

As recently as October the Venetian ambassador Suriano was claiming that at Philip's court Ruy Gómez and his friends 'rule everything'. Alba soon found, for example, that others were interfering with the appointments he had made in Italy. Suriano reported that 'the duke considers himself aggrieved, and his adherents say that he is come to obtain the observance of his privileges, and if denied them he will resign and go to Spain'. The black-mail was the familiar one, and fortunately for Alba it continued to work. The grandees who opposed him, mainly Ruy Gómez, Juan Manrique and the duke of Feria, found it difficult to stand up to the general's aggressive tactics. Alba went around browbeating the courtiers. He had a long interview with Suriano, and gave him a new variation on his theme. He told the ambassador that he was now 'old', and that it was time for him to retire. He then 'began to talk about the affairs of the world and of the need which Christendom would have of a good peace'. Europe's principal field of conflict, the Italian peninsula, was now 'pacified', thanks to Alba's armies and his network of influence. The duke felt he could reap his rewards, retire, and go off to his estates. Suriano was too shrewd an observer to accept that this could be Alba's last game. He reported, on the contrary, that

> the king holds him in respect and so do the other lords of the council, so that everything depends on him. If he remains here he will be master of everything. King Philip's confessor has said that 'the duke of Alba is more than king, and chooses to do everything'. The duke's apartments are frequented by the whole court.[3]

Alba's position was so strong that rumours hinted at the king considering him as a possible governor of the Netherlands. The duke was said to be culti-vating his links with the Flemish nobles in order to back up such a move.[4] There is nothing inherently unlikely in this, for Alba had spent many years in the company of the nobles, had socialised with them and fought at their side. It is intriguing to imagine what the future history of the country would have been like if he had held the reins and not Margaret of Parma, Philip's half-sister who eventually took over as governor. In the end, there were other developments that required the duke's services. The end of the war with France was followed by peace negotiations, a long process made longer by the wish of Philip II to settle once and for all the many issues that had dragged the emperor and France into continuous wars. Talks between the plenipoten-tiaries were begun in October 1558 in an abbey near Cambrai, then moved early the following year to the village of Cateau-Cambrésis. On Philip's side the negotiators were the prince of Orange, the duke of Alba, the bishop of Arras (Antoine Perrenot, later Cardinal Granvelle), Ruy Gómez and Viglius, president of the Council of State in Brussels.

The immense range of issues discussed at the talks affected the interests of every nation in western Europe, and historians have never doubted the transcendent nature of the peace agreement. Alba was a central figure in the negotiations. 'The conference here continues with great diligence,' the Venetian ambassador Tiepolo wrote from Cateau-Cambrésis in February 1559, 'for every day they remain at least three hours together. This morning the duke of Alba and the others went into the town to see the English ambassadors.' Ten days later there was a hitch. 'As the duke of Alba is seriously ill the renewal of the conference will be postponed.'[5] Alba informed Gonzalo Pérez that 'since yesterday afternoon I have had a high fever and last night I was gripped by shivering which lasted three hours, I hope that it is nothing'. The treaty and its aftermath occupied Alba during the entire first half of the year. In a private conversation with Tiepolo, Alba told him 'at great length that King Philip was content with his own and did not desire the possessions of others, and that just as he well knew how to wage war, so did he desire peace above all'.

The treaties that constituted the peace of Cateau-Cambrésis were signed by all parties on 3 April 1559. The agreement was greeted with celebrations, and there was an undoubted will to make it work. In the light of the battle at St Quentin as well as France's withdrawal from Italy, Spain was regarded as a victor. Many contemporaries took this view and subsequent historians have agreed with them. Though Philip II appeared to have the upper hand, he had no ambitions other than to achieve peace for his territories. Both sides made significant concessions, yet there were also gains. Most notably, France and Spain were confirmed as the major powers of Europe. Their friendship was confirmed by the proposal for a dynastic marriage between the ruling families. As sureties (or 'hostages') for agreement to the terms of the treaty, the French required the presence in Paris of the leading negotiators. In this way Alba found himself lodged at the French court together with the prince of Orange and the count of Egmont. The duke took the opportunity of his presence in Paris to talk frankly with French nobles about the political situation. The constable of France expressed the view that the new beliefs emanating from Geneva were a menace to stability in Scotland and in France, and suggested a working alliance between Philip II and French Catholics against heresy. Alba told Philip II that he saw no benefit in such an alliance.[6] The mere fact that the duke had spoken to the constable gave rise to hostile interpretations. The prince of Orange, who was sympathetic to the Protestants and not a party to the conversations, commented later to Cardinal Granvelle that he believed that Alba had in reality agreed on the alliance. The intention, Orange alleged, was to establish a Spanish-style Inquisition in France. Though the accusation was untrue, it reflected a growing tension over religious matters.

Perhaps the most significant corollary of the peace was the marriage arranged between the king of Spain and Elisabeth, daughter of Henry II and Catherine de' Medici. As part of the celebrations prior to the wedding, a grand tournament was held in Paris on 30 June, but the day ended tragically. Henry II insisted on taking part in one of the jousts, when the lance of his opponent, a captain of the Scottish guard, broke through his visor and entered his eye. The king was taken out, unconscious and gravely wounded. That afternoon Alba, Orange and two French nobles were allowed in to see him. A few days later Henry recovered consciousness and ordered the wedding to go ahead. The glittering ceremony, in which Alba stood in for Philip II, was held in the cathedral of Notre Dame on 9 July 1559. The king died the following day. Alba stayed to take part in the funeral at St Denis on 13 August, then prepared to pack his bags. 'The duke of Alba with all his attendants,' a diplomat reported, 'departed hence on the 17th on his way through France to Spain.' Exactly a week later, Philip II also left the Netherlands in a small fleet that headed back home. The king had been absent from Spain for over five long and eventful years.

The return to his homeland did not produce the results that Alba expected. As high steward he controlled the king's household as well as the public functions of the court. Exactly twenty years Philip's senior, he had aided and advised him at every step of his political career. As head of the powerful noble house of Toledo and Europe's foremost soldier, Alba had every reason to hope that his pre-eminence and his services would, on the king's return, guarantee him the leading place in the government.[7] This did not happen, for as we have seen in Spain itself there were forces undermining his position. Philip had a profound respect for the duke, but little in common with him in personality or in outlook, and always disliked being overawed by him. The duke's absence in Italy, moreover, had given his opponents and particularly Ruy Gómez a couple of years during which they were able to move into key posts in the Spanish administration. A serving soldier, no matter how eminent, could easily be outmanoeuvred by politicians.

Using the excuse of an attack of gout that affected him upon his arrival in Spain, the duke did not visit the royal court in Toledo until the first week of January 1560. He could not put off his absence much longer because he was required at the ceremonies that led up to the wedding of the king to Elisabeth of Valois. The ceremonial was performed in the palace of the duke del Infantado at Guadalajara, after which the royal couple moved to Toledo to reside in the Alcázar. No sooner did Alba return to the active life of the court than he realised that his long absence on the king's business had disadvantaged him in the struggle for positions of influence in Castile. He reacted angrily. 'The duke,' Tiepolo reported, 'gave it clearly to be understood that he would not go to the court if Ruy Gómez was there, and this has been the chief cause of Alba's absence until now. The king knows that he has too much need of Alba's counsel and authority.'[8] As we have seen from previous occasions, whenever he felt slighted or found that the court was not in his control, the duke would retire to his country estates to sulk. This did not offend Philip, who employed members of Alba's grouping equally with those attached to Ruy Gómez.

The king was also quite aware of the rivalries and interests involved. An incident at court in June 1560 occurred in his very presence. He was immersed in a consultation with Francisco de Eraso. The secretary, to ensure privacy, locked the door from the inside and left the key in it. Later, Alba turned up to see the king. Finding the door shut, he tried to use the key which gave him, as high steward, right of access throughout the palace. When it would not enter, he banged on the door. The king and Eraso went on with their business. Alba was left to wait outside for an hour, fuming among the other courtiers, until Eraso came out. 'Even the doors!' Alba complained angrily.[9] The king came out and tried to reason with him. Tiepolo reported that Alba 'prayed his Majesty to grant him leave to go home. The king did all he could to appease the duke, but in the end said that he would grant it to him for a few days'. The Venetian judged perceptively that 'because Alba exceeds all the other ministers in authority, so he wishes everything to depend upon himself alone, nor can he suffer others to have power equal to his'.[10] The duke retired to his estates as he had threatened. The incident seemed to demonstrate that Philip was relying more on the advice of the Ruy Gómez group, and Alba complained that decisions he had suggested in council were undone the following day when Eraso drew up the documents. Tensions in the royal council were constant throughout 1560, as everyone at court was well aware. 'I have often found him on his bed,' the French ambassador L'Aubespine reported of Alba that September, 'terribly depressed and lamenting the ill fortune of those who are in public affairs.'[11]

Over the next few years the rivalry of interests between the Alba and the Eboli groupings dominated most aspects of court politics. But the king, following his father's practice, allowed differences of opinion and policy to flourish. He was willing to learn from all sides.[12] Unpleasant incidents might occur, but he pretended not to notice. His secretary Gonzalo Pérez admired his ability to govern with a council where everyone was at each other's throat. 'To tell the truth,' he commented soon after the return to Toledo, 'I don't know how he was able to bring together sixteen councillors so different in character and in other respects, but I believe that His Majesty will surmount this and will know what to do.'[13] In the end the king relied on himself to be able to keep the balance between conflicting groups. Since it was the rule in government at that time for only the king to make decisions, differing opinions and advice could help rather than hinder efficiency.

The faction fighting in Spain was no petty matter, for it had repercussions on other areas of the monarchy. The struggle for influence in Italy was in some measure waged within the king's councils, where Ruy Gómez had been manœuvring himself into a position of advantage. The same applied to the Netherlands, where after Philip II's departure the chief minister was Cardinal Granvelle, a friend of Alba. The elite groupings of the period were bound together first by family ties and then by ties of loyalty to great houses. But, above all, they were proud of their service to the crown. Loyalty to the king usually overrode rivalries. Alba's brother-in-law Antonio de Toledo, Prior of León, was the duke's closest ally, yet also continued to be a leading official of the government in the years when the duke's star had waned. This fluidity blurred many of the differences between factions such as those of Eboli and Alba. They might in practice fight over every conceivable matter.[14] But it was more difficult to identify radical disagreement over principles.[15]

Alba's bad temper and arrogance were sometimes effective, for in practical terms no essential business could be conducted without him. When he went off to his estates after the incident of the doors, court business came (according to the Venetian ambassador) to a standstill. He remained sulking for two months like a spoilt child. When he came back, in October 1560, the ambassador could confirm that he 'occupies the chief place at this court'. During the weeks that he was away on his estate at Alba de Tormes, he took care to keep in close touch with the king. It is possible that his periodic absences from court helped, ironically, to give his views greater weight, for Philip felt more at ease reading advice than listening to it. And Alba gave a lot of written advice. In August he sent a long opinion of sixteen folios on the situation in northern Europe, and what the king should do about it. 'Your Majesty,' he said, 'is charged with the most onerous and difficult job that one can imagine.' From his personal experience he could see that the king could do nothing unless he maintained a military presence. 'Your Majesty must retain the Spanish infantry in Flanders [that is, stop the withdrawal demanded by the States General] and send them adequate money, and you should appoint a person of authority from Flanders to speak with the States and tranquillise them.'[16] The man he recommended for this task was the count of Hornes. In view of later developments, it was an interesting choice. At the same time, Alba wrote, the Spanish military presence in Italy must be reinforced. The Mediterranean, as it turned out, was the primary area of concern for the government in those months.

In June 1559, when he was still in Brussels, Philip had given his approval to a Spanish-Italian expeditionary force designed to capture Tripoli.[17] The expedition was the idea of the duke of Medinaceli, viceroy of Sicily, and Jean de La Valette, grand master of the Knights of Malta. Long delays transpired before the huge force finally set out from Syracuse in early December. Bad weather compelled them to shelter in Malta till late February 1560. They set out again in March and occupied the island of Djerba. The delay allowed the Turks in Istanbul to put together a relief fleet. The Christian ships, commanded by Admiral Gian Andrea Doria, who had just succeeded his uncle as head of Spain's Mediterranean fleet, were caught by the Turks in May on Djerba and half the fleet was sunk. The soldiers, led by their officers, fled in panic, while Doria and Medinaceli managed to escape. What was left of the force was besieged by the Turkish fleet. Over ten thousand men eventually surrendered in July, and were led in triumph a few days later through the streets of Istanbul.

The disaster stunned the court and all Europe. Spain had never suffered a military reverse of these dimensions in its entire history. On 2 June the Venetian ambassador reported that 'the king has remained almost the whole of the day in consultation with the duke of Alba, Juan Manrique, Antonio de Toledo, and Gutierre López de Padilla'.[18] In the wake of Djerba, the duke began to revise the situation of Spain's forces in the Mediterranean. In April 1561 he was in Cartagena, looking over the naval defences of the peninsula. His primary concern was to strengthen the forts and garrisons along the coast.[19] Other councillors, and the king himself, were more concerned about Spain's obvious weakness at sea, and they supported a massive new programme of shipbuilding in the yards available at Barcelona and Naples. In the midst of this military crisis the king suffered a domestic crisis in the spring of 1562 when his heir Don Carlos suffered an accident and fell into a coma. Alba was at hand to accompany the king when he dashed to his son's bedside in the town of Alcalá. Following a suggestion made by the duke,[20] the embalmed body of a local saint, the Franciscan Diego of Alcalá, was brought in from a local convent and the prince was made to touch it. Shortly after, he began to recover. In gratitude for the recovery, Philip subsequently obtained from the pope the official canonisation of Diego of Alcalá.

Though the Mediterranean remained the centre of attention in the Council of War, there were disquieting developments in the north of Europe. Throughout the winter of 1561–2 there were small, bloody, conflicts between Catholic and Protestant groups all over France. In March 1562 the killing of a group of Protestants at Vassy by the duke of Guise's men, was denounced as a 'massacre'. Religious fury spilled over into civil war. Instability in France would certainly affect the neighbouring Netherlands, and might touch Spain itself. To help the French government out of its difficulties, Philip sent some military support from Flanders to Queen Catherine de' Medici. In October Alba informed the French ambassador in Madrid, Saint-Sulpice, that military help would continue provided no further religious toleration of Protestants was permitted, since this might destabilise the Netherlands. 'It would almost be better,' Alba told him, in one of those pithy phrases that he habitually used, 'for the kingdom of France to destroy itself than to allow such a breach in questions of religion.'[21] Other Spanish ministers gave the ambassador the clear impression that they were quite happy to see a France weakened by dissension.[22]

At the same time the Netherlands also began to cause serious concern. The country was Spain's economic lifeline, as Philip and his ministers were well aware. Three-fourths of Spain's chief export, wool, went there to be marketed. Over four-fifths of the ships plying the trade route between the north and the peninsula were from the Netherlands. The loans which had helped to finance the late emperor's wars were largely negotiated there. This fortunate inheritance could be destabilised by dissension, civil and religious, or by the greed of neighbouring states. Cardinal Granvelle, whose advice weighed most with Margaret of Parma, favoured a firm hand against religious and political opposition. The chief nobles, however, saw Granvelle as the symbol of what they most opposed. Finally, in March 1563, three leading nobles – Orange, Lamoral of Egmont and Philippe de Montmorency, count of Hornes – sent an ultimatum to Philip. Granvelle, they said, must resign. They were leaving the Council of State until he did so. The crisis continued into the summer months, with Margaret determined to support the cardinal, and Philip trying vainly to placate the angry nobles from Spain.

Alba was directly involved in the problem. The anti-Granvelle campaign was backed in Madrid by the royal secretary Eraso, who as we have seen was allied to Ruy Gómez, while Granvelle was allied to Alba. Egmont and Orange looked to Ruy Gómez and Eraso for support; Granvelle looked to Alba. The split of opinion among his advisers was undoubtedly useful to Philip II, for it offered him a choice of different options to take. In the autumn of 1563 he was in the Crown of Aragon, presiding over the Cortes of those realms which were meeting in Monzón. In October 1563 Margaret of Parma's secretary arrived with a special message. She had finally given in to the pressure in Brussels, and now requested Philip's permission to sack Granvelle. There was no lack of voices to support the move. Eboli and Eraso were accompanying Philip, and they were in favour. Granvelle's most direct support, however, was not present, for Alba was away attending to urgent family business at his estates in Andalucía. Writing to García de Toledo from Madrid in August, the duke noted: 'the king will be at Monzón by the 3rd or 4th of next month. I have his permission to go and visit Huéscar, it is very important for me to go and see the vassals whom I have there.'[23] He was in Huéscar from the end of September, but kept in close touch with the king about what was happening, and was particularly attentive to Granvelle's situation.

'I arrived here on Sunday 12 September,' the king wrote from Monzón to the duke, whose advice he continued to require even when they were temporarily separated.[24] Alba and his wife had their noses buried in the business of their estates in Huéscar, which the family did not often visit because of its distance from their principal seat. The town, about ninety miles north of Granada, was almost wholly Morisco in population. Not surprisingly the duke felt uneasy in the different cultural environment. Huéscar, he wrote, is 'a place of mine that I am not sure is in this world'.[25] During his stay he obtained from the king the special favour of converting the estates into a dukedom, whose title was reserved exclusively for the prospective heir to the title of Alba. In this case the title was meant as a wedding gift to his son Fadrique, who in January 1562 had married María Pimentel, daughter of the count of Benavente. When he left Andalucía a few months later, in March 1564, Alba explained to his relative Cardinal Francisco Pacheco, who at that time was in charge of Spanish affairs in Rome: 'I have stopped in Huéscar longer than I intended, because I found many matters in the town requiring attention and others as concealed as though they were in Peru. They are the best vassals in the world and live in the finest and most temperate lands that I have seen in my life, but there are a number of restless scoundrels who go round causing trouble among the people. I have done what I could to restore good order, and am heading for Coria to leave the duchess at home.'[26]

As the marriage of Fadrique showed, the duke was very busy securing the foundations of his family's power in Spain. During the year 1564 he was also negotiating the marriage of his youngest son Diego, for whom the contract was drawn up in Pamplona in September. In February 1565 Diego was finally married in Lerín, Navarre, to Brianda Beaumont, one of the two identical twin daughters of the count of Lerín. She reunited in herself some of the highest titles of her kingdom, being not only countess of Lerín but also constable and hereditary chancellor of Navarre. Their first son was born in Lerín in November 1568. It turned out to be a significant marriage, for the son by Brianda eventually succeeded (in 1585) to the dukedom of Alba when the fifth duke, Fadrique, failed to produce an heir.

During the months that the duke was away on his estates, the king sought Alba's views on the situation in the Netherlands. In response to the information that Egmont, Hornes and Orange were pressing to have Cardinal Granvelle removed, Alba's reply was typically aggressive. 'Every time I see letters from those gentlemen in Flanders,' he fumed, 'I get so enraged that if I did not try to control myself Your Majesty would take me for a madman.'[27]

On no account, he advised, should Granvelle be removed. The duke did not hold back. He forecast that there would be serious troubles in Flanders, provoked by those in control in France: 'affairs on all sides are in a terrible state and the solutions are inadequate. I believe that the French want to stir up trouble for Your Majesty in the territories of Flanders.' He opposed any proposal for a meeting between Philip and the queen mother of France, because she was not to be trusted and would use a meeting only to bolster her own authority. He also opposed the idea of a visit to Spain by the count of Egmont. Reverting to his standard turn of phrase, he called for the heads of the three Flemish nobles to be cut off. In the weeks that followed he continued to oppose the withdrawal of Granvelle. When he did not have his secretary available, Alba wrote the letters himself. The king, in return, also answered in his own hand. It was a vigorous correspondence, but in the end availed little. The king did not accept Alba's advice, opting instead for a strategic withdrawal of the cardinal from his post in Brussels. In 1564 Granvelle gave out as an excuse that he had to visit his ailing mother, and left for his residence at Besançon. In his retirement, as he tended to his gardens and wandered round his magnificent library, the cardinal could ponder that his friendship with the duke of Alba had not been of very much use.

The dismissal of Granvelle did not necessarily indicate a victory of the Eboli grouping at Philip II's court, for the king was always careful to weigh advice before he made decisions. At about the same time that he removed Granvelle, he also promoted Granvelle's brother Chantonnay to be his ambassador at the court of the emperor, and Alba's friend the Basque Francés de Álava to be ambassador at the court of the king of France. The latter appointment was particularly important, not only for Spain but also for Alba, with whom the new ambassador maintained a continuous and close correspondence for the next eight years. The death of Catherine de' Medici's husband Henry II had produced extreme instability in Spain's most powerful neighbour and traditional enemy, France. The Protestants (Calvinist in belief, and known in France as 'Huguenots') were daily increasing in number. Their strength came in great measure from the support given by members of the aristocracy, notably the Bourbon family. After Henry's death the noble factions began to jostle each other for control of the monarchy. The young king Francis II reigned for barely a year, dying in 1560. His successor and brother Charles IX was only ten when he came to the throne. As queen mother, Catherine effectively controlled the government. But dynastic rivalry among the noble families, added to the passion excited by religion, was an explosive mixture that drew France into decades of civil war and threatened to affect Spain's interests directly.

Philip II wanted to persuade France to adopt a firm policy against the Huguenot leaders. He was drawing on his direct experience of what had happened in Germany when his father was unable to control the Lutheran princes. Catherine on her side wanted Spain's public support for her dynasty, menaced by conflicting noble interests. Both were aware of the very great gap that separated them. The French were actively in alliance with the Turks, and had ambitions in America; Spain was committed to obstruct the French in both these areas. In 1564–5 the queen mother made an unprecedented tour of the nation – it lasted nearly two years – with the intention of securing the loyalty of the provinces to Charles IX. The venue eventually selected for a meeting with the Spaniards was Bayonne, close to Spain's frontier. Catherine hoped to obtain a closer dynastic alliance with the Habsburgs through a marriage of her daughter Marguerite with Philip's son Carlos, as well as one between Charles IX and the daughter of the emperor.

While events in France were calling for more attention on the part of Spain, the problem of the Netherlands continued to be a top priority. Granvelle's departure had not solved the problems in Brussels, and early in 1565 the Council there sent Egmont to Spain to talk directly to the king. Lamoral of Egmont, forty-three years old, was the war hero of the Netherlands. He had served, like Alba, in campaigns in Germany, and was the architect of the victories at St Quentin and Gravelines. He arrived at the Spanish court on 20 February, and was lodged at his own request in the residence of the prince of Eboli. He was entertained generously by everybody, but the visit happened to coincide with a delicate moment in the rivalry between the political groupings at court.[28] Philip was about to make decisions that would seriously affect the Eboli interest, and Egmont's presence complicated matters. The count, for instance, had talks with the infante Carlos in which he apparently broached the possibility of a new war by the Netherlands and Spain against the French. The idea may have excited the imagination of the prince. Egmont also had confidential talks with the king, who eventually sent him on his way ('the happiest man in the world', were the count's own words) on 6 April.

The issues raised by Egmont, however, were far from being resolved and very soon blew up into a serious crisis. During the count's visit the king had discussed his proposals, contained in a fifteen-page memoir in French, with the members of the Council of State including Alba. The Flemish nobles wanted an increased role in the Brussels government, and moderation on the heresy laws. The king set about drafting an 'Instruction' which Egmont was to take back with him and give to Margaret. Philip had before him the report of Alba and other advisers in council, but the approach he adopted was his own. He set out to reassure and mollify, rather than make outright concessions.[29] He agreed, for example, on changes in the administration without specifying the changes in detail. On Egmont's proposal of a conference in the Netherlands to reconsider the heresy laws, he agreed but specified who should attend and that the meeting must not be public. The final Instruction, dated 2 April, was to be handed by Egmont to Margaret. Egmont saw and approved the text before his departure. The count was returning under the impression (which Philip had done his best to sustain) that the king was making concessions. He said as much to his colleagues when he arrived in Brussels. But on May 13 Philip signed letters for Margaret which touched on the religious question and expressly ordered the execution of six Anabaptists whose plea for clemency had been referred to him. The hopes of toleration vanished. There was a general outcry, and Egmont and the Flemish nobles protested that they had been tricked. Margaret, put under pressure, had to give way to them. She explained to Philip that the committee sanctioned by him had met and had recommended a policy of toleration, so that she was suspending executions for the time being.

After Egmont's departure the main business at court in spring 1565 was the meeting, sought by Catherine de' Medici, between the rulers of France and Spain. Philip was sceptical of the advantages to be gained, and from the first made it clear that he personally would not go. The event was instead given the official status of a reunion between Catherine and her daughter the queen of Spain. In March Philip decided that Eboli, who was due to accompany Elisabeth, might be too soft in his dealings with the French, and assigned Alba to take his place. Eboli felt that he was being edged out of his rightful role in state affairs, but knew that it would not help to complain to the king. Instead he called the French ambassador, Saint-Sulpice, and asked him to intercede with Philip.[30] Saint-Sulpice found Eboli prostrate on his bed with depression. The king would not change his mind. He informed Catherine, however, that he would cancel the meeting if any members of the Huguenot nobility were present.

Elisabeth's enthusiasm for the visit to her homeland and reunion with her mother was boundless. Philip gave her complete freedom to plan the journey as she wished. She took him at his word, and spent a fortune on clothes and jewels. Her chamberlain Juan Manrique in despair informed the king that 'the queen has spent most of the money on clothes which she has ordered at great cost'.[31] Early in May 1565 the royal party set out on its journey, taking the route through Soria, Pamplona and San Sebastián. 'Yesterday Her Majesty left Irún,' Alba reported from St Jean-de-Luz on 15 June, 'and arrived at the estuary where the king her brother and the queen were waiting for her. They got into boats and crossed over from the Spanish side, when they reached land they were received with great affection.'[32] The immense royal party then made its way to Bayonne.

Philip's emissaries at Bayonne were Alba and Don Juan Manrique. The latter was sympathetic to Eboli's point of view and could in some measure counter Alba's position, though in practice their reports to the king were signed by both and so represented common ground. The French nobles to whom they talked had differing views about the situation in France and the remedies required. Only the veteran soldier Blaise de Montluc, a fierce enemy of the Huguenots, saw eye to eye with Alba. The duke's report to Philip showed a rare sign of his dry humour. 'M de Montluc came to talk to me,' he wrote to the king, 'and since he is so vain it seemed to me that the way to get to him would be through his vanity so when I embraced him I said in his ear, "You are the one responsible for all this fuss here and for the two princesses meeting together".' Montluc responded positively and unburdened himself to the duke. In the same way the young king of France, Charles IX, confessed to Alba that 'taking up arms is not the solution, I would destroy my kingdom'. With the queen mother it was not so easy. Catherine at first refused to meet Alba, complained about Philip's apparent distrust, and threatened that 'this is the short-cut to war'.[33] The two emissaries had no option but to turn to Elisabeth, who was asked to bring her mother into the talks. Although Philip felt that allowing his wife into the meeting 'is not right', Elisabeth proved her worth as a parry to her mother's outbursts. The talks were conducted in French, though Alba spoke the language poorly and Catherine had a very heavy Italian accent.

The Spanish emissaries came to Bayonne to express their concern about events in France; they were also trying to formulate their own options. Agreement with France would clarify what could be done about the Netherlands and the Turks. Alba and Juan Manrique informed Philip that their intention was to 'find out the state in which matters of religion stand, and what the solution might be. It is time for Your Majesty to decide what should be done to resolve this problem, which could be the beginning of the end of this kingdom [of France] and cannot fail to be the beginning of the problem in all Your Majesty's territories.'[34] Alba was outspoken on the political issues affected by the religious question. In December 1561 he had already stressed to the French ambassador in Madrid, the bishop of Limoges, that his government should take firm measures, as Henry II had done, against the Huguenot leaders.[35] In conversations that Limoges had with both Alba and Philip II, he was left in no doubt that the Spaniards feared instability in France and its repercussions on the Netherlands.

In Bayonne Alba put forward the idea, in his talks with Blaise de Montluc and the rigid Catholics, that an immediate solution would be to 'cut off some heads', namely those of the Huguenot leaders the prince of Condé, admiral Gaspard Coligny, and the duke of Gramont. It was typical Alba language, but by no means a concrete proposal. His talks with Catherine were in reality much more diplomatic than those he had conducted with the military veteran Montluc. 'The Queen Mother,' he wrote to Philip, 'was highly suspicious that I had no other solution to propose than the immediate resort to arms, and came well armed with strong reasons and answers to show me that this was not the way.' 'France must be cleared of this vicious sect' of Huguenots, Alba insisted to the queen.[36] She replied sarcastically, 'Since you understand so well the evil from which France is suffering, tell me the remedy.' Alba parried: 'Madame, who knows better than yourself?' 'The king your master,' she retorted, 'knows better than I everything that passes in France. What means would he employ?' Alba criticised her current policy of coexistence between Catholics and Calvinists. With the policy, she said, 'a great deal of ground was gained'. That was not true, Alba replied, much ground was being lost. What did he suggest, she asked, a resort to arms? Alba told Catherine that he was opposed to any use of arms against the Protestants at present: 'I replied that at present I did not see the need, nor would Your Majesty advise it'.[37] The dialogue continued about other matters, and at one point became heated. When Elisabeth backed up Alba's point of view, her mother rounded on her: 'Vous estes devenue bien espagnole!' ('You've become a true Spaniard!'). Elisabeth answered calmly, 'I am a Spaniard, I admit; it is my duty.'

At one point Catherine emphasised her point by attacking the king of Spain's own policy of toleration in the Netherlands. 'Why does he not castigate those who are rebels against God' in his territories? It was an excellent point, and Alba did not know how to reply. The disagreement about how to achieve religious peace in France became so sharp, that Catherine summoned the papal legate to mediate between both sides. Eventually a compromise accord was reached, by which Catherine would call together the French clergy to discuss the reforms proposed by the Council of Trent, without entering into any debates over dogma. The agreement, however, was verbal and not written. It could not fail to arouse fears that the French Catholic leaders were allying themselves with Spain to carry out some terrible design.

The talks were not all devoted to business. A huge amount of money was spent by Catherine and the king on celebrations. At a special dinner given by the king some two thousand lords and ladies sat down to feast. The talks ended on 29 June, when a lavish tournament in costume was put on by the French. Charles IX dressed as a Trojan, while Duke Francis of Guise and his men dressed as 'Scottish savages'. On 1 July the royal party set off towards the Spanish frontier at Irún. Though Philip expressed to Alba his 'satisfaction' with his conduct of the meeting, no agreement nor even any convergence of views emerged from it. Alba was severely disappointed. He complained to a French cardinal of 'the little agreement that has come out of all this, the little hope that there was of achieving more, and my own dissatisfaction with what has been discussed so far'.[38] Two years later he repeated to the Spanish ambassador in Paris, Francés de Álava, his regret that Catherine had not accepted the advice he gave at the time: 'would to God the queen had taken the advice she received in Bayonne, and what was agreed there that she would do, for her affairs would now have turned out quite differently'.[39] The impression gained at the court in Madrid was that 'in short, nothing has been achieved'.

Catherine came away with the conviction that any firm action she took would be supported by Spain. 'But,' she told Álava, 'as you said to me the other day it is important to maintain great secrecy, for there are many in a state of turmoil for fear of what might happen to them.'[40] Since the talks were held completely in private, the Huguenots quickly came to the conclusion that some sinister plot had been hatched between the crown and Spain. Philip, however, had gained nothing from the meeting except vague words and considerable expense. Unable to rely firmly on the French crown, he was obliged to make his own political agreements with those French nobles whose interests coincided with his.

In the course of 1565 a significant change of policies and personnel began to take place in government. Ruy Gómez felt that the changes had begun in 1564, when the king appointed him as Steward to the household of prince Carlos. Philip explained at the time that he would not entrust his heir to anyone except the prince of Eboli. But Eboli felt, with reason, that his new duties would remove him to some extent from the politics of the court. His fears were justified. Replacing him for the talks at Bayonne was a clear pointer. Other changes in state personnel, notably the rise in influence of the Navarrese priest and lawyer Diego de Espinosa, also tended to weaken Eboli's position. In 1565 Diego de Espinosa became president of the Royal Council, accumulated further posts and in 1568 obtained through Philip the rank of cardinal. It was a meteoric career and destined to be short, but while it lasted he was the most powerful man in the monarchy after the king. His rise benefited all his friends, including many who happened to have connexions with the Toledo family. The situation helped Alba appreciably in Italy. In 1565 the new ambassador appointed to the papacy was Luis de Requesens, a friend of the king and also of Espinosa and Alba. At the same time García de Toledo, Alba's cousin and since 1564 supreme commander of the Mediterranean fleet, was named viceroy of Sicily.

For a few years more, while Espinosa was in charge at court and Alba's policy in the Netherlands appeared to be working, the Toledo family and its friends could count on maintaining their influence in Italy. In 1571 Alba's ally Granvelle was made viceroy of Naples, and Requesens became governor of Milan. The political allies of the Toledos were backed up by a whole troop of close relatives who occupied crucial positions and also accompanied the great personages of the family everywhere. Alba was able to obtain positions for his family in Italy. In 1565 one of the members of the clan wrote to Alba thanking him for help in obtaining the succession to the strategically important fortress of Santelmo in Naples. His letter to the duke expressed clearly the bonds of allegiance: 'I have received this grace from Your Excellency, from whom I am confident I shall receive even greater ones. Your Excellency can count on me always to be your servant, and follow your orders in all that is of Your Excellency's service, which I shall fulfil as your most faithful subject.'[41] Thereafter he became an integral part of Alba's retinue, subsequently accompanying him to the Netherlands.

The change of direction in Philip's policy, and the way in which he distanced himself from Eboli's approach to international problems, had as one of its consequences the disgrace of secretary Francisco de Eraso. Eraso, as we have seen, was the outstanding official in an administration that functioned largely through secretaries who controlled the access of information to the king. Since Philip's return to Spain in 1559 he had exercised a firm control over several aspects of policy and was also actively in touch with the parties in the Netherlands. Egmont and Orange found him sympathetic. Granvelle, by contrast, quickly found that Eraso was his enemy. The turbulent politics of the Netherlands were in this way directly linked to personal ambitions at the Spanish court. Early in 1565 an investigation (*visita*), of the sort which the king sprang from time to time on his officials (and which this time was carefully engineered by Eraso's enemies) was ordered into aspects of financial administration.[42] Eraso was one of the chief officials affected. Eboli was obliged to distance himself from him, and even given the job of announcing the verdicts early in April 1566. Eraso was fined a large sum and deprived of several of his offices. 'He resented it and complained bitterly,' because his friends (by implication, Ruy Gómez) had failed to support him.[43]

An agent of Alba in Madrid sent a report to the duchess, then in Alba de Tormes, about the reactions at court. 'The opinions that circulate,' he reported, 'are very strange. The very same people who used to speak ill of Eraso now speak ill of the investigation, and this doesn't surprise me because it is old hat. What they say is that there was a great deal of malice in the investigation, because they see disciplined many whom they took to be good, and untouched others whom they did not consider such. Eraso has gone home and wrote to His Majesty that he was going.'[44] Eraso still continued to play a role in the administration, until his death in 1570. But his change of functions signified a shift of balance in the court bureaucracy. Those now in charge tended to be less sympathetic to Eboli and in favour of the line being pushed by Alba and Granvelle.

Alba's leading role in the talks at Bayonne confirmed his position in the king's favour. It was, from every point of view, the highest that he had risen in the government of Philip II, which he had served faithfully for nearly twenty years. His success had been accompanied by the overshadowing of the prince of Eboli in the administration and the disgrace of Eboli's ally Eraso. Alba's men were occupying key posts in the monarchy, especially in Italy and in various ambassadorships. At court the duke was able to work on excellent terms with the king's most trusted secretary, Gonzalo Pérez. Ruy Gómez and his allies discreetly retired to the background. At crucial points, the king consulted only with Gonzalo Pérez and a couple of members (Antonio de Toledo and Alba) of the Council of State. This meant that Alba had a powerful role in influencing the way that the king was making decisions. All foreign ambassadors at court dealt directly with him if they wanted any matters to be settled speedily.

From around October 1565 there were strong rumours at court that Philip was going to Flanders. For months the advice to go there had been pressed on him by advisers. But, as a correspondent in Brussels complained in September to Granvelle, 'His Majesty does not have even one person with him who will tell him how important it is for him to come to these lands'.[45] The impression grew among those in the north that Philip or his advisers were indifferent. Ironically, the two opposing tendencies were agreed that the king should go to the Netherlands. The aggrieved Flemish nobles wanted him to deal with the situation personally. Granvelle, no friend of theirs, felt that Philip needed to go personally to see how the nobles were mismanaging affairs.

The king was undecided. In the summer of 1565, he eagerly welcomed fresh and direct reports made to him personally at Valsaín by one of his agents, the friar Lorenzo de Villavicencio, who had just returned from the Netherlands. In several audiences lasting up to three hours, Philip spoke alone and directly to the friar, quizzing him about both persons and events in Brussels. Villavicencio, a tireless writer, also heaped a number of memoranda upon the king, who looked at them with care and passed them for attention to his secretary Pérez. Though he did not share all the friar's views, the king was most impressed by his information. His reports appeared to be in accord with what was really happening. Late that summer, Philip received correspondence from Margaret in which the regent firmly supported concessions to the nobles and a measure of toleration. The king consulted closely with Pérez, and through him with Alba. 'There is so much to consider here and it is so important that we get it right,' he told the secretary.[46]

At the end of August the king and Pérez, with the active help of Villa-vicencio, drew up a policy document on the measures to be adopted in the Netherlands.[47] At crucial points, notably in religious matters, the influence of the friar was explicitly accepted. Philip had at last made up his mind. The policy was to be hard-line: no concessions on toleration, no increase in the political role of Egmont, Orange and the nobles. Philip arrived at this policy because the arguments of Villavicencio, Granvelle and – at one remove – Alba, made more sense to him. He was still not sure how to implement what he had decided to do. Other major preoccupations, principally the holding of provin-cial councils in the dioceses of Spain and the defence of Malta against the Turks, kept him very busy with work. He also, early in September, became ill with the severe headaches that periodically afflicted him. His instinct was to write to Margaret of Parma, telling her to take a firm line. Villavicencio, however, insisted that only his presence in the Netherlands would resolve matters. In the event, Philip decided to do both. From September onwards, the air was alive with rumours of the king's impending visit. His work in Spain done, Villavicencio returned to the north in October. In the same month, Philip wrote to Granvelle in his retirement at Besançon and invited him to go to Rome to represent his interests there. In mid-October, amid the beauty of the autumn woods at Valsaín, Philip signed and sent off to Margaret the letters which set out the policy he offered the Netherlands leaders.

The instructions arrived in Brussels in November. When the content of the king's letters was made known, there was uproar. The leading grandees Orange, Egmont and Hornes withdrew from the Council of State. There were protests in the provinces. Once again rumours swept the country that Philip intended to introduce the Spanish Inquisition. Nothing could have been further from his mind. He was convinced, he told Granvelle, that the Spanish model of Inquisition was unsuitable for export either to the Nether-lands or to Italy.[48] However, the continuous refusal of the king to make any concessions regarding toleration helped to unite dissatisfied groups against the government in Brussels, which was seen as a supine tool of Spanish policy.

In April 1566, some of the Calvinist-inclined lesser nobility of the Nether-lands, led by Hendrik de Brederode and Louis of Nassau (younger brother of the prince of Orange) at the head of some three hundred armed confederates presented to Margaret of Parma a 'Request' demanding toleration. The nobles were sneeringly dismissed as 'beggars' (*gueux*) by a minister at Margaret's side, but she was powerless to refuse their demands. On 9 April she issued an order modifying the application of the heresy laws. The leading Catholic clergy and officials, who felt a policy of total suppression to be unworkable, greeted this with satisfaction. That same week Orange, Egmont and Hornes presented an ultimatum to the regent that they would resign from the Council of State if the king did not give it a greater voice in government and if the policy of toleration were not continued. Once again, Margaret had to give in. It was agreed that two spokesmen, Floris de Montmorency, baron Montigny, and the marquis of Berghes, should go to Madrid to explain matters. Baron Montigny was the brother of Philippe de Montmorency, count of Hornes. He had been to Madrid in 1562 and knew his way around the politics of the court.

The support of moderate Catholics in Flanders for a policy of toleration was not wholly outrageous to Spanish opinion.[49] Philip himself had favoured moderation in England. The situation in Germany also supplied a precedent. There, as the king well knew from his personal experience, princes could decide the religion of their subjects. Philip could see the need for moderation instanced by his father's Interim, just as in England he had advised caution over the persecution of heresy. In the Netherlands, by contrast, he was now convinced that any concession over religion would lead to a rapid collapse into the situation that France was currently facing. The issue was rebellion, much more than heresy. 'The flames are spreading everywhere and if those realms [he was referring to France] do not make haste to quench them they could be consumed in them beyond remedy.'[50]

At the end of April 1566, long before any disorders had taken place, he was preparing for the possibility of military intervention in the Netherlands. 'Every day,' the French ambassador Fourquevaux noted, 'the Council of War meets over the matter of the Netherlands.'[51] Military commanders were coming and going every day in the palace. There were rumours that the preparations might be against the Turks, but Flanders seemed the most probable. What remained undecided was whether the king himself would go. In May 1566 several conservative advisers who favoured the firm repression of heresy were also firmly against the resort to an army. Both Cardinal Granvelle in Rome and Friar Villavicencio in Brussels argued that the presence of the king would be sufficient to remedy matters. Philip accordingly confirmed his intention to go in person.

Events, however, delayed him. Significant changes had taken place at court. In April 1566 his principal secretary Gonzalo Pérez died. His responsibilities were, informally from the summer of 1566 and formally from December 1567, divided between his son (illegitimate, since Gonzalo was a priest) Antonio Pérez, and Gabriel de Zayas, a nominee of Alba. These changes very quickly modified Alba's advantageous position in the administration. The duke favoured Zayas as successor to all the spheres of business that used to be handled by Gonzalo Pérez. But the rise of Antonio Pérez, who made no secret of his hostility to Alba, opened the way to a dilution of his influence in policy-making. Alba also had to contend with the increasing influence of one of his old opponents, the first duke of Feria, Gómez Suárez de Figueroa.

In the midst of this flurry of changes, Montigny and Berghes arrived in June from Flanders. It was an unpropitious time to show up, for Philip was about to retire with the whole court to Valsaín. He left the whole apparatus of government behind in Madrid, but summoned select officials. Over several days, he had talks with the Council of State and other selected ministers. At a crucial meeting of the council on 22 July, a range of options was suggested to the king, who was left to make his own decision. Four days later he announced his course of action. He would go to the Netherlands in the spring, a decision that met a basic demand of many Netherlanders. His next resolution was not so palatable. He rejected categorically the demands made by Egmont, Orange and the nobles. The information he was receiving from the Netherlands could hardly have led Philip to make any other decision. Precisely in July, he heard from a correspondent that Hendrik de Brederode and the *Gueux* were raising men for an insurrection, and that Calvinist preachers from France and Geneva were entering the country and preaching sedition.[52] The great nobles were doing nothing to stop this. Letters which arrived from Margaret on 21 July told the same story. The king must either act firmly, the regent urged, or concede to the demands. This was more than enough to concentrate the king's mind. For over a year, ever since Egmont's visit, he had allowed events to take their course. Now, it appeared, was the time to call a halt.

The Council of State convened every day in the last week of July. On the 31st the king wrote to Margaret. His instructions were, on the face of it, an attempt at moderation. The laws against heresy had to be enforced, but with various modifications. A general pardon would be issued, but religious offences were excluded. No sooner had the letters gone than Philip regretted even his few concessions. In a small legal ceremony, witnessed only by the officiating notary together with Alba and two other councillors, on 9 August he retracted the offer of a pardon, on the grounds that he had issued it under duress. Shortly after, he instructed Margaret to raise troops in Germany. During that summer he was kept informed of the recruitment of soldiers by the Calvinist nobles. By August 1566 he had clarified the issues to himself. In a letter to his ambassador in Rome, Luis de Requesens, he explained that if he went north it must be with an army, because 'it would have no impact nor offer any solution, if it were not with a show of force'. 'If possible,' he stated, 'I shall attempt to settle affairs of religion in those states without the use of arms, because I know that it would be their total destruction to resort to them. But if matters cannot be settled as I wish without using arms, then I am determined to resort to them.'[53]

On 3 September a sheaf of letters from Margaret arrived at Valsaín. They reported widespread anti-religious riots and destruction of images in the cities of the Netherlands. In Ypres cathedral the Calvinists had blasphemed in the pulpit and had then spent all day sacking the building. In west Flanders alone some four hundred churches were sacked.[54] After this, a shocked Philip was in no doubt that a state of rebellion existed. The Spanish public shared his views. In the streets of Madrid anger against Netherlanders was so great that one of them said, 'we dare not show our faces'.[55] But the king was still hesitant. Not until 22 September was a special meeting of the council convened. There was now no doubt at all that an army had to be sent in. The day after the council meeting Philip looked relaxed and confident.[56]

By October the troops raised in Italy and elsewhere were estimated at forty-eight thousand men. In a special Council meeting on 29 September the argument for armed intervention was reconfirmed.[57] The king, exceptionally, presided over the session, in order to avoid disputes between the councillors.[58] The prince of Eboli, supported by the duke of Feria, argued against the king going to the Netherlands or sending an army there. He suggested that in view of the impending danger of a rebellion, Philip should send a representative (possibly Eboli) who would attempt to reconcile the factions there and respect the religious practices and constitution of the country. Alba, supported by the former Eboli adherent Juan Manrique (who had now changed sides) and by Cardinal Espinosa, felt that the time for clemency and negotiation had passed. He advised that 'the disorder be crushed as soon as it appears', by sending an army that would punish the main instigators, pardon the rest, and prepare the way for a visit by the king, who would distribute pardons and favours and thereby consolidate his position. The meeting went on late into the night, and was ended by the king when tempers began to run short. The next day the king confirmed that his view coincided with that of Alba, and he reiterated the September decision to go to the Netherlands with an army. He now insisted on immediate action, 'before the snows block the route'.

There was still considerable doubt as to who would command the army. Among the names mentioned were those of the duke of Feria, prince Carlos (aged twenty-one), and the king's half-brother Don Juan of Austria (aged only nineteen). At the end of November Alba reluctantly agreed to accept the task, and received his commission on 1 December. There remained the task of explaining to the world what was involved in sending an army. It was decided to minimise the ideological aspect, which was at that time inflaming political problems in France and elsewhere, by emphasising only the issues of law and order. When all appropriate military preparations had been made, Alba explained to the French ambassador that 'in this question of Flanders the issue is not one of taking steps against their religion but simply against rebels'.[59] He said the same thing to the nuncio. Lest this might appear to be showing too little concern for the cause of the faith, he reassured the nuncio some weeks later that all the talk about subduing rebellion was simply a cover for the real motive: to protect true religion.[60] By offering in this way differing explanations to the king of France and to the pope, Philip and Alba hoped to keep them both happy.[61]

The new commander promptly set to work, with typical efficiency, to arrange all the logistics for his expedition. Once again he was back in the driving seat. His surviving personal papers show how he himself took a hand in all the necessary details.[62] He explored the possibility of taking the troops through France if the winter snows made it impossible to cross the Alpine passes. They could go by sea to Marseille or Toulon and then follow the Rhône northwards in order to cut across to Franche-Comté. In March 1567, however, Charles IX, nervous about the impact of a Spanish presence on his already strife-torn territory, refused permission for any troops to cross France. Normally Alba would have put in hand rapid and urgent measures to decide on an alternative route. But it still took four more months before he was able to leave Spain, on what was supposed to be an urgent expedition. Why was there a delay?

The fact is that there was continued opposition to sending the duke as general. He was not the king's first choice for command of the army.[63] Advisers were deeply divided over who should go. According to the Imperial ambassador, 'there was a great dispute and difference of views over which commander would be sent to Flanders'.[64] Some felt that Don Carlos was a possibility, but recognised that he was too young. The name of the duke of Medinaceli was mentioned. Philip would have preferred the duke of Parma – Margaret's husband Ottavio Farnese – or the duke of Savoy. Both were respected by the Netherlanders, the former because his wife was governor and the latter because he had commanded the forces that won the victory of St Quentin. Possibly more important, they were not Spaniards and not party to the current struggles and intrigues. When he failed to enlist their support, Philip turned instinctively to Alba. Three weeks after the 29 October debate, however, Montigny and Berghes were still urging that Ruy Gómez be sent to the Netherlands. Even after Alba's appointment was made public, Eboli continued trying to change the decision, though when the appointment appeared firm the duke's rivals may have accepted it as a good opportunity to get him out of the way.

There were problems about finding money for the expedition, but they were resolved when the Indies fleet, which arrived in September, brought a large amount of silver for the crown. The bulk of the financing was achieved by seizing an even greater amount of silver from the merchants of Seville, by way of an involuntary loan. Italian financiers covered other costs. The delays certainly affected the drafting of Alba's instructions, which did not receive their final form until 1 March. The antagonisms provoked by the matter reached such fever point that finally in mid-March 1567 other courtiers intervened and persuaded Eboli and Alba to stage a formal public reconciliation at which they embraced each other and promised to work together.[65] When spring 1567 came the only certainty was that an army would be going, and that Alba would be leading it. It was bruited about that the force would be a massive one, sufficient to dissuade any possible opposition. The nuncio heard a figure of 55,000 men from Alba's own lips; a noble in the Netherlands heard a figure of 66,000. Knowledge that the duke would be coming north with an army helped powerfully to concentrate the minds of the Catholic leadership in the Netherlands. Some remained openly scornful. 'What can an army do?' Egmont asked Margaret, 'Kill 200,000 Netherlanders?'[66] During the winter and early spring Margaret and her officials, with the help of Orange, Egmont and other aristocrats, used troops to eliminate the centres of Calvinist sedition. In April 1567 Brederode fled. Margaret sent an emissary to report to Philip that armed intervention was not now necessary. It was too late; the Council had already decided there was no other option. On 15 April Alba went to Aranjuez for a final consultation with Philip.

On 16 April Alba took his leave of the king and also of Don Carlos, whose hand he kissed. The prince, however, became angry and said that he was the one who should be going to the Netherlands, as Philip had promised, and not Alba.[67] He worked himself up into one of his rages, drew his dagger and threatened the duke: 'you must not go to Flanders, or I shall kill you'.[68] Alba seized the prince's hand and held him until a gentleman came into the room to help. There were no further incidents, and Alba left for Cartagena. A few weeks later, on 26 June, Philip soothed Don Carlos and Don Juan by promising that they would accompany him on his forthcoming voyage to the Netherlands, whose final details were being prepared. The prince continued to occupy a place in the story, for Montigny and Berghes were aware of his hostility to Alba and attempted to win him over to their side. After all, he was heir apparent and would be the next ruler of Spain. They hinted to the king that the prince should be appointed governor of their country. This would be in complete conformity with a promise that Philip himself had made publicly to the Netherlanders in 1559. Alba was instinctively suspicious of the activities of the two Netherlanders, but it would be some time before he could act against them.

The very day that Margaret's emissary arrived at court, Alba set sail from Cartagena in the fleet of Andrea Doria, which also transported nearly eight thousand soldiers from Spain who would take the place of the tercios to be taken from Italy and sent to Flanders. The duke went in a distinguished company. Among the passengers was a young noble from a junior branch of the great Mendoza family. Bernardino de Mendoza, twenty-six years old at the time, formed part of the duke's immediate team and was sent by him, as soon as they arrived in Italy, to solicit the pope's blessing for the expedition. Thereafter Mendoza went to the Netherlands, where he was destined to serve for the next ten years as a soldier and diplomat under all the Spanish governors, devoting his leisure hours to the preparation of a history of the tumults in that country.[69] Alba was also given charge of a very special passenger: the archbishop of Toledo. After seven years of house arrest by the Inquisition in lodgings in Valladolid,[70] Bartolomé Carranza was at last being allowed to go to Rome to see the pope. He had arrived at the port on 31 December, and was put up at the fortress in Cartagena until the fleet could sail. 'The archbishop of Toledo,' Alba wrote to Cardinal Espinosa, with wry humour, 'has been going out of his mind since yesterday thinking that because we spent last night embarking we did not intend to take him with us. They tell me that every hour we delay seems like a year to the archbishop.'[71] After nearly four months of waiting in port, Carranza's patience was rewarded. 'In order to lose no more time,' the duke informed Philip on 26 April 1567, 'I have decided to leave tonight.' In the darkness before dawn, the great fleet of forty galleys sailed out to sea and made their way northwards up the coastline.

4   The Council of Troubles, 1567–1572

Every day my head is assaulted with doubts over whether the guilty should die.

Brussels, April 1568

Alba was sixty years old when he was chosen as commander for the Netherlands. Both diplomats and painters of the time coincide in the way they describe him. 'In person he was tall, thin, erect, with a small head, a long visage, lean yellow cheek, dark twinkling eyes, a dust complexion, black bristling hair, and a long sable-silvered beard, descending in two waving streams upon his breast'.[1] Despite his austere, well-regulated life the years had taken a toll of his health, and the gout which affected all the leading men of the age did not spare him. 'The duke my lord,' an official of the family wrote to the duchess from Madrid early in 1566, 'is in good health although two days ago he stayed in bed because of infirmity in his legs. He conducted business from bed all day, got up for supper and ate well and happily, which is saying a great deal for His Excellency to be able to do so, burdened as he is with work.'[2] Nine months later, at the end of November, his health was no better: 'For the last four months the gout has had me tied down, unable to move without a stick, and I fear that this business will last all my life, although it is true that my regret arises because I have had good health so far.'[3] Illness did not stop him attending to state business. It was, however, an unfortunate time for Spain's only army captain to be laid low, for he was about to embark on the most decisive military commitment of his entire career.

There were hostile voices on all sides, and from the beginning there were members of the king's council who worked to undermine his operation. Exactly a month after Alba's departure from Cartagena, the prince of Eboli told the French ambassador that 'the duke is not wanted in the Netherlands, both the good and the bad fear him'.[4] Alba's reputation for brutality in the Italian campaigns had preceded him, and his enemies expected no mercy. But this time there was no talk of enemies, only of restoring order among the king's own subjects. The duke was going simply to prepare the way for the king, whose decision to travel to Flanders was firm. Alba understood that a small army must accompany the king in order to stabilise the situation. At no time had he lent support to the idea of a punitive force, *without the king,* being sent to the north.[5]

It had been the duke's intention to go accompanied by his son Fadrique. The practice in his family had always been to take the sons on campaign to give them the necessary experience to carry on the military tradition. After the death in 1548 of his son García, Alba devoted himself wholeheartedly to promoting Fadrique as a worthy heir, and he had already done his best to advance his son's interests in Italy. But Fadrique, marquis of Coria as he then was, became involved in a matter that was ultimately to carry very serious consequences for himself and his father. An irrepressible pursuer of women, he also married with frequency. In May 1551, as we have seen, he married a daughter of the duke of Cardona, Guiomar de Aragón y Folch de Cardona, who died in January 1557 without issue. Subsequently in January 1563 he married María Josefa Pimentel, daughter of the count of Benavente, who also died without issue. In 1566, no doubt anticipating another war campaign abroad, he made a promise of marriage to a court lady of the queen, Magdalena de Guzmán, in order to have sexual relations with her. Magdalena was not an innocent victim, and had already a few years before been married to a son of Hernán Cortés. At that time, a betrothal or exchange of promises, known as *verba de futuro,* was sufficient to constitute a marriage. There existed, however, a second part to the procedure, called *verba de presenti,* by which a couple had to repeat the vows personally in the presence of a priest. This completed the ceremony in the eyes of the Church. Fadrique changed his mind after the betrothal, and refused to go through with the second part. Magdalena complained directly to the queen, who intervened with the king. She was persuaded to withdraw to a convent in Toledo. Fadrique was arrested and in November 1566 confined to the castle prison of la Mota de Medina.

In February 1567 the king allowed him to be released from strict confinement, but a decree of 20 May sentenced him to three years' military service in the fort of Oran on the North African coast. His son and heir was consequently not at the duke's side when he set sail for Flanders that spring. Alba felt the absence deeply, and continued to make efforts on his son's behalf. Finally on 7 April 1568 at Alba's request the king allowed Fadrique to serve in Flanders, by way of fulfilling his punishment.[6] He was to go directly there from Oran, without returning to Spain. The incident continued to cast a shadow over Philip's relations with the duke, who in the meantime was comforted by the presence and aid of his natural son Don Hernando de Toledo.[7] Hernando, born in 1527, had risen to the highest ranks in the monarchy through his undeniable merits but also through the patronage of his father. He served with the duke in the Naples campaign, and in 1556 received the title of grand prior of Castile of the Order of St John of Jerusalem. The headship of this order formed part of the patrimony of the house of Alba, and Antonio de Toledo was simultaneously given the rank of grand prior of León. In 1566 Hernando was one of the military commanders sent to relieve the siege of Malta. After completing this duty successfully, he opted to accompany his father to Flanders, where he served from 1567 to 1570 as the duke's chief cavalry commander. The duke lived for his sons, and Hernando's company was a profound solace to him. But it never made up for the absence of his legitimate son and heir, and there appears to have been both rivalry and dislike between the two military sons of the duke.

Doria's ships proceeded slowly, hindered in part by poor weather. Off Cap de Creus, on the Catalan coast, Alba was reported to be ill with gout pains in one foot. The vessels finally put in at Genoa, where Alba had consultations with the ruling elite and with the Venetian ambassador. By the time he arrived in Milan the army was almost ready. Eventually a force of 10,500 troops, of which 1,250 were cavalry and the rest infantry, set out from Asti in the duchy of Montferrato, on 25 June 1567. The four regiments of Lombardy, Sardinia, Sicily and Naples, comprised a total of up to nine thousand men. They were generally known as 'tercios', a term that had become standard from around 1536 and tended to mean a regiment of ten companies under a *maestre de campo* (field marshal). Each company consisted of roughly three hundred men, while two of the ten companies were made up entirely of musketeers (*arcabuceros*).[8] The regiments were commanded respectively by Sancho de Lodiono, Gonzalo de Bracamonte, Julián Romero,[9] and Alfonso de Ulloa, all distinguished and experienced captains. The soldiers were nearly all Castilians. The cavalry force was under the command of the prior Don Hernando. Chiappino Vitelli, marquis of Cetona, a veteran of the wars in Italy, was appointed infantry commander; and another Italian, Gabriel Serbelloni, was placed in command of the artillery. The soldiers took their wages with them: five hundred mules, according to a report from one of the officers, carried the cash.

The route chosen for the march had been studied and approved by the king's agents in 1566. Subsequently known as the Spanish Road, because it was for some forty years the regular route taken by the Spanish armies, it had been known and used long before by travellers and traders of every nation.[10] Cardinal Granvelle had recommended it to the king a few years before, and Alba had also used it to get to the Netherlands from Italy. Nobody, however,

had envisaged taking a whole army along the route; clearly there were problems in moving a large body of soldiers through potentially hostile territory.
Because he was unable to obtain permission to cross French territory, at the
end of 1566 Philip sent envoys to other states bordering the route, namely
Lorraine, Savoy and Switzerland, to ask for permission for the peaceful
passage of his men.

At the end of June the troops had crossed the mountainous part of their
route, through the Mount Cénis pass, and descended to the cultivated plains
around Chambéry, then the capital of Savoy. Even at this late stage, according
to the Imperial ambassador in his memoirs, there was an attempt to stop
the army. The king reacted to Margaret of Parma's warning that 'she greatly
feared that the arrival of the Spaniards would cause new riots in Flanders',[11]
and ordered a short halt. The doubts passed, the army moved on again. The
summer months should have been ideal dry weather for the movement of
men, horses and artillery, but in fact it rained a great part of the time. Alba
wished to avoid having his men sleep on damp ground, and was forced to
seek lodging for them in the settlements along the road.

The movement of the army created great alarm in all the countries
bordering the route. There were fears in Switzerland that an attack was
planned against Geneva, the centre of Calvinism. The French authorities
raised troops in the Lyonnais and fortified the frontier with Luxembourg.
Royal troops under Marshal Tavannes kept watch from the French side of the
frontier while Alba passed along the Burgundian border, but made no move
to contact him or greet him. Above all, the French Protestants feared that the
Spanish troops present on their frontiers were the fulfilment of a secret plot to
crush them, agreed at Bayonne between Alba and Catherine de' Medici. In
reality, the plot in 1567 was Huguenot rather than Catholic, and it aimed to
overthrow the Valois dynasty. Even as the duke began his long march to the
north, the great Huguenot nobles in France, led by the prince of Condé and
admiral Coligny, abandoned the royal court and went to the provinces, where
they put into effect a conspiracy to seize the royal family and gain possession
of the major cities of the realm.[12] The civil war that ensued in those months
and went on until March the following year, focused the attention of all
Europe and very conveniently took some of the spotlight off Alba's operation.
Over the next five years, the existence of a state of war in France continued to
be the most important factor affecting events in the Netherlands. In many
respects, events in the two countries seemed in fact to be part of a single
struggle. At least, that was how the French Huguenots perceived the situation,
as Alba did subsequently.

In the first week of July the Spanish troops were at last on home ground
when they entered Franche-Comté, territory of Philip II, where they had to

pass through thickly wooded countryside. In the last week of the month they entered the territory of Lorraine. The prior Don Hernando went to Nancy to pay his respects to the duke of Lorraine, who made a journey out with his court on 30 July to visit the army. The troops staged a march-past for the duke, who dined with Alba and his officers.[13] The French soldier and chronicler Brantôme, who had served with Spanish forces in Africa in 1564 and been present at the Bayonne talks in 1565, was at this time serving in the French royal army but could not resist making a trip to visit Alba's men. He greeted old comrades, including Alba, and has left us a famous description of the impressive tercios and the no less impressive number of women who came with them: 'four hundred courtesans on horse, as fair and gallant as princesses, as well as eight hundred on foot'.[14] The day after the duke of Lorraine's visit, a French noble came to the camp to salute the Spaniards on behalf of the governor of Metz, a fortress under French control. Alba had no reason to harbour good memories of the place, which was the scene of Charles V's last debacle in Germany.

During the long march that lasted two months, the soldiers would have had ample time to ask themselves why they were there. If we can trust the testimony of a gentleman soldier, Baltasar de Vargas, who served in the tercios of Naples and wrote an extended piece of doggerel as his contribution to the enterprise,[15] the objective was straightforward. The excesses and rebellions of 1566 made it necessary to punish the Calvinist heretics. The expedition was directed specifically against heresy, Vargas believed, though that did not implicate all the Netherlanders, for many of the nobles and people had remained faithful to the king. It appeared that the Spanish troops had been well prepared in advance for the attitude they were meant to adopt once they arrived.

In fact, the Spanish government had taken care to leave everyone in doubt about the exact purpose of the army. The Netherlanders did not understand what it might achieve. They had always prided themselves on being free subjects of the king, unlike the Neapolitans who (they felt) had been occupied by force. The reference came up frequently in later years. The emperor Maximilian II, Philip's brother-in-law, himself reminded Philip that 'anyone who thinks he can control and govern Flanders like Italy, is very much deceived'.[16] The duke of Alba, observers guessed, was there to restore order, arrest dissidents and check the growth of heresy. But the situation, according to Margaret of Parma, was under control, so why was an army needed? It was in any case the first time that heresy in another country had ever appeared to be a concern of the Spanish crown.

Whether they liked it or not, the Spaniards would be accused of obsession with heresy. Already in 1566 a pamphlet entitled *Les subtils moyens par le Cardinal Granvelle inventez pour instituer l'abhominable Inquisition* was circulating in the Netherlands, accusing Granvelle and his Spanish masters of wishing to introduce the famous tribunal there. Most of western Europe already had a fixed image of the bloodthirsty Holy Office. A legend about it had long been active in Italy, and the Venetian ambassadors in Spain helped to provide substance to the picture. In 1557 ambassador Badoero spoke of the terror caused by its procedure. In 1563 ambassador Tiepolo said that everyone shuddered at its name, as it had total authority over the property, life, honour and even the souls of men. 'The king,' he wrote, 'favours it, the better to keep the people under control.'[17] Even as Alba was leading his troops through the forested valleys of the Spanish Road, two Spanish Protestants were running off the presses in nearby Heidelberg the first edition of a book that would became a powerful weapon against Spanish imperialism in Europe. The *Sanctae Inquisitionis Hispanicae Artes*, published in 1567 and written jointly by two Spanish Protestant exiles, Casiodoro de Reina and Antonio del Corro,[18] supplied for perhaps the first time a full description of the functioning of the Inquisition and its persecution of Protestants in Spain. Alba was coming, the rumours now said, with the Inquisition. In subsequent months Philip II repeated time and again that he had no intention or interest in introducing the Holy Office to the Netherlands. At the very time that magistrates in Antwerp were objecting to the possibility of a Spanish tribunal, they themselves were executing heretics. The Antwerp courts between 1557 and 1562 executed 103 heretics,[19] more than died in the whole of Spain during that period. Nevertheless, rumours of Spain's alleged intentions continued to be a useful legend employed to discredit Spain and encourage resistance to the military intervention.

As Alba approached the frontier of the Netherlands, the nobility of the provinces looked for their own individual solutions to the threat of armed force. On 8 August, Alba reported to Antonio de Toledo his safe arrival at Thionville in Luxembourg, and how he had received a secret visit from a man 'sent by the count of Egmont, confidentially and with the utmost secrecy to find out what my intentions were'.[20] Several nobles of the Netherlands also came out to greet him, among them Philip, baron of Noircarmes, who had played an important part in crushing the Calvinist rebels during the weeks after the image-breaking. On August 16 the duke was at Tirlemont, where a few days later 'the leading nobles came to kiss the hands of His Excellency, among them the count of Hornes, the son of the prince of Orange, Egmont and others'.[21] There was no reason for the nobles to be satisfied with the arrival of an invasion army, and the encounter had all the signs of acute tension. The meeting between Egmont and Alba was notably strained. When the latter saw Egmont coming, bringing with him a gift of horses for the duke, Alba exclaimed jokingly in reference to himself, 'You see before you a great heretic!', and embraced him. Egmont embraced the duke and replied in equally joking terms.[22] The situation was too serious for them to address each other in normal discourse, as they had done in the old days.

In the afternoon of Friday, 22 August, Alba entered Brussels at the head of units of his army. Egmont accompanied him as far as the city entrance and then made his way home. The magistrates of Brussels stayed indoors and made no move to greet him. There was also extreme tension throughout the Netherlands; the people who felt they had most to fear were packing their bags and leaving. The entry of an army in peacetime, into a territory where there was no longer any apparent threat of disorder, could only be seen as a menace. Against whom was it directed? What were the duke's orders? Among the leaders of the Netherlands the reaction was one of anger and fear.

Alba went straight to the governor's palace to pay his respects to Margaret of Parma, who received him with the chief members of the Council of State at her side. She exchanged courtesies but her aspect was grim. She had tried her best to stop him coming. As late as 12 July she had sent a plea to the king, written urgently and therefore in Italian, her only working language, to warn him that sending Alba would have disastrous consequences, since he was hated by all and would draw down further hatred on Spain.[23] Nobody was pleased to see the troops. At mass on Sunday in the governor's palace, Margaret's confessor preached the sermon; he criticised the presence of the soldiers and referred to the Spaniards as 'traitors and thieves'. The hostility in the capital was palpable. Alba had no hesitation in reporting to Madrid that the king should not regret being unable to come this year, 'because in the light of many things that I have seen since I arrived in these states, your coming is not for the moment advisable'. On Monday there was a formal meeting between the governor and Alba, in which the duke was supposed to explain his mission and present his credentials.[24] It proved to be a dialogue of the deaf. Margaret demanded to know why Alba was there, and he responded that she knew very well, from the king's letters to her, why he was there. She then asked what her instructions were. Alba replied that there were none, for 'I have told you that I have not come here to change anything but only to carry out your orders'. She apologised for the conduct of some of the nobles, in particular the prince of Orange, but demanded that the troops must leave. The duke replied firmly: 'Madame, I have told Your Excellency that I have come here to assist you.' Eventually Margaret insisted that she wished to resign. She had already written to her brother expressing this desire, and coming events confirmed her in her decision.

Alba took steps to make sure that units of the army were suitably billeted at crucial points. Several tercios had already been sent off to occupy the principal garrisons; those from Naples, for example, were sent to Ghent, while the troops from Lombardy remained in the capital. The duke came armed with few precise instructions, and in the belief that he would soon be followed by the king, whose decision to go in person to Flanders had been put off several times. Philip, meanwhile, was waiting for news from Alba. At last, on the night of 21 August, he heard for the first time of Alba's safe arrival in Brussels. By then it was obviously too late to sail, for the unstable weather conditions would not allow it. In September the royal visit was cancelled, but the king was still waiting for further reports from the duke. There had been two preconditions for his going, the king later informed the pope.[25] First, he had to hear of Alba's arrival; but the duke had been delayed. Second, Alba had to carry out 'certain acts which must precede my departure'. These acts were to include the arrest of Egmont, Hornes, Orange and other nobles. The strategy, explained the king, was 'first to use the severity of justice, then afterwards use clemency and kindness'. The former had to be done in his absence, the latter in his presence. From the moment of his arrival, Alba had clearly in his mind the king's instructions to carry out 'the punishment that we have always considered should be effected before my arrival'.[26]

One of the duke's first steps at implementing 'severity of justice' was to set up, on 5 September, a special court called the 'Council of Troubles', to judge those implicated in the events of the preceding year. Leading judges of the country were appointed as members, though the real executive officials were only two, both Spaniards, Luis del Río and Juan de Vargas. Even their decisions were not final but had to be personally sanctioned by Alba alone. The court held its first session two weeks later, on 20 September. Several days before that, on 9 September, Alba began the great repression by securing the arrest of Egmont, Hornes and a number of other Flemish notables. Simultaneous arrests were made throughout the country, in Antwerp, Mechelen and Louvain.

The arrest of Egmont, the great war hero of the Netherlands, and onetime companion of both Alba and the king, was not unexpected. The count had received warnings long before Alba's arrival.[27] That summer a noble who had just returned from Madrid[28] visited him and reported that 'there are very bad stories told about you in Spain'. When Egmont laughed at him, he repeated that 'birds in the field sing much more sweetly than those in cages', and warned that he should leave the country. Whether through valour or excess of confidence, Egmont stayed. He went out to greet Alba when he arrived, and was treated with great courtesy and respect by the Italian generals, notably Chiappino Vitelli and Gabriele de Serbelloni. Among the Spaniards, many admired Egmont and tried to save him. On the night of 8 September, as his wife the countess afterwards related, a Spanish officer (whom she thought to be Julián Romero) came secretly to their house and urged her husband to leave at once. The count's admirers also included Alba's son the prior Don Hernando. On 9 September he gave a lunch to which Egmont, Hornes and many other nobles were invited. Hornes had been persuaded to return to the capital only two days before, after receiving reassurances from the Spaniards. During the lunch a message came from Alba, inviting the gentlemen to visit him at his residence after the meal, to advise him about the new citadel he was planning to construct in Antwerp. The prior, who was seated next to Egmont, whispered in his ear: 'Leave this place, Count, at once; take the fastest horse in your stable and make your escape without a moment's delay.' Egmont rose from his seat and went into the next room, determined to accept the advice. But Philip de Noircarmes followed him and dissuaded him from doing so.

The lunch finished at 4 o'clock, after which the nobles went to Alba's residence, where they proceeded to take part in discussing the plans for the citadel with the duke and his engineers. The meeting broke up just before 7 in the evening. Sancho Dávila, captain of Alba's guard, asked Egmont to stay behind for a moment. When the two were alone, Dávila informed him that he was under arrest, and asked for his sword; at the same time, a company of musketeers entered and surrounded the count. Hornes was arrested outside in the courtyard as he was leaving the meeting. Both were immediately detained in separate rooms in the same residence, where they remained for two weeks, denied all exterior contact. On 23 September both were removed to the castle in Ghent. In a letter to the king immediately after their arrest, Alba explained that 'I have put off carrying out this business for so many days in order to seize all of them in one blow'.[29]

Fear reigned in Brussels. A member of the duke's circle informed the duchess of Alba that 'affairs here are as quiet and tranquil as though nothing had happened. Tomorrow the duke my lord leaves for Antwerp where I think he will be ten or twelve days to begin the fortification of the citadel'.[30] A week after the arrests Alba informed Philip that

> no one dares to ask me if I have authority for what I am doing. I refuse to present my authority, saying only that I have to do what is in Your Majesty's service, and that I do not have to offer any explanation if I do not wish. In this way they are stopped in their tracks. Today I have begun to look at the reports and confessions. Many things are emerging, and I am convinced that there will be a lot of clear evidence to justify the trial of the accused. . . . As for religion, Your Majesty can be sure that it is entirely uprooted and that it needs to be planted again, not even in England was it so ruined.[31]

The arrests were a decisive step in more senses than one. After the detention of the chief nobles, many who feared the possibility of arrest felt they could breathe more freely, for no action was taken against them. Confident that his strategy of fear was the right one, Alba did not contemplate a prolonged series of measures. The letters he sent out on 14 September confirm that he felt the essential task had been done. To Chantonnay, Philip's ambassador in Vienna and brother of Granvelle, he regretted the need to arrest 'two gentlemen such as these, whom I have always loved and respected as if they were my own brothers'. To the king he wrote that 'till now both great and small show satisfaction with what has been done. I am told that some people are leaving the country but am making no effort to arrest them because I feel that the pacification of these states cannot be achieved by cutting off heads'. To Requesens, Philip's ambassador in Rome and later his successor in the Netherlands, he confirmed that arrests were kept to a minimum: 'His Majesty's intention is not to shed blood, nor by nature do I favour it, and if this business could be resolved in some other way we would take it, because the intention is not to cut down this vine but to prune it. It grieves me profoundly that matters have reached the stage they are in.'[32] These statements, written in confidence to the highest personages of the monarchy, were obviously an accurate summing up of Alba's perspective at that moment. Everything had gone smoothly, there had been no trouble and no bloodshed, and in consequence there was no need for extreme measures of any sort. The conclusion is an important one, for it belies the frequent assumption that the duke came to the Netherlands intent on a bloody repression.

By October, what had at first seemed to be a troublesome situation had been reduced to order. The unqualified success of the operation, however, did not mean that the way forward was very clear. Many people had been taken into custody, and Alba's difficulty now was in deciding how to alternate between severity and clemency. 'The prisons are so full,' he commented, 'that I don't know where to put the detained and I am now busy making more space for them. I did not want executions but neither did I want them to go unpunished or become outlaws. I am trying to find a path somewhere between these three options.' From Spain, Philip could almost see the end in sight. 'I am thoroughly pleased and satisfied with everything you are doing', he wrote in reply to Alba's letter of 9 September. 'I cannot but stress that you have greatly satisfied me.'[33] 'With the energy and vigour you are applying to affairs, I feel that their resolution is in sight . . . Here too the arrest was made at the opportune time of M. de Montigny, whom I ordered taken to the castle of Segovia . . . After the imprisonment of Montigny, I also ordered the arrest of Vandenesse and his transfer to the same castle.'[34] Jacques de Vandenesse was a gentleman of the king's chamber, a native of Hainault who was in close touch with Egmont and Orange and kept them informed of events at court. He had been rather too free at court in his criticisms 'against the duke of Alba and against the Spaniards', and was arrested when it was found he had been passing out confidential information.

At the court of Madrid the French ambassador Fourquevaux observed: 'they say here that there is no further need of soft words to the Flemings, but rather of harshness and the bloody sword'.[35] It was a striking phrase, but not quite true, for in Brussels the duke had made no firm move towards a policy of severity. The Council of Troubles had barely been set in motion, and would take several months to impact. While the arrests went on Alba had time to centre his attention on the broader consequences of the repression. He felt – correctly, as it turned out – that the problems in the country were being provoked by influences from Geneva, from France and from Germany. All of these could be controlled through the efficient use of arms. In October he went so far as to offer his services to invade France with an army and polish off the Huguenot nobles in a quick action that would be 'a matter of a few days'. 'If it were summer,' he assured the king of Spain optimistically, 'Your Majesty can be sure that right now it would all be over.'[36] There is every reason to conclude that if the threat from outside the Netherlands had been resolved, Alba would not have felt the need to step up repression inside the country.

For Alba, the political problems in France and the Netherlands were closely connected and required a military solution. Reflecting now on the issues raised by the arrest of the counts, he felt that use of the army against potential rebels was inescapable. 'For princes to go to war against their subjects', he assured Philip, 'is something that should be avoided if possible, and Your Majesty knows very well that when you asked my views about it I gave them to you this year.' 'But,' he added forcefully, 'if not going to war against them means the ruin of religion in the kingdom and the state, then war must be considered a lesser evil. With war there is the risk of losing but also of winning, and it is the only way to be sure of winning.' The chain of reasoning led back to his own trusted convictions: that war could solve all problems. War had terrible consequences, but could also be a necessary surgery. In perhaps the most memorable phrase he ever penned, Alba assured the king that events in France were at a critical stage when the French crown must consider whether to wage war against the Huguenot nobility, for 'it is better that a kingdom be laid waste and ruined through war for God and for the king, than maintained intact for the devil and his heretical horde'.[37]

In November the king wrote to Alba: 'you have a free hand'.[38] He forwarded to Alba for his consideration some papers from Lorenzo de Villavicencio, who maintained that Alba's task was now done. The situation, Villavicencio insisted to the king, could not be resolved with an army. Nor must force be used against the Netherlanders, for that would unite them all against Spain. They would fight to defend what was theirs. His words were strangely prophetic: 'Don't let Your Majesty be persuaded that the Flemings are beasts and drunks, for they are human beings and if not so now they will be so one day, standing together and in their own land and with neighbours who will help them; and even if they kill one of ours and we kill ten of theirs, in the end they will finish us'. Spaniards could not be allowed to govern in the country, 'for they neither know the language nor understand the laws and customs'. The only solution was for the king to go there at once.[39] It was one of the tragedies of this complex situation that Philip ignored Villavicencio's advice and simply sent the documents on to Alba. He did the same three months later when he received papers from a Flemish adviser containing similar advice.[40] In November Margaret of Parma sent a firm letter to Philip II, advising the use of clemency rather than the rigour that Alba seemed to be contemplating. 'Otherwise, my lord,' she wrote, 'if severity is used the good will certainly suffer along with the bad and it will be imposible to avoid the ruin and total destruction of this country.'[41] Nevertheless the duke was allowed to make his own decisions on how to act.

The festive winter season was far from being festive in Brussels. Margaret of Parma had resigned her post. She presided over her last session of the Council of State on 16 December 1567, before leaving Brussels on the 30th, after swearing in Alba to succeed her. The duke and officials accompanied her as far as Namur, from where her group headed south towards Italy. Alba's appointment as governor was meant to be temporary, until the king's arrival, for his official status was captain-general of the army. He was lodged in a wing of the governor's palace where the king had once stayed. He chose to reside there, he wrote to the king on a freezing night in January 1568, 'in order to have at hand the administrative and financial councils, to which I can arrive by the heated staircase, where I am now writing with a good supply of wood in the stove. I am enjoying this cold in Your Majesty's service'.

There was a lot of business to be done, but Alba's position was unenviable. He had not come with the intention of running the government, and therefore brought no civilian administrators with him. He necessarily had to direct affairs that were in the hands of Netherlands officials whom he did not know and whose methods he frequently disagreed with. It was a formula guaranteed to create dissatisfaction on both sides, especially among Netherlanders who felt that all the decisions were being made by Spaniards.

> I am working as fast as is possible in this world to get through the business of the rebels. I hope that very soon everything will be settled in order to make the first executions, for up to now I have not wished to shed a drop of blood in order not to begin with people of low condition and be

1. Antonis Mor van Dashorst, *The Duke of Alba*. The Dutch artist Antonis Mor
(?1516–?1576) specialised in formal portraits and was a court painter to Philip II. After
travelling through much of Europe fulfilling commissions, he lived in Antwerp from the
1560s, where (probably around 1568) he painted this solemn portrayal of an ageing duke,
whose beard was beginning to show obvious strands of white.

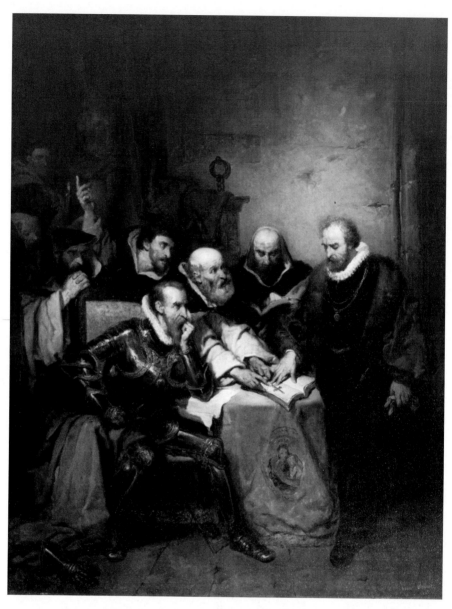

2. Louis Gallait, *The Duke of Alva Administering an Oath*, 1835. Alba's Council of Troubles in the Netherlands (nicknamed Council of Blood) had two Spanish members, one of them being Vargas, depicted here taking his oath as member of the council. Vargas was notorious for his complete ignorance of the languages spoken in the Netherlands.

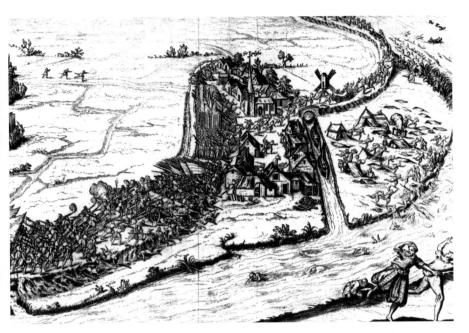

3. Frans Hogenberg, *The Battle of Jemmingen, c.* 1583. On 21 July 1568 at the town of Jemmingen (now Jemgum) in the northern Netherlands, near Emden, Alba's army inflicted a crushing defeat on the troops of Count Louis of Nassau, who escaped by jumping into the river Ems. The Dutchman Frans Hogenberg was probably the most distinguished engraver of that time. This plate appeared in Michael Eytzinger's *De Leone Belgico* (1583).

4. Frans Hogenberg, *Execution of the Garrison of the Town of Haarlem, c.* 1583. When the town of Haarlem surrendered to the Spanish troops in 1573 after a long siege, Alba respected a promise to spare the civilian population, but ordered the systematic execution of virtually the entire defending army, numbering over two thousand. This grim scene is taken from Michael Eytzinger's *De Leone Belgico* (1583).

5. Antonis Mor van Dashorst, *Fernando Alvarez de Toledo, 3rd Duke of Alba*, 1549. Antonis Mor was in demand by the emperor Charles V and also painted leading members of European royalty. This impressive portrait of the duke presents a mature, confident soldier, who played a key role in the emperor's victory over the Protestants at Mühlberg in 1547.

6. Eugène Isabey, *Arrival of the Duke of Alba in Rotterdam*, 1844. Rotterdam was among the few cities in the northern Netherlands to remain loyal to the Spaniards at the start of the revolt in 1572. This magnificent oil on canvas imagines how the city may have greeted Alba when the duke came to visit. Eugène Isabey was court painter to Louis-Philippe of France.

7. Pieter Brueghel the Elder, *The Magpie on the Gallows*, 1568. Painted in Brussels in the year after the arrival of Alba in the Netherlands, and a few months before his own death, this superb and enigmatic comment on peasant life contained the warning that loose tongues (symbolised by the magpie) could lead to the gallows.

8. Willem Jacobszoon Delff, *The Throne of the Duke of Alba*, 1622. In reaction against the political repression instigated by Alba, from 1569 pamphleteers began to issue leaflets that presented him as a monster. The duke was depicted as a sinister bearded figure seated on his throne of judgment (the 'throne of Alba', as the text of the prints described it), dispensing cruel sentences against a defenceless people. The same theme of the 'throne' was used in this early seventeenth-century print by the Delft engraver.

King Philip of Spain, following the advice
Of the bishop and the inquisitor,
Has brought great sorrow to the Netherlands.

Two monks journeyed to Spain
And complained that they
Were chased from their churches.

The Pope has presented Alva with the sword.
Granvelle and the Duchess of Parma participate.
Oh woe Netherlands, now in a critical situation.

With money and goods the Pope supports him
So that the Papists would maintain
The upper hand with force and fire.

9. Alva's Mission to the Netherlands and the Effects of his Tyranny (A series of four prints), artist unknown, 1572. This series of four prints, examples of Protestant propaganda, illustrate the reasons for, and the consequences of, Alba's mission to the Netherlands. (Translations of the Dutch and French text are taken from Tanis and Horst 1993.)

The ships fall into disrepair and the seamen are
  helpless.
The merchant can sell no merchandise.
The Whore of Babylon is merry with the Duke
  of Alva.

The peddler is condemned to poverty.
He cannot sell his goods because of
Alva's beheading, taxation, and stealing.

He seizes with force the wealth
Of the country and has caused many
Innocent people to be hanged and burned.

He has also taken the lives of Egmond and
  Hoorne
And suppressed the whole nobility.
This is lamented by burghers and peasants.

10. Jean-Auguste-Dominique Ingres, *The Duke of Alba Receiving the Pope's Blessing in the Cathedral of St.-Gudule, Brussels,* 1815. The Catholic Church saw Alba as a champion against heresy. This work was a preparatory sketch for a painting commissioned by the then duke of Alba that was never completed.

criticised for picking on those least able to defend themselves. The queen of England [Elizabeth] says she is amazed that there has been no punishment of some great noble, and I believe that she is not the only one. I have made every effort to justify the recourse to punishment and in examining the matter I have seen that it can be done, bearing in mind that those who are implicated have not acted with arms in their hands but have proceeded always as servants of Your Majesty. I have satisfied myself over what they deserve, the example should be made almost immediately, and I consider it more effective if done in cold blood. What would have happened if we had not captured them?[42]

Of the leading dissidents who escaped from Alba's hands, only William of Orange remained. Tall, dark-haired, with a small moustache and a short peaked beard, the prince of Orange-Nassau was aged thirty-five at the moment he was left in the role of defender of his country.[43] German by origin, his family seat was just across the frontier from the Netherlands, at Dillenburg. A comrade-in-arms of Philip during the latter's years abroad in mid-century, he never made a secret of his concern for the privileges of his class or of his dislike for religious dogmatism. Widowed in 1558, in 1561 he married Anne, the Lutheran daughter of the late Maurice of Saxony. The marriage, celebrated in Leipzig,[44] gave him a useful link with the princes of the Holy Roman Empire. When news came of Alba's departure from Spain, Orange opportunely took refuge in Germany in April 1567. He had already been warned by his secret agent at the Spanish court,[45] that Alba had instructions to arrest him on arriving in the Netherlands. He also received a warning letter from the elderly Landgrave Philip of Hesse, who after Mühlberg had been a prisoner in Spanish custody. 'I know the duke of Alba and the Spaniards,' Philip wrote to the prince, 'and how they dealt with me.' Before he left, Orange tried to persuade Egmont to join him in resisting the Spaniards. 'Cousin,' he told Egmont, 'if you take arms, I will join with you; if not, I must leave you and quit the country. Do you forget how the duke of Alba used to say to Charles the Fifth: "Hombres muertos no hazen guerra: dead men make no war"? I will not wait for their justice nor trust to their kindness.'[46] When Granvelle, at the time Philip's ambassador in Rome, heard that Orange had evaded Alba's clutches, he commented perceptively that 'until he is within the trap, the duke of Alba has captured nothing'.[47]

It became clear to Orange that the only way to regain the Netherlands was by the use of an army. On 6 April 1568 at Dillenburg he issued a commission to his brother count Louis of Nassau to raise men in the name of Philip, to defend 'the freedom and liberty of everyone in his religion and conscience', and the 'privileges' of the country, against the 'slavery, sorrow and misery' introduced by the Spaniards. He sponsored small invasions from three directions. Jean de Montigny, seigneur of Villars, invaded from near Maastricht on 20 April with some 3,000 men, but no towns came to their support. Five days later his forces were annihilated by a column of Spanish tercios before Dalheim and he was taken prisoner. His formal confession in May gave details of plans for rebellion and of those involved. Another small force of some 2,500 French Huguenots under their commander the sieur de Cocqueville invaded from France, but was driven back and in July was destroyed by troops sent by the king of France; only 300 men escaped. The third invasion force, under Louis of Nassau, crossed on 24 April into Friesland. On 23 May at Heiligerlee it defeated an army under the count of Aremberg, stadholder of the province, who was killed in the battle. There was no doubt in Alba's mind that a serious rebellion was in progress. Louis of Nassau's proclamations, issued in German in the name of the prince of Orange, promised to 'liberate religion and overthrow the Spanish Inquisition and government'.

Captured prisoners gave details of Orange's links with Protestants in several countries. On 28 May Alba issued an edict banishing William of Orange and his associates, and confiscating their property. He had already in February seized Orange's teenage son and heir, Philip Willem, and sent him to Spain, where he was brought up as a good Catholic. The invasions could not fail to affect the fate of the prisoners in Alba's hands, and set in motion the full machinery of repression. On 1 June eighteen rebel nobles were executed in the market square of Brussels. The next day Villars and two others were also executed. In the afternoon of Saturday 5 June 1568, in the main public square of Brussels, which was bounded on all sides by three thousand Spanish troops, the counts of Egmont and Hornes were beheaded for high treason. Alba watched the terrible events from the window of the governor's palace, and could not restrain his own emotion. According to one report, he shed tears 'as large as peas'.[48] The duke's formal report to his king was dry and terse: 'the punishment was carried out in the manner that Your Majesty will see from the enclosed dispatches. Your Majesty is today lord of these states'. At the same time he expressed his surprise at the apparent calm with which the executions had been received. 'Nobody has uttered a word to say that it was done unjustly. I always feared that no matter how much we justified the trials there would be an outcry, and there is none.'[49]

The deaths shocked opinion throughout Europe. Not since the execution of Thomas More in England a generation before had a state execution provoked such universal and unanimous condemnation. Philip's ambassador in Vienna could not fail to report to his master the completely negative reaction in Germany where, he said, the Protestant princes were spreading the rumour that Spain was preparing to invade the Empire. 'Both sides,' he wrote, in reference to both Catholics and Protestants, 'resent the presence of Spaniards in Flanders and there is growing bitterness against them and the sentence carried out by the duke of Alba.'[50] In Brussels, the people dipped their handkerchiefs in the blood on the scaffold, and thousands went to pay their respects to Egmont's body in the convent where it was preserved. The two nobles, as knights of the Golden Fleece, could be tried only by their peers. But Philip, grand master of the Order, had cleared the way for the trial by a special patent which he had drawn up in April 1567 and sent to Alba in December that year.[51] There is no doubt that Philip considered Egmont responsible for much of the trouble in Flanders. The decision to act, however, lay exclusively in Alba's hands, even though (according to some) he may have been reluctant to proceed to execution.[52] Philip expressed his regret formally to Alba. 'I very deeply regret that the offences of the counts were so serious that they called for the punishment that has been carried out.'[53]

High officials of the Spanish empire were equally shocked. Luis de Requesens, who succeeded Alba as governor, commented some time later to Philip II that the duke 'shed too much blood'. In Brussels he asked for Alba's own account, and the duke told him that in order to decide on the fate of the two counts he had asked for the confidential written vote of each of the six members of the Council of Troubles. Of the six members, five voted in favour of execution. Requesens criticised this procedure as illegal, for each judge should have voted openly in the presence of the others. The secret vote, he felt, implied that a condemnation was required. Alba told Requesens that he had not pressed the judges further, and that his signature alone was put on the death warrant.[54]

Alba had now to deal with Louis of Nassau's forces, amounting to some twelve thousand men, camped in the area of Groningen. In mid-July the duke reached the area, at the head of an army of about fifteen thousand. In an initial skirmish Louis lost three hundred of his men, but decided to make a stand at Jemmingen (known today as Jemgum), a small town on the left bank of the river Ems, near its junction with the river Dollard. The streams surrounded a narrow peninsula, within which Louis placed his army, facing the Spanish positions. They could only approach him along a narrow road, which he guarded with his artillery. To his rear, reached by the same road, was his only exit, towards Jemmingen. From Alba's point of view, it appeared that Louis had unwittingly hemmed himself between the Spanish troops and the river Ems. On the morning of 21 July, the duke ordered an attack.

Louis's men were attempting to open the sea dykes to let in the water, but they were too late. Their artillery barely had time to fire, and his men turned to flight. The action, which lasted from about ten in the morning to one o'clock, 'was not a battle but a massacre'.[55] Writing his despatch at noon, Alba reported that 'according to the reports there are at least seven thousand enemy dead, counting both those killed and those drowned in the river; count Louis escaped naked, his effects were found floating in the water and were brought to me'.[56] Those not lucky enough to save themselves in the Ems, were pursued through the fields and slaughtered. Sixteen artillery pieces were taken. Possibly less than eighty Spaniards died in this action, which the duke may have been right to term 'a very great victory'. The victorious soldiers made their way back to Groningen, pillaging as they went; the sky turned red with the flames from burning houses. Riding in the rear of his army, Alba was furious at the indiscipline of his men. He ordered the guilty to be executed, and shortly afterwards ordered the dissolution of the unit responsible, the tercio of Sardinia which had come with him from Asti.

A final effort to turn the tide was made by the prince of Orange, who invaded Brabant early in October 1568 from the direction of Trier with a huge army of thirty thousand men. Two months before the invasion he issued a proclamation that 'only when Alba's bloodthirstiness has been overpowered, can the provinces hope to recover their purity of justice and their prosperity'. But Orange's army was too large, too untrained, and above all it was unpaid. The towns, unsure of which way to declare themselves, did not dare to give their support. Alba applied the strategy that best suited the situation and that he had used to advantage in Italy: he simply waited. Instead of engaging Orange in battle, as some advised, he withdrew his men always just out of range, hoping that the invaders would spend their energies and their supplies. His tactics in the campaign were faultless, and more brilliantly executed than any of his famed 'victories'. No one has described the operation better than Motley.

The campaign lasted little more than a month. Twenty-nine times the Prince changed his encampment, and at every remove the Duke was still behind him, as close and seemingly as impalpable as his shadow. Thrice they were within cannon-shot of each other; twice without a single trench or rampart between them. The country people refused the Prince supplies, for they trembled at the vengeance of the Governor. Alva had caused the irons to be removed from all the mills, so that not a bushel of corn could be ground in the whole province. The country thus afforded but little forage for the thirty thousand soldiers of the Prince. The troops, already discontented, were clamorous for pay and plunder. During one mutinous demonstration, the Prince's sword was shot from his side, and it was with difficulty that a general outbreak was suppressed. The soldiery were maddened and tantalised by the tactics of Alba. They found themselves constantly in the presence of an enemy, who seemed to court a battle at one moment and to vanish like a phantom at the next. They felt the winter approaching, and became daily more dissatisfied with the irritating hardships to which they were exposed.[57]

One important skirmish took place on 20 October, principally because the commanders in charge, Don Fadrique and Chiappino Vitelli, took advantage of an exposed rearguard and cut the enemy force to pieces. But Alba refused to extend the skirmish into a battle. The prince of Orange was joined by a small force of French Huguenots, but that did not improve his situation. Not a single town opened its gates to greet him, and in the meantime his soldiers were close to mutiny. In mid-November he and his forces retreated southwards into French territory. Virtually without the loss of a single soldier, the duke had defeated a huge army of invasion and had inflicted losses of up to 8,000 men. He returned proud and confident to Brussels, where the city gave itself over to festivities in his honour.

The triumph, however, was only one side of the picture. The next three years would be forever associated with what Netherlanders remember even today as 'the tyranny of Alba'. The primary instrument of repression was the Council of Troubles, a body that had no legal standing but that elevated itself above all the normal tribunals and institutions. Day by day, throughout the provinces, suspects were being arrested and imprisoned and their property confiscated. Those indicted included dissident preachers, the iconoclasts of 1566, members of the Calvinist groups, and gentry suspected of rebellion. The total number of detainees is difficult to assess. What is certain is that the members of the Council of Troubles worked vigorously, trying some 12,000 cases between 1567 and 1573. Over 1,000 persons were eventually executed, and up to 9,000 were punished with confiscation of some or all of their property.[58] Alba participated in all the decisions since he literally *was* the Council, whose members could not arrive at conclusions without his approval. 'I am proceeding as fast as I can,' he informed the king, 'not a day passes without me spending seven hours, morning and afternoon, in the Council.'[59] 'We are rounding up the sackers of churches, the ministers of the heretical groups, and those who took up arms against Your Majesty,' he reported in April 1568; 'I have ordered all these to be executed.'[60] In one day alone in March that year, five hundred arrests were made. Indictments were also drawn up against some of the principal towns that were accused of rebellion because of the events of 1566. They were fined and in some cases their officials were arrested. The cities and nobility accepted the scourge meekly and passively. They had neither the soldiers nor the leadership to resist. Hundreds of people had already fled the country before the army's arrival. The exodus, which took place mainly between 1567 and 1568, eventually totalled around sixty thousand, most of whom went to the neighbouring German states.

The impact of those years has often been grotesquely inflated, above all in the classic pages of Motley, who affirmed that 'the whole country became a charnel house, the death-bell tolled hourly in every village. Columns and stakes in every street, the doorposts of private houses, the fences in the fields, were laden with human carcasses, strangled, burned, beheaded. Thus the Netherlands were crushed.'[61] That image lingers on in the popular memory and in history books, and must be vigorously rejected. At the same time, however, it should be stressed that the terror and suffering imposed by the foreign army and its collaborators did make a deep impression. Alba himself recognised that the repression 'has caused great fear throughout the country among those who feel guilty, an infinite number have fled'.[62] In order to reduce the emigration, he proposed publishing reassurances that it was not his intention to arrest everybody. As his secretary Albornoz explained (in a phrase borrowed from his master): 'it is not His Majesty's intention to cut down this vine, only prune it'.[63] The fact remains that Alba pruned drastically, and not without reason his name came to be associated forever with the workings of the dreaded tribunal.

The severity in the Netherlands, instead of solving a crucial problem, elicited bitter criticism from every major European state. Alba, however, was unrepentant regarding his tough policy. The population, he explained early in 1568, must remain in a state of fear, 'so that every individual has the feeling that one fine night or morning the house will fall in on him'.[64] There seems to have been no doubt in the duke's mind that he was simply obeying the king's instructions. 'Concerning the chastisement that Your Majesty wished me to inflict on these people, Your Majesty has mentioned it to me so many times that I have the impression you wish it to be done, and I agree that it is very necessary and now more than ever.' There was apparently a complete coincidence between king and general about the need to punsh the heretics and the rebels. At the same time, Alba was keeping in mind Philip's suggestion 'whether it would be desirable to bring some order into these states and join them under a single system of law and practice', that is, introduce some unity into the very disunited Netherlands.[65] Charles V had gone some way to achieve this, but it seemed now to be an ideal moment to take further measures.[66]

Since he had been sent to deal with a presumed situation of heresy, the duke could not fail to deal with heretical publications. In March 1569 a round-up was made of all suspicious books. In Tournai, where the Calvinists had been strong, over five hundred books were seized and later burnt in a public bonfire.[67] At the same time, the duke helped to introduce a system for censoring books, similar to those which other European states were beginning to launch. In popular parlance the Council of Troubles, which had suddenly brought fear and death into thousands of homes, became known as the Council of Blood. The scale of the terror was well known to many in Spain. A study published there in 1577 estimated, with considerable accuracy, the number of executed to be 1,700 persons.[68] The total of executions, however, was of lesser import. The real shock of the repression was that it was backed by a foreign army, and chose its victims from every social class and every community in the country.

Few of those implicated escaped. 'I have agents everywhere seeking out the guilty,' the duke boasted. There was no room for the type of coexistence between troops and population that some of the Spaniards who came with Alba might have hoped for.[69] Alba specifically intended to terrorise in order to deter, and aimed to cause the maximum impact among the common people. The small fish, he explained to the king in June 1568, should be dealt with before the big fish. 'I have always felt that one should go from lesser to greater in this, so as to cause more alarm.' By the end of 1568 the liberties of the Netherlands were non-existent. The failure of the prince of Orange brought about a slump in his reputation. He had no option but to turn for help to the French Calvinist leaders, and in August 1568 signed a formal treaty of alliance with the prince of Condé and Admiral Coligny.

The repression would have been much tougher if Alba had had the services of reliable officials, but he had to work within limits and with the personnel available. It was difficult, he informed the king, to bring to justice all those implicated as rebels, and even more difficult to execute them all; he was therefore resorting to the more practical policy of confiscating property and imposing fines. 'I shall begin to arrest some of the most guilty and wealthy individuals in order to press them to pay a fine, because it would be impossible to execute all those who have offended against God and Your Majesty.'[70] Once the preliminary executions had been carried out, the remaining victims should be squeezed for money. 'It seems to me that now is the time to do away with the knife and see if we can induce some people to pay a fine, which would give us a good bit of money.'[71] Where fines were involved, however, officials took most of the money to pay for their costs, so that it might not be worth implementing that particular policy. It was one among the many frustrations he came up against.

Another was the problem of dealing with heretics. A letter to Cardinal Diego de Espinosa, who happened to be Spain's Inquisitor General, sums up Alba's pent-up frustration: 'give me an Inquisition, and you'll see what I can do!'[72] It was a chilling comment on what might have been. Alba's regime had already in three years executed ten times more people than the Inquisition of Spain was to execute in the entire reign of Philip II.[73] It had in that time seized more heretical books than the Spanish Inquisition seized in its entire history. With a Spanish-type Inquisition to support him the duke might have been more efficient, but he could scarcely have been more brutal. He continued to believe that the problem of heresy must be dealt with in the most rigorous way possible, and kept complaining that the clergy in the Netherlands were not active enough. In May 1571 he wrote to cardinal Pacheco in Rome: 'I beg you to tell His Holiness that I am trying to have some ministers of the [papal] Inquisition appointed here, because the bishops are not as efficient as I would like at a time when there is dire need for punishment; they think that preaching is enough, but I would also like punishment. . . . The other day I sent two ministers to Deventer, they burned nine people. Every day we are discovering and punishing, but a great number of people have also been reclaimed.'[74]

Though there was outrage throughout Europe at Spain's policy, the king had no misgivings. He wrote to his ambassador in France that he was 'surprised at the sinister interpretation' put on events in Flanders by the French court, where the Huguenots had considerable influence. His policy was exclusively 'concerned with punishing rebels and not with religion'. 'I have never written or said otherwise.'[75] He was not about to launch an anti-heresy crusade, he said. Moreover, after the successful repression it was time to arrive at a settlement. In February 1569 he wrote to Alba: 'let us talk about the general pardon, since I feel that it is now time to concede it'.[76] The duke, however, was in the midst of a situation where evidence was turning up every day relating to the implication of people in the recent events. He was in no mood to hear about a premature pardon, and felt irritated that other advisers of the king, such as his friend Granvelle, were supporting it. 'Your Majesty informs me,' he wrote back in March, 'that Cardinal Granvelle has written to you that a general pardon is appropriate because it will be more beneficial than a policy of confiscations. Your Majesty should write to ask his advice about how this may be done so that I can be apprised and attempt to carry it out. I personally see no other way than that which I have communicated to Your Majesty in my letters, and the moment when the pardon can be issued is as I have written to Your Majesty, and not before.' The experience of the past, he emphasised, with a side swipe at Granvelle, was no guide to the wholly new circumstances of the present.[77]

In Germany the criticism, on the part of both Catholics and Protestants, was particularly strong, since the Netherlands had always had close links with the Holy Roman Empire. Philip tended to pay special attention to German views. His long stay there had given him good insight into the complexity of

German politics. Above all, he needed the emperor Maximilian II's support if he was to continue being able to recruit German soldiers – valued above those of any other nation – for his armies in Flanders and Milan. He periodically sent money[78] to help Maximilian's war effort against the Turks. Through his ambassador Chantonnay, Granvelle's brother, he kept Maximilian in close touch with his policy in the Netherlands. In May 1568 he explained that he was going to perform his duty there even if 'the whole world should fall in on me'.[79] The execution of Egmont and Hornes, however, stretched relations between the two branches of the Habsburg family to breaking-point. The emperor's ambassador in Madrid, Dietrichstein, delivered to the king in August a firmly-worded letter from his master.[80] So strong was the feeling among the German princes that the emperor on their behalf sent his younger brother, the archduke Charles of Styria, to try and mediate with the king.

During these months the duke's age and poor health were beginning to tell. In August 1568 Albornoz reported that 'you cannot believe how ailing the duke is and how much he needs a rest'. Six months later he was much the same, 'with a slight improvement but still very old and exhausted'.[81] His frequent depressions affected the way he arrived at decisions. 'He is so desperate,' said Albornoz, 'that he is likely to leave it all and go off, because he says that he is in no state to go either forwards or backwards.' It is very likely that his state of health was beginning to affect his judgment. Alba admitted to Gabriel de Zayas twelve months later, in September 1569, that if the king did not withdraw him before that coming winter, the winter would finish him off, 'because I really feel that the air of this country affects me so seriously that it is destroying me'. Albornoz could not refrain from writing to Zayas: 'it is an outrage to keep a man of well over sixty years in Flanders against his will, it is something done only to criminals'.[82]

The duke turned for support to his sons. At the end of November 1568 Alba professed to García de Toledo his belief that the prince of Orange must be stopped if the security of the Netherlands and indeed of the monarchy was to be preserved. It was a fair deduction, resulting not only from Orange's military attacks but also from what he knew about the support being offered to Orange in France. However, who could stop Orange? Alba had no doubts on the matter, for since 1568 he could count on the services of Fadrique, who had been allowed by the king to join his father in the Netherlands.

When Fadrique arrived in the country his first care was to write to the duke, apologising for the trouble that he had undoubtedly caused his father:

I had a thousand things to write to your lordship, in particular about the matters in my past about which you will have had many reports, all of them so hostile to me that I fear that my apology and penitence arrive a bit late, and so I shall not offer them here but wait until when please God we see each other, and so I beg your lordship to believe about me only that which in all truth I certify to you, for I have done nothing that is unworthy of the parents I have and the upbringing I have received from you.[83]

The arrival of his son and heir assumes no significance in any of the modern accounts of the duke's government of the Netherlands. In fact, for Alba this seems to have changed everything. He doted on Fadrique and had done everything to make sure his son was a success. The punishment decreed in 1567 was a bitter blow, for which he never quite forgave the king. Now at last father and son were reunited. On a freezing cold November's day in 1568, full of satisfaction at the military action in which Fadrique and his detachment had destroyed the rearguard of the prince of Orange's troops, the duke wrote to tell García de Toledo that the warmth of the reunion more than made up for the bitter weather:

> Don Fadrique has been such a help to me that I swear by all the oaths I can as a Christian and a gentleman that I have observed in him what I never expected to see in any man. I entrusted the whole army to him, and went out into the field only to hear his account. I confess that I am crazy with happiness to see how the action turned out and in special to see how Don Fadrique fared, for I thought that with him the long tradition of the heads of our family being soldiers would come to an end, and I see that it is quite the contrary.[84]

After the successful drive against Louis of Nassau, it seemed obvious that the required man to come to Alba's aid was Don Fadrique. My own head, the duke confessed to García de Toledo, is 'weak and old', and because this was so he was putting full military control in the hands of his son. It was a fateful decision that left its mark on events in the Netherlands. Meanwhile the duke's health did not improve. In January 1569 it was his principal complaint when writing to Cardinal Espinosa that 'not a single night that I go to bed do I think that I can ever get up again'. However, everything should be in order by the following May, he hoped; his only wish now was to be recalled, for his work was done. 'The business here, Sir,' the duke reported to Philip in the spring of 1569, 'is finished, thanks be to God.'[85]

The shock tactics, the arrests and repression, the executions and the defeat of invasion attempts, all combined to overawe any possible opposition, and stunned the population into submission. The duke used the reprieve to prepare administrative measures that were intended to improve government in the country, notably in legal matters and in the reform of bishoprics. The most important changes he proposed were in taxation, and it was at this point that the acquiescence so far achieved began to dissolve. The troops and garrisons had to be paid for, since the king did not intend to pay for them out of Spain's resources. Accordingly, in March 1569 Alba convened the estates of all the provinces in the Netherlands and asked them to agree to three new taxes, known as the Tenth, Twentieth and Hundredth Pennies.[86] The last of these was a once-only imposition of 1 per cent on property and income, and the estates saw no problem in agreeing to it. It was promptly collected, without problems.

The other two taxes were a different matter, for they were intended to be permanent. The Twentieth Penny was to be a 5 per cent tax on sale of property, and the Tenth Penny was intended, in the manner of the famous Castilian tax the alcabala, to be a 10 per cent tax on sales of commodities; both were to be administered by the government in Brussels, not by the provinces. The estates refused to agree to taxes that would be out of their control and deprive them of financial power. The duke threatened, and made concessions in the nature of the taxes. But the estates were stubborn. In the event, neither the Tenth nor the Twentieth Penny was ever levied. Alba could manage to survive with the yield of the Hundredth Penny, and succeeded up to 1571 in making the military operation almost self-supporting.[87] But there were clashes looming ahead.

The months of 1569 passed, with continuing tranquillity in the provinces. As the cold of the autumn crept into his bones, the duke inevitably returned to the theme of his health. 'If it is not Your Majesty's pleasure to recall me from here this winter,' he told Philip, 'God will surely do so.'[88] He insisted early in 1570 that he could now safely go home, since he had done his job. 'I see nothing that might cause Your Majesty to be anxious, and much reason for satisfaction and contentment,' he wrote.[89] The situation seemed so promising that on 16 July 1570 Alba eventually published the pardon to which he had been opposed a few months before. 'On the 13th this month,' he wrote to the king from Antwerp, 'I arrived in this town and on the 16th the general pardon was announced, to the great satisfaction of the people, though those who run the government were not so happy since they wanted no exceptions whatever.'[90] The ceremony was held in the main square, with bishops, dignitaries and councillors seated at his side as he stood up to read the document. With the exception of six categories of offenders, pardon was extended to all others who made their peace with the Church and received absolution.

Immediately after issuing the pardon, Alba took a break from his duties in order to travel southwards to meet the new queen of Spain, the emperor Maximilian II's daughter Anna.[91] Twenty-two years younger than Philip II, she had been born in Spain in 1549 when Maximilian governed the realm during Philip's European tour. It had been planned many years before that she should marry Philip's son Don Carlos, but the death first of the prince and then of Philip's own wife Elisabeth Valois, led to a change of plan and it was decided that she should marry her middle-aged uncle. It appeared to be a glaring mismatch, but matters turned out quite the reverse and she and her husband the king experienced ten years of undeniable happiness together. Anna accompanied her father to the Imperial Diet at Speyer and travelled from there down the Rhine to Cologne, where she was met in August by Alba, who escorted her to the Netherlands. Bad weather delayed the sailing for six weeks, time which the queen spent touring Antwerp. She eventually sailed from Vlissingen on 25 September. Hernando de Toledo, who had been summoned by the king to take up the post of viceroy of Catalonia, formed part of her escort.

The issue of the general pardon in July seemed almost to represent the end of the whole affair. Alba felt he could congratulate himself on having achieved what no other general in history had ever achieved: the pacification of a whole province, 'and without losing a single man, because I can assure you that in the two campaigns [the engagements against the troops of Louis of Nassau, and against those commanded by the prince of Orange] barely a hundred soldiers died'.[92] The duke's optimism was shortlived, however, for reactions to the pardon were far from favourable, either from the people of the country it was meant to pacify or from the officials who were meant to administer it. Moreover, the work of punishment was still continuing. Three months after the pardon, the count of Montigny, who had been arrested two years before during his visit to Spain and on whom sentence of death was issued in Brussels in March 1970, was executed furtively in the gloomy castle of Simancas.[93] The execution was approved by the king's council in Spain, but inexplicably it was decided to inform the count's wife that her husband had died from natural causes. Then on 1 November the same year the vengeance of heaven itself seemed to descend on the Netherlands. Storm winds off the north coast raised the water level and swept the sea inland: dykes were broken, towns and fields flooded, and hundreds of lives lost.[94]

A tired Alba, glowing with the satisfaction of a job he considered well done, had time to express his own personal complaints. He was unwell and needed to go home, his expenses had not yet been met. He unburdened himself to Diego de Espinosa in a letter that revealed every side of his situation: his fidelity, his health, his achievements, his troubles, his son, his unending grievances.

I was the one who advised His Majesty to adopt this policy, so honourable and so befitting a prince like him. I accepted coming to carry it out, committing my sixty years and my infirmities to the difficult journey. I arrived to find affairs in such ruin, and so hopeless to remedy, that they appeared not simply difficulties but impossibilities. When I came His Majesty wished to prove me as God proved Abraham, not allowing my eldest son and heir to come with me, in such a way that the whole world could see the disfavour in which His Majesty held me. There have been very many other trials but the latest has been for His Majesty to repay the service I have rendered him in a manner that no other person in the world would repay, not even my enemies.[95]

When he was in better mood and health, however, the tone of his letters changed. In September 1571 the king had appointed the duke of Medinaceli to take up the post of governor in Brussels, and at the same time take over the military command. Waiting in Brussels for his replacement, Alba yearned for the solace of his home and his family. And how were the fiestas in Alba de Tormes, he asked his son Hernando de Toledo? One event in the festivities had always been a mock marriage: 'write to me in detail about how the celebrations in Alba went, and if they carried out the marriage as if it were of a woman whose spouse is absent in America, and saying that I can say that the duchess is certainly like the wife of a man absent in America'.[96]

With the affairs of the Netherlands apparently under control, and until his recall could be effected, Alba became the key person to regulate Spain's position in northern Europe. The chief problem, as always, was France. The Huguenots had the support of over half the French aristocracy and could count on sizeable armies. Inevitably both the prince of Orange and Louis of Nassau served in the Huguenot ranks and cultivated links with the French nobility, whose help they hoped to obtain. Alba retaliated by sending military units to support the king, Charles IX, in 1567 and 1569. But the volatile situation in England also had to be handled with caution. Philip refused to be dragged into the dangerous schemes implicating Mary of Scots. She had fled into England from Scotland in 1568 and put herself under Elizabeth's protection. Mary, half French in origin, was a key figure in the politics of some of the Catholic nobles of France, and Philip had no intention of furthering their ambitions. Even more significant was his refusal to support the abortive rebellion which a group of Catholic earls in the north of England carried out at the end of 1569. Interference in English politics promised little benefit to Spain, which only wanted from Elizabeth her neutrality, and security of the seas. Alba kept in touch with the situation and refused to get drawn into any commitment to the English plotters.

While apparently serious threats to the queen were emerging in England, Philip limited himself to supporting Alba's concern for good trade relations. The duke had always been a firm supporter of the English alliance, which he considered preferable to any alliance with France. He backed Philip's policy of impeding papal moves to excommunicate Elizabeth. Above all, he highly prized the commercial links of England with the Netherlands. Despite these good intentions, friendship with England was irreparably disturbed at the end of 1568. In November five small Spanish pay-ships were sailing up-Channel to deliver bullion to the duke of Alba's army. Threatened by a storm, they took refuge on the English coast. Elizabeth impounded the ships and then seized the precious cargo. A break with England seemed inevitable. The tension was exacerbated in the same year by the expulsion of the English ambassador to Madrid, for undiplomatic remarks about the pope. Early in 1569 the Spanish authorities, in retaliation for the seizure of the pay-ships, embargoed all English ships and property in the Netherlands and in Spain. The English did the same to Spanish property in England. In January 1570 Philip informed Alba that 'we are in a virtual state of war', since English corsairs continued to attack Spanish shipping. The following month the pope issued his excommunication of the English queen.

The publication of the bull infuriated Philip. Alba's reaction was expressed firmly in a letter to Spain's ambassador in Rome, Juan de Zúñiga. The pope, he claimed, was both badly informed and mistaken. 'I do not believe that whoever advised this action at this time has acted from good motives or understands the real state of affairs right now.' The advice was so bad that he suspected it might have come from the French. The bull was quite simply an invitation to English Catholics to rebel against their ruler, a policy that Alba considered both reprehensible and dangerous. There was certainly a problem in England but the bull 'does not heal the wound and in fact renders it inevitably mortal. To do this at this time is the total ruin and destruction of affairs.'[97] He advised moderation, so as not to drive Elizabeth into French hands. This, rather than any pro-English sentiment, lay behind his advice of 'war with the whole world, but peace with England'.[98] Philip's wish to stay friends with England was also motivated by fear of complications with France. In May 1570 he instructed his ambassador in France to tell the English ambassador that 'on my side, I shall not break the ancient friendship and alliance between us'.[99]

The situation in England caused complications for Alba because of the machinations of an Italian adventurer named Ridolfi. In 1571, with the support of Mary of Scots, Ridolfi devised a plan to overthrow Elizabeth, proclaim Mary as queen, and send in a force from the Netherlands to support a rising by the Catholic nobles. Alba distrusted Ridolfi, and gave detailed reasons why he did not consider it advisable to encourage the Italian. Throughout July and August his letters to the king insisted that Ridolfi was not to be trusted, and that his plan would only exacerbate rather than resolve the situation. The outcome would be a destructive war that would resolve nothing.[100] Philip made it clear that he was not interested in Ridolfi's ideas,[101] though as the months went by he tended to come round to seeing its good points. In Madrid although the councillors of State were enthusiastically in favour,[102] they stressed that nothing could be done until the king gave his formal support. This he did not do. He made no explicit statement committing himself to action,[103] though he was certainly anxious that the plotters in England should take the initiative.

At every point Alba resisted the pressures from Madrid. He felt that the king's advisers were, as usual, both stupid and uninformed, and in particular he resented the pressure from his enemy the duke of Feria, a leading proponent of the conspiracies. He was convinced that a military adventure in England was both unsound and dangerous, and in any case he strongly opposed any embroilment with England at a time when the security of the Netherlands required defence against the real enemy, France. It is likely that Ridolfi was a double agent in the pay of England's chief minister, the anti-Spanish Sir William Cecil. At any rate, the plot was revealed by Cecil's spies in September 1571. The nation's leading nobleman, the duke of Norfolk, was arrested for his apparent implication, and later executed. Spain's ambassador De Spes was expelled from the country. There was still no open rupture with Spain. But the plot had decisive consequences. It broke once and for all England's traditional pro-Spanish connection; it pushed Elizabeth towards an alliance with France; and it confirmed the emergence of a pro-Protestant foreign policy in the English Privy Council. Looking back on these events two years later, Alba felt convinced that the Ridolfi plot had had disastrous consequences for Spain, in encouraging Elizabeth to extend her aid to the Dutch rebels during 1572, when the whole situation in the north took a fatal turn for the worse as far as Spain was concerned.

In the six years that Alba had been in the Netherlands he was inevitably in touch with what went on with the rest of the monarchy, but his absence meant that he played no part in some of the most crucial events of the century. It was a period when the threat from Islam in the Mediterranean was at its height. Within the Iberian peninsula there was a serious uprising of the Moriscos in Andalucia in 1569, coinciding with a sharp increase in north African piracy. Armies were raised in Spain to deal with the Moriscos, but they were commanded by others – notably Luis de Requesens and Don Juan of Austria – and not by the king's principal general, Alba. The greatest military event of the century also took place without Alba's presence: the battle of Lepanto.

Turkish naval forces had been carrying out extensive attacks against Christian powers in the Mediterranean and in the summer of 1570 occupied most of the island of Cyprus. A Holy League against the Turks was signed between Spain, the papacy and Venice in May 1571. When the Christian naval forces eventually assembled at their rendezvous in Messina in the summer of 1571, they totalled over two hundred galleys, the greatest assembly of ships ever concentrated in the waters of western Europe. All the nobles and warriors of the West vied with each other to take part in the great expedition, which was put under the overall command of the 24-year-old Don Juan of Austria. At sunrise on 7 October the western fleet came upon the enemy, at the entrance to the gulf of Lepanto, off the Greek coast. It was perhaps the most remarkable land battle ever to have been fought at sea, and ended in a memorable victory for the Christians.

From the start, Alba had opposed and objected to the idea of a Holy League.[104] In October 1570 he explained to Antonio de Toledo why he took this attitude: the League gave too much power to the pope; it would cost money that was better spent on the urgent needs of the business in the Netherlands; and it gave too much attention to the Turks when the real threat to Europe came from heresy. The Holy League would achieve little, for military decisions could only be made by soldiers not by diplomats and cardinals: 'on this matter anyone who is not a soldier would have not the slightest idea what to do'. One should not trust Venice or France. The Church had its objectives wrong: 'it is not the Turks who harass her now, but heretics'.[105] Nor did he take kindly to the appointment of Marcantonio Colonna, ally of his enemy the Jesuit head Francisco de Borja, as commander of the papal fleet in the expedition. From every conceivable point of view, Alba looked askance at the famous expedition. When it was all over, he dutifully congratulated Don Juan of Austria on the great achievement. But his essential views had not changed, and they were shared, moreover, by other prominent servants of the Spanish crown – notably Cardinal Granvelle – who did not think that one event such as the battle of Lepanto could bring security to the West, or eliminate the threat from Muslim power. They felt France and the Netherlands were the major problems because of their complete instability. As Alba commented to Juan de Zúñiga, Philip's ambassador in Rome, if the objective was to destroy Turkish power then the key lay in a collaboration between the emperor in Vienna and the king of Spain.[106] It was not enough to rely on the Italians.

The duke's opposition to the Lepanto campaign arose in part out of his anxiety over the financing of the Netherlands operation. In the course of the year 1571 the money he had managed to raise with the new taxes was beginning to run out, and there was still no progress towards agreement on the Tenth Penny. In July that year he decided to force the matter. He declared that he would begin to collect the Tenth Penny on 1 August whether or not the estates consented. No help was forthcoming from Spain as the king was tied down with other commitments. Alba therefore began to use the army to put his plans into effect. The authorities in the Netherlands replied with what was tantamount to a general strike. They sent protests to the government in Spain, shops closed their businesses, and refusal to pay the army-enforced tax became widespread. As shops closed, people went out of work. Discontent spread. The provinces were closer to rebellion than they had ever been since 1566.

Alba's health during these months seemed to be deteriorating rapidly. His secretary Albornoz informed the duchess in May 1571 that

> the duke woke up last Saturday, the 7th, in a poor state, after having slept badly in the night. He ate some chicken but with no appetite for it and did not drink anything. At 5 in the afternoon he began to be short of breath, his fingernails changed colour and he began to have bouts of shivering and then of sweating. As it was getting dark I asked him to lie down, he did so and the sweating took over, he was all night with fever but supped on some boiled lettuce and drank water. The next day he woke up a bit better but not completely so, and in the afternoon he got pain in his foot and that is how he is now.[107]

Alba had passed five years in the north, five long years in which he had done his duty but had not received even the elementary grace of being allowed to go home. 'When I think about my case my rage is so great that it makes me lose my judgment', he confessed in May 1571. Living side by side with the duke and sharing all his humours and miseries, Albornoz could not refrain from commenting sourly to the Alba family agent in Madrid, the Luxemburger Dr Milio, that 'five years away from home can kill you, and can certainly drive you blind'.[108] At long last, however, by December 1571 the end appeared to be in sight. Alba received news that the duke of Medinaceli was about to set sail from Laredo for the Netherlands. An attack of gout deprived him of sleep for several days, but he managed to recover, and started packing his bags.

The comfort he looked for was no sooner within his grasp than it was snatched away.

A group of Calvinist exiles who had been based in England, known as the Sea Beggars (*Gueux de Mer*), led by the Liège nobleman Lumey de la Marck, seized the offshore port of Brill on 1 April 1572. For the first time it gave the Calvinists a base from which to attack the Spaniards. Alba was confident he could contain their activities. But his attempts to collect the Tenth Penny had aroused fierce opposition in the towns. They now collaborated with the exiles, who received the open support of Orange. Just two weeks after the capture of Brill, on 14 April the prince issued a proclamation from Dillenburg calling on the people, in the name of the king, to rise against 'cruel, bloodthirsty, foreign oppressors' and their taxes and inquisitors. With the prince of Orange's firm support, the cause of rebellion acquired a leader. Early in the morning of 24 May 1572, the town of Mons in Hainault opened its gates to a small force under Louis of Nassau which invaded the Netherlands from France with the help of Huguenot nobles.

The coming of the Sea Beggars seemed for the moment to be less relevant than the situation in France, where events gave far greater cause for concern. Exposure of the Ridolfi plot persuaded Elizabeth to agree on a formal alliance with the French in April 1572 (the treaty of Blois). The accord appeared to be extremely damaging to Spanish interests. The young king Charles IX was at this period strongly influenced by the Admiral of France, the Huguenot Gaspard de Coligny. He also had meetings with Louis of Nassau, who attempted to persuade him to form an alliance against Spain. A marriage had been arranged between the king's sister Marguerite and the Protestant king of Navarre, Henry of Bourbon. French diplomats tried to extend the marriage arrangements to include one between the king's younger brother François, duke of Alençon (later, duke of Anjou), and Elizabeth. The latter, now thirty-eight years old, refused to think seriously about marrying someone twenty-two years younger than herself.[109] Despite this, the scenario opening up for Philip and Alba was a frightening international Protestant front, backed by France.

'There have been no other speeches but war with Spain', the English envoy wrote home from the French court at Blois.[110] Admiral Coligny was pressing Charles IX to intervene in favour of the rebels in the Netherlands. Spain was in no doubt about the reality of this threat. Nor was Queen Elizabeth, who had good information of what was going on and did not intend to get drawn into a conflict with Spain. Neither did she relish the idea of France dominating the Netherlands. In June 1572 she promptly withdrew from the alliance made at Blois. Charles IX was faced by the unappetising alternatives of acting alone against Spain, or pulling back and betraying his Huguenot allies. There remained a third alternative: to break with the Huguenots. It was the solution pressed on him by his mother Catherine de' Medici.

Subsequent events are well known. All the great leaders of France, both Protestant and Catholic, were gathered in Paris for the marriage of Henry of Navarre to the princess Marguerite on 18 August 1572. On the morning of 22 August an attempt was made by gunshot on the life of Admiral Coligny of France, who was gravely wounded. The Spanish representative reported to his king that there were wild rumours everywhere about who could have been responsible. 'A first reaction,' he wrote, 'was that the duke of Alba had ordered him killed.'[111] His own view, which turned out to be correct, was that the royal court had instigated the assassination attempt. Two days later, on St

Bartholomew's Eve, Coligny was brutally murdered as he lay wounded. His death was made the signal for the massacre of some three thousand Huguenots in Paris and a further twenty-five thousand or more in various parts of the country.

The news shocked Protestants in Europe. The emperor Maximilian, who was not committed to either side on religious matters, protested to the papal legate that the sword was no answer to religious differences. Among Spain's leaders, by contrast, the news brought nothing but joy, for they confirmed the elimination of those French leaders who had supported Orange. The first firm details of the event reached Madrid on 6 September, when the king was residing in the monastery of St Jerónimo. Philip had always entertained an unjustifiably firm image of what had really been agreed at Bayonne, and saw the events as a fulfilment of that meeting. His ambassador Diego de Zúñiga, writing from Paris, made it clear that Catherine and the king were responsible, but that the killing of so many Protestants had not been part of the plan.[112] On the day after Coligny's murder, Catherine wrote in her own hand to Philip, who replied at once to congratulate her on 'this glorious event'. He also wrote to Zúñiga with his reactions to 'the good news'. 'I had one of the greatest moments of satisfaction that I have had in all my life, and will have yet another if you continue writing to me of what is happening in the other parts of that realm. If things go as they did today it will set the seal on the whole business.'[113] The French ambassador, Saint-Gouard, was invited to visit him the day after he received the news, and reported to his king: 'He began to laugh, with signs of extreme pleasure and satisfaction . . . He said he had to admit that he owed his Low Countries of Flanders to Your Majesty.'[114]

5   Revolt in the Netherlands, 1572–1578

Nobody in the world desires the way of leniency more than I, but I have a special detestation of heretics and traitors.

Amsterdam, 31 August 1573

The Sea Beggars arrived in a country that was ripe to receive them. The winter of 1571–2 was harsh and a late frost destroyed fruit trees and crops. The hazards of climate, however, were as nothing compared to the distress created by widespread resistance to the Tenth Penny. If they had to pay a tax on their goods, traders felt, they preferred to shut shop. In many towns it was reported, 'the brewers refused to brew, and the bakers to bake'. People were thrown out of work, augmenting the poor on the streets. The problem was made worse by a crisis in the textile industry in those months. City authorities distributed outdoor relief in order to avoid disorders. Although at this time there were many different causes of distress, resentment tended to focus on the Tenth Penny.[1] Faced by the equivalent of a general strike against his proposals, Alba was left fuming. So far, he informed the king in February 1572, he had proceeded with moderation. For the moment, 'I shall follow the way of leniency so long as I am in good health, and when not I shall take the other'.[2] It was during this crisis that in March the citizens of Ghent found copies of the 'Paternoster of Ghent' scattered in their streets, directed against Alba.[3] It began:

Our Devil, who doth in Brussels dwell
cursed be thy name in heaven and in hell

and ended with the prayer:

Grant that this Devil may soon depart
and with him his Council, false and bloody
who make murder and rapine their daily study;
and all his savage wardogs of Spain
Oh send them back to the Devil their father again. Amen.

The early successes of the Sea Beggars were very much more than a straw in the wind; they quickly began to develop into a general revolt of the northern Netherlands. When other towns realised that the Beggars were occupying Brill in the name of the prince of Orange, they invited them in. On Easter Sunday of 1572 the port of Vlissingen was persuaded to join the rebels. It was an important gain, for it commanded access to the Scheldt. On 21 May the port of Enkhuizen joined the Beggars. By the summer most of the towns of Holland and Zealand, with the exception of Amsterdam and Rotterdam, had given their obedience to Orange. At the same time a small force of exiles invaded from the duchy of Cleve. Led by count Willem van den Bergh, husband of Orange's sister, they seized the town of Zutphen and occupied parts of Gelderland and Overijssel. In all, there were five different invasions during 1572. They were backed up principally by the king of France, Charles IX, who under the influence of Admiral Coligny, had promised to help Louis of Nassau and the Orangist cause. The rebels' main drive came from the south: on 24 May a force led by Louis of Nassau seized the key fortress of Mons. The prince of Orange was in Frankfurt enlisting men and purchasing supplies, and personally crossed into the province of Limburg on 7 July at the head of a force of some twenty thousand men. The situation had changed considerably since his last invasion attempt, and he was able to occupy several towns. In the same month of July a force of English and French volunteers captured Sluys and Bruges.

Alba was in dire straits. His immediate problem was money. He could not retake Brill easily because it was extremely difficult to transport cannon across the water. On 26 April he wrote to the king, in controlled terms, that 'I am continuing with preparations to remedy the situation, but don't know how I can do it without money'. He was much more outspoken, however, in a letter to Antonio de Toledo, to whom he made it plain that he was quite desperate. 'Affairs over here,' he confessed, 'are in a much sorrier state than I communicate to His Majesty.' There were problems about money and equipment, but most of all he could not refrain from lamenting his personal position. 'What I am saying could almost be taken as a last testament, for in testaments men lose their fear of facing the world.' He had spent all he had, and had not been repaid; the consequences would be fatal for his house, 'because apart from my arrears, since I arrived here I have had to spend more than 250,000 crowns'. And finally there was the question of when he could leave. 'In truth I do not know how it is possible that I am alive and so I believe that I am not . . . I have been through five years and it is now the sixth, keeping me here has been like an exile or a prison sentence.'[4]

He repeated his complaints to Espinosa. 'Making me come here to cut off heads as I have done, and then having the same punisher remain as judge for

so long, is something no one has had to do. If his aim was simply to gain experience, it would have been better for His Majesty not to have done it, because
he has lost a great deal thereby and will lose more every day.'[5] During the
months of 1572 he had made a remarkable effort to increase the number of
men in the army of Flanders. Between April and August a force of around
13,000 men was raised to a wartime level of 67,000.[6] This was a serious financial commitment, and also required adequate commanding officers at the top.
But neither his years nor his health made it possible for him to direct
the necessary military operations. He therefore put them in the hands of
Fadrique, who led the troops into Holland.

Louis of Nassau's occupation of Mons at the end of May opened up a
second front, which Alba was forced to take care of personally. Fortunately for
him, in July the Spaniards in the Mons area, commanded by Don Fadrique
and Chiappino Vitelli, eliminated a detachment being sent to help count
Louis. The force of six thousand, sent by the French king and the Huguenot
leader admiral Coligny, was under the command of the seigneur de Genlis,
Jean de Hangest. It was cut to pieces on 17 July by Spanish troops, just south
of Mons. Only thirty men survived and were captured, among them Genlis.
A letter was found on him, from Charles IX to Louis of Nassau, reassuring
the count that he intended to use his armies to free the Netherlands from its
oppressors. Alba's aide Albornoz wrote to the royal secretary Zayas that 'I have
in my possession a letter from the king of France which would leave you
open-mouthed with astonishment if you could see it.'[7]

The threat of French intervention was all too real. Alba left Brussels on 26
August and arrived before Mons on the first day of September. The day after
his departure from Brussels, the prince of Orange with his army crossed the
river Maas, entered Brabant, and had the satisfaction of seeing the main
towns, notably Mechelen and Oudenaarde, open their gates to him. Both
Orange and Alba were evidently taken by surprise when news of St
Bartholomew's night filtered through. The few gains that the prince had
made were at once thrown into doubt. He appeared before Alba's camp on 9
September and made attempts to relieve Mons, but they were fruitless.
Deprived of French support, he withdrew his forces three days later, after a
surprise night attack led by Don Fadrique cost the lives of six hundred of
his men. Alba, meanwhile, was overjoyed at the news of the events of St
Bartholomew's night. 'It has given me great satisfaction', he commented, 'to
see what has been done to those heretics.' He almost felt he could claim the
credit of the action for himself: 'I recall many times having said exactly this
to Her Majesty in Bayonne and I see that she has been true to her word.'[8]
Alba's only doubt was over the motive for the massacre. He suspected,
and rightly, that the Huguenots had been eliminated for political and not for

religious reasons. His satisfaction was complete when Mons capitulated on 19 September.

The apparently clean sweep made of Huguenots in France encouraged Philip II to expect that the main threat to the Netherlands, which had always emerged from France alone, would disappear. In September he repeated to Alba his satisfaction with the events in Paris, and expressly gave the duke permission to execute the Huguenot prisoners captured in the action in July, before the fall of Mons. His words were pitiless. 'The sooner you uproot such evil weeds from the face of the earth,' he wrote to Alba, 'the less reason you will have to fear that more bad fruit be produced as in the past, and so if you have not already despatched them from this world I shall be grateful if you would do so at once and let me know.'[9] The execution of the same Huguenot prisoners was also explicitly requested of the duke by the king of France, Charles IX, who had sent the troops in the first place but now, after the events of St Bartholomew's night, wished to demonstrate to Alba that the letter found on Genlis was a misunderstanding. Genlis and the prisoners were duly executed some time later,[10] but the decisions taken after the fall of Mons were much milder than the two kings might have expected. All the Huguenot nobles and soldiers, together with all the local Protestants, were allowed to leave. Around seventy persons were condemned to death for collaborating in the 'rebellion' of the town, and it appears that they were duly executed, from mid-December onwards. The executions and subsequent repression in the town were left under the direction of baron Philip de Noircarmes, whose disagreeable reputation was enhanced by his activities there.

Alba's replacement as governor had by now arrived. Juan de la Cerda, duke of Medinaceli, a friend of Ruy Goméz, had served as viceroy of Sicily and then of Navarre. From the start he was dogged by bad luck. His fleet sailed from the northern coast of Spain on 1 May but was forced back by bad weather and resumed its voyage two weeks later. In the Channel it was harassed by the Dutch, who destroyed many of the ships. The duke arrived at his destination only on 13 June, bringing with him a force of infantry. He was in time to take part in the early phases of the campaign to reduce the towns that were actively supporting the prince of Orange. He was at Mons when it surrendered to Alba, and received with the greatest courtesy count Louis of Nassau, who was allowed to withdraw along with other supporters of the Reformed religion. Nassau was ill and had to be carried out on a litter. Alba turned to Medinaceli and said, 'Today we have won a great victory!' The latter, according to one account, replied: 'We have lost an even greater one, by losing the hearts of the people!'[11] If Medinaceli really made such a statement, it would have been because he was paying attention to the views of the many Netherlands advisers who turned to him because they had failed to influence Alba. The difference of opinion between the two dukes intensified in the weeks that followed.

Although after the Paris massacre the Orangist towns could no longer count on international support, and were usually small and poorly defended, they had the advantage of being many in number. In the summer of 1572 around fifty had declared for the prince.[12] Alba could not split up his forces to reduce each of them. He therefore opted for a policy of selective brutality. The first to receive the brunt of this treatment was the town of Mechelen, before which Don Fadrique's forces camped in the first week of October. The troops in the army – principally Castilians, Belgians and Germans – had not been paid for some time, and at Mons they had by the terms of surrender been deprived of the right to sack.

Mechelen's offence was that it had accepted an Orangist garrison but had previously refused to accept a government one. The Orangist garrison withdrew peacefully when the town was seen to be indefensible, but Alba considered that also to be treasonable, for the town should have handed over the Orangists. Even after the burghers had decided to admit Alba's troops, shots were fired from the walls: this was considered unpardonable. When Mechelen eventually let his troops in, Fadrique with Alba's approval took the decision to let the troops sack at will, even though it was a solidly Catholic town. The havoc and killing that ensued were such that both Spanish and Netherlands officials openly expressed their abhorrence. Recalling the events four years later, one of the latter commented that 'one could say a lot more about it if the horror did not make one's hair stand on end!'[13] An Italian, aware that Alba had made a deliberate decision to allow the pillaging because his troops had not been paid, reported that the atrocities had lasted four days, and commented: 'with this sacking and no doubt in the hope of others, the duke of Alba can satisfy the Spaniards for some days more without them asking for wages'.[14] The excesses had the desired result: other Orangist towns quickly offered to accept the Spaniards. The duke pursued what remained of Orange's forces northwards into Gelderland. The prince gave up the effort, dismissed his troops and took refuge in Holland.

The brutality had been effective, and Alba had no qualms about repeating it. Protests over Mechelen, however, were so strong that he felt it wise to issue a statement justifying the action. The city, he claimed, had received hostile troops but not admitted those of the government; it had allowed his men to be fired upon; and it had let the enemy troops retire in safety. There were other significant successes for the Spanish on the sea coast in those weeks, notably the brilliant march made at the end of October by Cristóbal de Mondragón and a force of 3,000 Spaniards through the estuary of the Scheldt when the tide was out, in order to relieve the town of Goes. As they advanced at night through the channel the water rose above their shoulders and they had to carry their arms and supplies on their heads, but pressed on successfully for five hours before treading dry land. Nevertheless, the feat did not stop the advance of the Beggars, whose brutality was no less than that of the Spaniards and served to terrify hesitant towns into opening their gates to them.

The new governor of the Netherlands had little sympathy with the pitiless methods employed at Mechelen. Once in Flanders, he quickly saw that the situation was desperate and that Alba's position was completely untenable. The latter in his turn resented Medinaceli's interference, though he gave little hint of this in his letters to Madrid, where his support was waning and where he was now accused of following his own whims rather than the wishes of the king. The French ambassador in Madrid, evidently drawing on information from Ruy Gómez, reported that the duke was blamed by councillors for wanting war when the court wanted peace.[15] Alba never wavered. That spring he happened to have a talk with the recent Imperial ambassador to Spain, Hans Khevenhüller, who was passing through Brussels on his way to Vienna. Khevenhüller criticised his policy, but the duke accepted the criticism in good spirit and simply reaffirmed the need for a policy of harshness. 'Severity was the only solution to the riots,' the duke told him, 'and many eminent men were of the same opinion, saying that once the severity began it was necessary to continue it, for if the fire is not put out at the start it will gain strength and in order to put it out more fierce and efficient methods are needed.'[16]

Medinaceli, on the other hand, seemed inclined to adopt the Netherlanders' viewpoint. 'Excessive rigour, the misconduct of some officers and soldiers, and the Tenth Penny, are the cause of all the ills,' he affirmed to a correspondent of Granvelle, 'and not heresy or rebellion.' He held up for emulation the policy of Charles V, who had pacified the Comuneros of Spain through clemency and had limited punishment of the rebellion of Ghent to 'a few people'. 'He told me,' the same correspondent reported, 'that it was ill done to have banished so many people, thereby depopulating the towns.'[17] It was an argument to which the Netherlanders listened with satisfaction, and to which Philip was being obliged to turn. At this point Medinaceli accompanied Alba to the siege of Nijmegen, while Don Fadrique was sent off to reduce the northeast. At Zutphen Fadrique encountered resistance, and decided with Alba's permission to set another example. On 11 November his army broke into the town and perpetrated one of the most coldblooded massacres of the war. A noble in a neighbouring town reported to Louis of Nassau that 'last Sunday a great sound of shrieks and killing was heard from Zutphen, but we do not know what has taken place'.[18] Alba's own report to Philip II was more specific. His son, he wrote, entered the town and 'they cut the throats of everyone they found and many burghers, because Don Fadrique had orders from me not to leave a soul alive and also to burn down part of the town'.[19] Fadrique's report to his father provided some details: 'Today I ordered the execution of 150 of these scoundrels and for tomorrow I have over 300, among them many citizens of Mons and Frenchmen who when that town surrendered took an oath not to fight again.'[20] The neighbouring Orangist towns rapidly submitted to the troops. 'Gelderland and Overijssel,' Alba informed the king, 'were conquered after the fall of Zutphen and the terror which that induced in them.'

Medinaceli could not accept the need for these bloody methods; he was determined to stop the war and issue a general pardon along lines approved of in principle by the king. But when he and Alba met in November to discuss the situation, no agreement was possible. Medinaceli insisted that the pardon would encourage 'the innocent'. Alba replied grimly 'that he did not know who the innocent were. If His Excellency knew, could he tell him?'[21] Medinaceli complained to the king that he was not allowed to see correspondence, and that his views were ignored. When it was plain that their views were irreconcilable, Medinaceli told Alba that there was no point to further contact between them. He stood up, went off to his tent, and the next day left the field without taking leave of Alba. His letters to Philip stated that he felt his presence to be superfluous. On 28 November Alba wrote to the king with his own version of what had happened, assuring Philip that he had done his best to maintain good relations with the governor. 'Because of the good relations that I have always had with the duke I have attempted to do it, though he has complained to me about some things. I have always given him an account of all matters and have always made decisions together with him, though I really do not know if I have satisfied him.'[22] It was ironic that Alba, who had for so long insisted that he return home, should now be clinging on to his command, refusing to let his replacement as governor make decisions or have access to information. Unlike Medinaceli, he saw the situation in purely military terms and felt that he was the only person who could deal with it. Instead of leaving the Netherlands, he stayed on.

'The split between Alba and the duke of Medina has been taken very badly here,' a friend in Madrid reported to Hernando de Toledo, the viceroy of Catalonia; and from Madrid secretary Zayas wrote to Alba sympathising with him and condemning Medinaceli's attitude. The open policy differences called into question Philip II's entire objectives in the Netherlands and exposed divisions there among the Spaniards, many of whom disagreed strongly with Alba and looked to his successor for a radical change.[23] In Madrid Ruy Gómez was quick to distance himself from the problem and the disputes among councillors. Medinaceli had been the choice of the king himself, he said, and of the Constable of Castile: 'no one can ever say that I had a part in selecting him'.[24]

The next town to be victim of the policy of systematic brutality was Naarden. The small town lay on the route that Don Fadrique's troops were taking towards Amsterdam. On 22 November Fadrique sent a small company to Naarden to demand its surrender. During the talks, a stray shot was fired at the troops from the town. The burghers delayed their answer, but eventually agreed with the commander Julián Romero that they would surrender if their lives and property were respected. Neither Romero nor Fadrique had any intention of observing their promise. Romero ordered the citizens to abandon their arms and attend a mass meeting in the church (a Catholic one) of the local hospital; around five hundred obeyed the request. He then sent an official to inform them that they were to die. Troops were sent in and they were all massacred.[25] The soldiers then began a systematic butchery of the entire population, including women and children. 'The Spanish infantry scaled the walls,' Alba informed the king in one of his most terrible letters, 'and slit the throats of burghers and soldiers without a single man escaping, then they set fire to the town at two or three points . . . I am very satisfied that an example has been set in such a villanous town with such great heretics.'[26] The whole town, he claimed in a decree issued at the time, had been guilty of the crime of *lèse majesté*. For a long time afterwards the town of Naarden ceased to exist. Philip congratulated Alba, saying that Fadrique had shown himself to be his father's son.

Winter had now truly set in, and the Spanish troops were unused to the conditions that faced them. Alba was in Amsterdam, the only large city to refuse entry to the Sea Beggars, and he made it his headquarters for the campaign. In an incident which took place in the waters beyond the city, Spanish troops engaged a number of Dutch seamen. They had to fight on the frozen surface of the sea and were easily beaten off by the Dutch, who used skates to move on the ice. 'It is the greatest novelty you ever heard of,' Alba exclaimed, 'to fight a skirmish of muskets on the frozen sea.' The engagement cost many Spanish lives, and the duke was forced to purchase skates so that his men could learn this method of waging war. Subduing opposition was unfortunately taking much longer than expected. 'It is, Sir,' he wrote to the king, 'the most bloody war to have been seen in many years, in the last nine months we have been going with our weapons in our hands surrounded constantly by enemies.'[27] From the beginning of December he was totally confined to bed with his illness, unable to move. Only from mid-January 1573 was he able to get out of bed in the afternoon. The illness kept him in bed until April, and prevented him playing any part at all in the campaign, which remained wholly in the hands of Fadrique. That month he received a package of fresh lemons sent from Spain by the duchess. He felt much better, and was able to walk far enough to go to mass at the church beside his house.

From his sick-bed he kept in touch with Fadrique's movements, which now concentrated on the town of Haarlem, besieged from early December. Though some of the town's magistrates favoured surrender and sent emissaries to Alba, the majority were driven by the example of Naarden to resist at whatever cost, since the word of the Spanish commanders could not be trusted. On 11 December Fadrique had about 30,000 men investing the town. Alba felt that another lesson would have to be given, and regretted it. 'I shall be sorry in my heart and soul if the town has to be taken by storm, but they are matters we cannot control. When towns that do not surrender have to be conquered, severity is unavoidable.'

To the surprise of the Spaniards who thought the place would fall in a week, Haarlem resisted, and brilliantly.[28] An assault just before Christmas was vigorously repulsed, with the loss of many Spanish lives. Julián Romero lost an eye in the action, and Alba suffered two casualties in the members of his family who always accompanied him: Rodrigo de Toledo was killed and Hernando de Toledo wounded in the arm. The duke reluctantly expressed his admiration for the defenders, who continued to hold out week after week. The citizens worked feverishly to throw up a second stone rampart in case the main walls should give way. When a second general assault was ordered by Fadrique during the night of 31 January, the dismayed soldiers found that the storming of the main fortifications was little gain, for a second stone wall rose before their eyes. The city could not be taken. The only recourse was to starve it out.

The Spaniards were also paying a price, for around one thousand of their men died in the weeks of siege. A Spanish captain in the trenches, suffering through the campaign and the freezing winter of 1572–3, confessed that 'I don't understand this war nor do I believe that anyone understands it, those who pay the price are the poor soldiers of whom none escapes.' In the first week of January he wrote:

> Here we suffer an incredible travail, for apart from the terrible weather and lack of food we are on guard 28 hours out of 48 so that there is no time to look after ourselves. God help us . . . The weather is the most awful that has been seen here in 600 years, every day they drag soldiers out of the trenches half-dead . . . The enemy and the weather are murdering our men, and not a few of them.

He expressed dismay that the king did not seem to realise how terrible the situation was: 'it is amazing that there is no one to inform the king of the dreadful state in which things are. . . The way things are going I do not think that it will be possible to take this country.'[29]

The heroic resistance of Haarlem encouraged both sides to make it their standing ground. Though Fadrique at one phase thought of raising the siege, his father soon dissuaded him. 'If you strike camp without the town surrendering,' the duke wrote, 'I shall disown you as son, if you die in the siege I shall go personally to take your place, though I am ill and bed-ridden, and if both of us fail then your mother will come from Spain to achieve in the war what her son has not had the valour or patience to achieve.'[30] The prince of Orange did all he could to send men and food to the city, but the Spaniards frustrated every move and wiped out attacking forces. The near-starving defenders made repeated attacks on the besiegers, and in one action in March succeeded in capturing cannon and supplies. In May, however, the Spaniards succeeded in gaining control of the lake that had been Haarlem's only relief route.

By now over three thousand defenders had perished. In the first week of July 1573 the prince of Orange managed to put together a force of around five thousand that approached the town from the south. Its movements were unfortunately known to the Spaniards, who had captured pigeons bearing information about its plans. Fadrique's troops lay in wait as the force approached by night, and overwhelmed it. Alba was informed that around three thousand of the insurgents died in the action. Haarlem's last hope had disappeared. The desperate city, facing death either from starvation or massacre, finally surrendered on 12 July, after receiving written assurances of mercy. This time there was no massacre of civilians, but Alba wrote immediately to his son that the entire garrison (mainly Belgians, English and French) should be put to death, and some of the burghers as well. 'Not a single person must escape,' the duke said to the French envoy.[31] The instructions were carried out. On entering Haarlem, the Spaniards methodically cut the throats of the entire garrison, some two thousand persons, in cold blood.[32] When the executioners' arms grew tired, they bound the remaining prisoners back to back and threw them in the river to drown. Only the Germans, some six hundred, were set free, on condition they did not serve against the king. Around fifty of the burghers were taken into custody, and several of them executed; very many citizens inevitably died during the fury of the occupation.

The recovery of Haarlem was a profound relief to the king, who was ill in bed at San Lorenzo when he received the news on 24 July. His secretary, who read him the despatch, reported that to the king 'the news of Haarlem has been better medicine than a great many doctors'.[33] But many Spanish advisers were horrified at the cruelty employed. The king's secretary Gabriel de Zayas, who handled most of the relevant correspondence and was in principle a supporter of Alba, was faced with the unenviable task of sending on to the king bitter criticisms from Spanish officials. Even Julián Romero complained to Zayas of 'the abhorrence in which the name of the house of Alba is held', a comment evidently directed against Fadrique but also by extension against other members of the Alba clan who went everywhere with the duke. 'Cursed be the Tenth Penny and whoever invented it, since it is the cause of all this.'[34] Alba's own secretary Albornoz was forced to admit to Zayas that the people of the Netherlands 'spit when they hear the name' of the duke. One of Philip's secretaries, Esteban Prats, who was sending regular reports to the king, warned him that the only way forward was to 'suspend the policy of severity', and issue a general pardon; 'to think that there is any other way of achieving the peace and tranquillity of this people, is to believe the impossible', for the rebels had superior forces and could always count on outside help. Rigour had failed, despite 'having executed over three thousand people in just over five years and exiled another 19,000'.[35] Hated by the Netherlanders, and increasingly estranged from the officials who governed the country in the name of the king,[36] Alba felt himself more and more isolated.

Granvelle, now viceroy of Naples, also saw no victory in Haarlem. He commented in September: 'I have never ceased to plead with the duke of Alba that he change his policy and resort to clemency, because for seven years he has seen from his own experience that the policy of severity is not the most suitable one'.[37] A few days later he came back to the same theme. 'We are still losing. The hatred that the country has for those who now rule is greater than you can imagine.' The whole of Alba's regime, he summed up, amounted to 'many millions ill-spent, and the complete ruin of those provinces'.[38] In Milan the viceroy, Luis de Requesens, also strongly disapproved of what had happened at Haarlem. He had already had occasion to disagree strongly with the duke's methods. 'Mercy,' he urged, 'is very necessary.'[39]

Alba's satisfaction at the fall of Haarlem was quickly followed by the bad news that the victorious tercios had mutinied. Haarlem's written agreement to surrender meant that the town could not be sacked. For the serving soldiers there was nothing to celebrate. Thousands of them had died during the siege, almost as many as within the city; they had moreover put up with eight months of foul weather and lack of pay. Julián Romero with his tercio was among the mutineers. Alba felt the blow personally, and said so to the king. 'I find myself in the greatest predicament of my life, for all my plans have come to nothing and in the forty years that I have been a commander I have never experienced what I now see before me, such a dangerous and unacceptable situation that I don't know what to think or how to resolve it, because without money I see no solution. It is the first time that Spaniards have acted in this way with me.'[40] In an effort to pressurise the king to send the required money to pay the soldiers, he stated that he had offered himself to the men as a hostage until they were paid.

Alba accepted the responsibility towards his men that befits a general and drew up a printed address, bearing the date 13 August, which he directed to them from Amsterdam. His efforts and those of his lieutenant Chiappino Vitelli managed to raise enough money to pay a proportion of the soldiers' wages. The mutiny collapsed after eighteen days. As soon as the soldiers had dispersed Don Fadrique arrested the ringleaders and had them shot, twenty at a time. The brutality appeared to have worked, but in reality sowed the seed for much greater disaster, because the soldiers never again trusted their commanders, and when a couple of years later the same problems arose they swore to remember 'what happened at Haarlem', and promised 'not to trust as we trusted the duke of Alba and his son Don Fadrique', especially the latter who 'made his promises but the words and promises were carried away by the wind'.[41]

One of the least commented on aspects of Alba's regime in the Netherlands is the way in which it quickly lost the support of Spaniards who were there, whatever their political views. It was not only unpaid soldiers who complained about the governor. Many of Alba's own advisers also turned against him. The duke was by nature extremely obdurate, and always nurtured the idea that he alone was right, but at the beginning his unfailing courtesy induced him to listen to the advice of others. He would welcome their ideas and often put them into practice. In the early period of his government, therefore, he could count on the cooperation of many prominent persons who were not necessarily sympathetic to his methods. Perhaps the best known of these was the Spanish humanist Benito Arias Montano.

A product of the Erasmian generation at the university of Alcalá, theologian at Trent, chaplain to Philip II and the most distinguished Hebraist in Spain, Montano was sent by the king to Antwerp in 1568 to prepare a new multilingual edition of the Bible. Since Montano had good contacts there, the king also asked Alba to consult with him for advice. It was an effective collaboration. Montano wrote to a government minister in Madrid that 'when I am here in Antwerp nearly every afternoon we talk alone, and when I am in Brussels we talk in the morning, at lunch and for two hours after lunch, and in the evening between two and four hours. He has a discretion, memory, judgment and discrimination that excite my admiration.'[42] Montano became a firm supporter of the duke, viewing the early arrests, executions and military campaigns as the only practical way to settle the disturbances. He saw the hand of God in the victory at Jemmingen, and suggested to the duke that a statue should be raised to commemorate it.[43] He also knew a sculptor, he said, who could do the job. Alba was taken by the idea, and arranged for the enemy cannon captured at Jemmingen to be melted down for the sculptor, Jacques Jonghelinck. The result was an over-life-size bronze statue of the duke that was erected in the market square at Antwerp, showing him trampling down rebellion. An inscription in Latin, composed by Montano, said: 'To Fernando Álvarez de Toledo, duke of Alba, governor of the Netherlands under Philip the Second, for having extinguished sedition, chastised rebellion, restored religion, secured justice, established peace; to the King's most faithful minister this monument is erected.'

The collaboration between Montano and the governor extended into matters of culture. In accordance with the directives of the king, Alba was interested in reforming aspects of education and printing in the Netherlands. In September 1569 Montano became one of a committee appointed to look into these issues, and his friend the printer Plantin was adopted as official publisher to the king. Montano and Alba also worked closely in preparing a new method of censorship, and sponsored a catalogue of prohibited books that was published by Christophe Plantin at Antwerp in 1569. Philip II felt that there were lessons to be learnt from the method of censorship adopted in Flanders, for he informed Alba at the end of 1569 that Montano's catalogue 'will serve as the model for making one like it here, and a copy has been given to those of the Inquisition with this end'.[44]

Even while working with the duke, Montano continued his close links with friends in the Netherlands. In September 1569, for example, the university of Louvain sent a delegation to the duke to ask that he withdraw Spanish troops from the university. Montano came with the professors. The spokesman of the delegation made a long and tedious speech before Alba. The duke had just spent three weeks ill in bed, and it was his first day up; he was weak and seemed not to be listening. Montano cut into the proceedings and told him that if the petition were rejected the spokesman would have to repeat the speech. Alba was highly amused by the threat; in the words of his secretary, 'the duke could not refrain from laughing', and agreed that the troops be withdrawn.[45]

In the event, the erection of a statue to Alba turned out to be a serious mistake. Observers in Brussels, Italy and Madrid criticised it as an unprecedented act of arrogance, which of course it was. 'Even the Spaniards take it ill that the duke should wish to sing his own praises,' a Jesuit reported later. 'There is no topic more talked about in the king's court than this.'[46] No general in recent times had ever raised a statue to himself. The figures that the statue was trampling down, moreover, could be viewed as the people of the Netherlands. It provoked the first significant outburst of propaganda directed against the duke and the Spaniards. The most successful of the satirical illustrations, which first appeared in 1569, was titled 'The throne of the duke of Alba'. The first illustrated satires on the statue appeared in 1571.[47] In an age when illiteracy was high and pictures spoke more than words, the message of the satires hit home. The statue did not long outlive the duke's regime. When Luis de Requesens was appointed as his successor, one of the first instructions he received in 1574 from the king was to remove the hated statue. The French historian De Thou, who saw it after it was pulled down, was 'as much struck by the beauty of the work as by the insane pride of him who ordered it to be made'.[48] Fortunately, Jonghelinck's artistic work was not wholly wiped out. A bronze bust of the duke which he sculpted at the same time, just over a metre high and conveying perfectly the stern aspect of the duke, survives today in the Frick Collection.

Affected like everybody else by the deteriorating situation, Montano soon revised his opinion of the duke's methods. He agreed with other critics that the Tenth Penny was at the root of the problem, and wrote to the king expressing his opposition to it. 'The affairs of this government', he noted in August 1571, 'are now in quite a different state from what they were a year ago.'[49] His opinion was extremely important, for the king respected him (he was later appointed as librarian of the Escorial) and paid heed to his advice. A year later, when Montano returned to Brussels from visits to Spain and Rome, he was called to consult with the duke at Nijmegen. The situation struck him as appalling. 'What I have found here is total disaster,' he informed the king's secretary Ovando, 'and my heart breaks to see things so changed.' In February 1573 he wrote to Zayas that 'there is nothing but division, disagreement and quarrels. The duke of Alba is more affected than you would believe, it is to be expected when so many cares and problems are piled on old age and infirmity.'[50] Montano was by now convinced that the methods applied by the duke were self-defeating and informed the king that only leniency would work: 'ten times more and twice that will be gained through this policy than through force and fear'. The king asked Montano to consult with the Netherlanders to find out 'which is the true solution that should be applied'.[51] Philip treated with respect the reports he received from the illustrious scholar. Montano's reports greatly helped to make the king change his policies in the Netherlands. He would discuss Montano's reports with his secretary Baltasar Gracián as they walked up and down the length of the great library in the Escorial.[52]

A yet more significant defector than Montano was Alba's friend, correspondent and colleague Francés de Álava. Álava was a Basque soldier and diplomat, who had served in all parts of Europe and from 1562 to 1570 was Philip II's ambassador at the French court. A rigidly conservative traditionalist, he supported the protection of the Catholic faith but also felt that Catholics should attempt to live at peace with their enemies, whether Muslim or Protestant. He ran a small network of spies who gathered information in northern Europe, and he also favoured the use of assassination as a possible political weapon. Alba relied on him for a constant stream of information about events in France. After several years observing the evolution of Alba's policies in the Netherlands, Álava felt obliged to advise the king that the use of force had been a failure, and that different methods should be used. He passed through Brussels and Antwerp in 1572 and was able to observe conditions for himself. He spoke directly with Netherlands officials, including Philip de Noircarmes and Charles, count of Berlaymont, who denounced the Tenth Penny and the duke's policies. He also spoke with the duke, and found him intractable. In his report to the king, Álava painted a bleak picture of the situation, said the Tenth Penny could not be enforced, and that the entire country wanted the duke to leave: 'the whole people agree on "Out, out, out!"'[53] Two years later he repeated to the king that in the Netherlands all was

> hatred for your officials and for the Spanish infantry which was meant to help restrain the people. Addressing Your Majesty with due humility and respect, it appears that this situation cannot be settled or solved by force. In my modest judgment, a different policy should have been attempted on the many good occasions that there have been, and though it would appear in part to prejudice Your Majesty's reputation and name, the truth is that most rulers have had to take the path, one of pardon and compromise.[54]

Alba's methods were not working. Opposition among the people of the Netherlands was hardening, not weakening. The military toll was appalling. To add to the misery of conditions and climate, the soldiers suffered a high death-rate. The taking of Haarlem, for example, may have cost the besiegers some ten thousand men. Finally, the burden on the exchequer was insupportable. The current debt in Flanders was around four million ducats, or two-thirds of the entire available income of the government of Spain.[55] To this had to be added the current costs of the campaign, which was over 600,000 ducats a month, the biggest single burden on the treasury. The monthly expense in Flanders was over ten times the cost of defence in the peninsula, and twenty times the cost of the royal household and government.

For different reasons, Alba was equally desperate about the war. In February 1573 he wrote to Zayas, appealing for a diversion of resources away from the Mediterranean and towards the north. 'I beat my head against the wall when I hear them talk of the cost here! It is not the Turks who are troubling Christendom but the heretics, and these are already within our gates . . . For the love of God, ask for the new supplies that I have detailed to His Majesty, because what is at stake is nothing less than the survival of his states.' Throughout the year, he continued to rage, plead, and rail against those in authority in Madrid. 'Until those who serve in his councils are dead or sacked,' he complained to Zayas in April, 'His Majesty will achieve nothing here. The truth is, Sir, I can't go on.'[56] One of his most gloomy letters to the king, written while he awaited Medinaceli's arrival, shows the duke fighting against the shadows that seemed to advance on all sides:

> Even if the sky should fall in on me and the king's own hand put an end to me, I would not believe it because I already have clearly in his own hand his satisfaction with the way in which I have served him here. I fear that those over here may return to the old game and my anxiety is such that really I don't know what to do with myself, I feel old, ill and poor, and Your Majesty would not believe how I have pledged my patrimony on this long and expensive campaign, and above all fearing the machinations over there of those who bear me no goodwill.[57]

In sending the duke of Medinaceli to Brussels, Philip had made it clear that he no longer backed Alba and was seeking an alternative solution. But the ailing Alba, profoundly immersed in the military policies he was implementing through his son Fadrique, had no wish to be dragged away from the task he had in hand, and moreover refused to accept the interference of the new governor. His insistence on retaining control was not to the king's liking, and Philip did not consider Alba indispensable to the campaign in the Netherlands. In July 1573 he wrote to Medinaceli that 'the delay of the duke of Alba in leaving those states after your arrival cannot be justified by the needs of the war, and is now so lengthy that it cannot fail to cause understandable dissatisfaction and irritation. It has caused me much regret and concern'.[58] When it became clear that the governor could make no headway either with the duke or on his own account, the king decided to withdraw Medinaceli and at the same time make sure that Alba would leave. He had already warned Alba explicitly. 'I shall never have enough money to satisfy your greed but I can easily find you a successor able and faithful enough to bring to an end, through moderation and clemency, a war that you have been unable to end by arms or by severity.'[59]

Medinaceli returned to Spain by land, through France. Meanwhile the king was struggling to find an adequate successor to Alba as military commander. On 30 January 1573 he had signed and despatched an order appointing his old friend Luis de Requesens, grand commander of Castile and currently governor of Milan, to the Netherlands command. Requesens had been in fragile health for many months and was aghast at being asked to take on this cross. He confided to his brother Juan de Zúñiga that Flanders was 'lost', that 'I am no soldier', and that he understood neither French nor Dutch, the two languages of the country. In short, 'I find a thousand reasons for not accepting'.[60] When six months later he had made no move to obey, the king insisted that he accept without question.[61] The months were passing and the situation in the north was rapidly slipping out of Spain's control.

The futility of extreme measures was shown by the fact that, in the same month as Haarlem's surrender, the little town of Alkmaar refused to open its gates to the army of Flanders. The burghers had already refused to allow in the troops of Orange, and hoped to remain neutral, but when the Spaniards challenged them they were overcome by fear and could not decide what to do. After a stormy meeting of the citizens a group forced the issue and let in Orange's men. The Spaniards, however, were held up by the mutiny among their troops and could not begin a siege until 21 August, when Don Fadrique presented himself before the town. It was a wholly unequal contest, with Alkmaar's eight hundred soldiers and thirteen hundred citizens capable of bearing arms, against an army of sixteen thousand. The town was completely cut off by land; it was impossible, Alba told the king, for a sparrow to enter or leave it.

The defiance of the little town angered the duke. Ill and impatient, he could think only in terms of repeating the methods of Naarden and Haarlem. 'If Alkmaar is taken by storm,' he wrote to the king on 30 August, 'I have decided not to leave a single person alive but to have all their throats cut since they have not profited from the example of Haarlem where all the burghers were pardoned except for just over forty who are in prison and five or six whom I had beheaded . . . Maybe with the example of cruelty the other towns will give in.'[62] As though to justify this fearful decision, he claimed that he had spoken to others who were also of the opinion that Alkmaar should be taught a lesson and that every living person there should be put to the sword. His intemperate reaction, and the easy acceptance of the word 'cruelty', were as we have seen typical of the duke, but also showed that he was not thinking clearly and not consulting with others sufficiently.

Events turned out quite differently from what he had expected. On 18 September, after a twelve-hour cannonade against the town, Don Fadrique ordered an attack. The citizens mounted the walls and resisted fiercely, so that after four hours the army was forced to withdraw, leaving over a thousand dead. The attack was repeated the following day, but with equally poor results. On 22 September, using quite different language to that which he had used previously, Alba told the king that 'if Alkmaar is not taken in two or three days I don't intend to waste more time with it'.

Neither Orange nor the town leaders had any real hope that they could resist the army. They therefore suggested that in the final resort, if no other help were available, they would open the dykes that kept the sea out of their fields, thereby flooding the whole countryside and with it the Spaniards. There was strong opposition to the idea, which, if put into practice, would destroy the livelihood of the peasants. Some of the sluices, however, had already been opened and were inundating the area. The Spaniards' cannon became bogged down in mud, a situation aggravated by constant rain. Fadrique faced a grim prospect. Like his father, he was seriously unwell with gout, and had to be carried everywhere by his soldiers in a chair. When he learnt from captured enemy correspondence that the intention was to open all the dykes, he realised he could do no more. On 8 October he raised the siege. After seven weeks of resistance, the little town of Alkmaar had beaten off the Spaniards. The saying grew up among the Netherlanders that 'victory began at Alkmaar' ('van Alkmaar de Victorie'). According to an English officer who was serving in the campaigns, the Spaniards 'lost divers of their best captains and at least 1,600 of their bravest soldiers'.[63] The duke tried to explain the reverse to his king. Apart from the threat of the dykes, he wrote, 'the weather has been the most terrible ever seen; for a whole month and a half it has done nothing but rain, so that everywhere in the camp you had to walk with water up to your knees, while the soldiers had to keep guard barefoot and the artillery was water-logged, and Don Fadrique even while being carried in his chair (because since Haarlem he cannot stand upright) almost had to swim as well. I decided, with the written approval of all the officers there, to withdraw the army'.[64]

Three days after the raising of the siege of Alkmaar the northerners achieved another success. On 11 October a small fleet of Orange's supporters sailed into the Zuider Zee, defeated the Spanish vessels there, and captured their commander, the count of Boussu, stadholder of Holland and Zealand. The reverses by land and sea were certainly fatal to Alba's spirits. His reputation as a commander plummeted. He had by now fallen out with his closest colleagues in the Netherlands, and preferred to rely only on Spaniards. He looked forward, he told the king, to the day when the council in Flanders could be run only by Spaniards or Italians. Months of frustration spilled over into the angry letter he wrote to Antonio de Toledo from Amsterdam at the end of October. 'I am the most dissatisfied man in the country, seeing the way that I have been dealt with in the last three years, treating me as a subordinate to the duke of Medina and the Grand Commander [Requesens], to diminish my authority'. The restrictions put on him were, he maintained, 'the principal reason for the disturbances that there are today in these states'.

It did not help that Requesens, who should have arrived in August, had not yet shown his face. The duke felt he was alone, without help, without money. 'For the love of God,' he pleaded, 'remove me from this post and get me out of here, and if it cannot be done by sending someone then shoot me and remove me that way. Nor do I want you to send me more work to do, I don't wish to see any or hear of any.' He was both unwell and weary, and prepared himself for the journey home. It was some comfort, albeit small, to receive expressions of goodwill from his son the prior Don Hernando, who had wished to return to Flanders when the present troubles broke out. 'I would have done so when the revolutions in those states commenced except that it was too late because the king had me occupied in matters I could not leave.'[65]

In the late autumn of 1573 the new governor of the Netherlands, Luis de Requesens, travelled up the Spanish Road with two companies of Italian troops. He entered Brussels on 17 November, and formally took over from Alba on the 29th. The duke did his best to persuade Requesens that the war must go on, that there should be no question of talks or negotiations and that the only effective method was the use of arms. His experience, he said, convinced him that there was no other way. He reported that he had advised the king to 'lay waste in Holland all the land that our people could not occupy'.[66] The new governor was horrified at this typical soldier's solution. 'Since the very first day,' he was to comment later, 'I have had the water up to my teeth.'[67] Alba, meanwhile, was anxious to leave a country where all his plans had collapsed in ruins. For the greater part of the year he had been confined to his bed, and at the end of November he was so ill that he did not leave it for ten days. His aides feared that he might be too unwell to leave. The French envoy in Brussels confided to his king that Alba's confinement may have been not only because of gout, but because the duke did not wish to show his face in public after the reverses he had suffered. Indeed, reported the ambassador, the duke 'had aroused such great hatred in the hearts of everybody, that they would have celebrated his departure with fireworks if they dared'.[68]

On 18 December Alba at last departed from Brussels. The complaints in his letters that he had been retained there for several months against his will cannot be taken seriously. Even while clamouring to be recalled, Alba had refused to leave as soon as the revolt of 1572 occurred, since he felt that he was obliged to crush it. The arrival of the duke of Medinaceli did not make him any more inclined to leave his post; in fact quite the reverse. He was more than ever determined not to leave the situation in the hands of somebody he judged to be incompetent. Only with the arrival of Requesens did the king at last have an opportunity to try a new approach to the problems of the north.

When Alba left, he took his team as well as his policies with him. Five companies of infantry escorted the group. Three days after leaving Brussels he reached Namur, where he was held up for nine days by gastric problems. But he was in no hurry, since he also had to wait for Don Fadrique who was attending to unfinished business in Brussels. On New Year's Day 1574 the duke and his group reached Virton, where they were caught up by Fadrique, Albornoz and by the duke's nephew Hernando de Toledo. Alba breathed a sigh of relief that he was at last about to leave the territory of the Netherlands. On 3 January they hoped to enter the duchy of Lorraine, crossing it in about nine days and reaching Franche-Comté. 'You would not believe,' he wrote, 'how bad the roads are, but then after all for someone who has just left prison everything can appear very good.' His feeling of liberation was tempered by fears that what he felt he had achieved might be overturned, so that he used the leisure hours of his journey southwards, to fight a rearguard action on his own behalf. Reluctant to lose control of decision making in Brussels, he did his best to make sure that his policies would be continued. Fearing that his face-to-face conversations with Luis de Requesens had not been enough, he sent off a long letter of advice from Virton to the governor. At the same time, in preparation for his reception in Spain, he sent off letters to the king summarising, explaining and justifying his conduct in the Netherlands.

Alba's letter of 2 January 1574, written to the king while he was resting in Virton, was a remarkable and revealing summary of his term of office in the Netherlands.[69] Many things had changed during the seven years he had been there, and he now felt he could see events in true perspective. When he first came, he explained to the king, he considered the situation to be one of rebellion, and had accordingly limited his task to that purely political aspect. He had not tackled the problem of heresy, to the great scandal of many Catholics. Many people had been denounced as heretics and therefore arrested, but no systematic action had been taken against beliefs. The Netherlanders, he affirmed, 'continued in this liberty of conscience and freedom from enquiry into their lives until the year 1570, when Your Majesty's pardon was issued'. When the prince of Orange first invaded, he received no support, because people thought that liberty of conscience was permanent. In the pardon, dissidents were given three months to conform, and he had prolonged the period of grace for a further two months. Only when he began to take action, did the rebels ally themselves with Orange. He had concluded that the problem of rebellion was at heart one of heresy. 'The rebellions, both that of '66 and that of '72, are one and the same and in both the objective has been the same one of religion. The fire was burning secretly under the earth until the punishments revealed the flame.' He had no doubt, he wrote, that 'the objective of all the rebels has always been religion'. What had seemed to be a political issue was in reality ideological; the struggle against rebellion was a struggle against heresy. His conviction differed from that of many other

Spanish advisers of the king, as later discussions would show, but his opinion remained firm.

Having done his best to explain his ideas and motives to his successor as governor and to his king, the duke resumed his journey southwards, taking rests whenever the pain in his limbs made it necessary. When he could not walk his servants carried him in the litter. Don Fadrique was in no better physical condition. The melancholy aspect of the group must have contrasted sharply with the warm reception the travellers were given when they entered Dole, capital of Franche Comté, on 18 January. 'They do not treat us as dead men,' observed a relieved Albornoz, 'and in truth we are not.' They followed the Spanish Road back down through the mountains, and into Italy. In February they arrived in Turin, where the ailing duke was greeted with full honour by the elite of Savoy. The next major city was Alessandria, where they had to stop for four days because Alba was suffering a high fever. Eventually, on 24 February, they entered the city of Genoa. 'The journey has been very long and my health much deteriorated,' the duke wrote to Requesens.

In the port of Genoa Spain's entire Mediterranean fleet and its admirals were waiting to transport him. There was some doubt over whether Alba should sail with the Genoese admiral Juan Andrea Doria, or with the Spanish commander Alonso de Leyva and his galleys. Eventually Don Juan of Austria, who was also in attendance, decided that Doria should undertake the crossing. In the small hours of 3 March the duke and his party sailed out of Genoa harbour in six vessels under the command of Doria. He was ill during the voyage, but when the ships arrived at the Catalan coast he was relieved to be home at last. 'Today just before three o'clock,' he wrote on 5 March to his brother-in-law Antonio de Toledo, while his galley rode the sea before Palamós, 'I arrived here, with the most beautiful weather that I have ever seen in my life.'[70]

His first stop was Barcelona, where his son the prior Don Hernando was viceroy, and then on to Madrid. On the trip he wrote from Fresno informing the king that he hoped to be at court in the last week of March. From Madrid the Venetian ambassador reported that 'six days ago [that is, 28 March 1574] the duke of Alba arrived here, towards whom the king showed no unusual sign whatever, neither of satisfaction nor the reverse. The duke is in excellent health, and bears his years well.'[71]

He never left the peninsula again. Alba had come home, by no means in disgrace and fully determined to fight the Flanders battle where in his view it might be done more effectively: in Spain. Withdrawn from the active front[72] because his superiors thought that his policies were mistaken, he refused to accept their reasons, and continued to fight vigorously in defence of his ideas. For the first – and by no means the last – time in European history, a country's leading general was forced to defend himself against the politicians.

His family had reason to be grateful not only for his return but also for what he brought with him. Like other nobles who served in the empire, the duke enriched himself with the literature and art he got to know and admire outside Spain. For a quarter of a century he had pursued Renaissance culture both in Italy and the Netherlands. 'Not a day passes,' Titian had written to Aretino many years before, from Augsburg in 1550, 'that the duke of Alba does not talk to me about the divine Aretino, because he esteems you greatly and says that he wants to be your agent with His Majesty.' At Augsburg both the duke and Prince Philip pestered Titian with requests for paintings. In 1573, when preparing to leave Brussels, Alba was still corresponding with the venerable painter over the possibility of new paintings.[73] Over the years he built up a substantial collection of works by the master. The years in the Netherlands were those that most benefited the family palace at Alba. Flemish tapestries, paintings and art objects made their way regularly southwards towards Alba de Tormes, while the duke dutifully paid the bills for them in Brussels.[74] At the same time, the duke made some efforts to promote aspects of culture that touched his family. An admirer and friend of Luis de Granada, he patronised the publication at Antwerp of fourteen volumes of the famous preacher's works, in a specially ornate edition asked for by the duchess.

It was a different Spain to which the duke returned, and there were still battles to be fought. But they were in a sphere in which the duke had usually been far from comfortable, the fluctuating sea of court politics. There were also important developments that signalled a change of direction among the active personnel. Between 1572 and 1573 familiar faces had disappeared from the political scene. The death in September 1572 of Diego de Espinosa removed a die-hard conservative who had coincided with Alba's views and had helped him considerably. Philip had raised him to positions of eminence because he admired his efficiency, but he soon came to disagree with the cardinal's work-methods. Espinosa often executed decisions verbally instead of putting them on paper. This made for speed, but Philip felt that this method cut out the possibility of reflection. He also disapproved of the cardinal's discourteous attitude towards the grandees. In a brief exchange over a matter concerning Flanders, Philip called the cardinal a liar. The incident almost literally killed Espinosa.[75] He died on 5 September 1572, of apoplexy during an illness.

Espinosa bequeathed to the king the services of his private secretary, the priest Mateo Vázquez de Leca. Twenty-four hours after the cardinal's death, Vázquez entered the royal service. Swarthy, plump and balding, Vázquez was of Corsican origin. Educated by the Jesuits in Seville (where one of his school-mates was the young Cervantes), his pious, fatherly demeanour won the confidence of all. He gained the trust of the king and became his 'arch-secre-tary', but also earned the rivalry of secretary Antonio Pérez. At the same time he attracted the hostility of the princess of Eboli, who more than once had referred to him (because of his complexion) as 'this Moorish dog'.

Ruy Gómez de Silva died shortly after Espinosa, on 29 July 1573; with him the Eboli group lost its spokesman. Friends of Alba commented on Philip's genuine and evident grief for the man who had been his friend and adviser for two decades.[76] Ruy Gómez's wife, the ever-active Anna de Mendoza, princess of Eboli, tactfully withdrew to a convent. 'If she has done so out of zeal for religion', an Alba family friend commented, 'she has done well to do penitence for the many bad things she has done to many people.'[77] The same correspondent commented subsequently to Albornoz about the princess: 'His Excellency [Alba] and his affairs have lost the most malign and malevolent enemy any man ever had, for although she appeared harmless there was no defenceless target against which she did not shoot.'[78]

The disappearance of Espinosa and Ruy Gómez worked neither for nor against Alba's interests. The duke had served loyally in the Netherlands and was by no means – as we have already pointed out – returning to Spain in disgrace. But the power-vacuum in Madrid created problems and produced serious tensions in political circles. Nobody summed up the situation better than the prior Hernando de Toledo, who informed Alba that 'the Holy Ghost will not be found here no matter how many masses the king orders said'.[79] Alba, of course, was still powerful, and could not afford to neglect his duties and his responsibilities to the king. Throughout 1574 he went back and forth from Alba de Tormes to Madrid, trying to put some order into the business of his estates while also keeping track of policy decisions in the court. In May Hernando reminded him with some insistence from Madrid that he should not be absent too much: 'Your Excellency is much required in this court for many reasons that Your Excellency should think about, and it seems to us that Your Excellency delays.'[80]

During the year 1574 the king was preparing to follow through his deci-sion to abandon the discredited policies adopted in Flanders. The reports he received from the duke of Medinaceli on the latter's return to Spain were of crucial importance for his change of heart. According to the king's biographer Cabrera de Córdoba, 'after Medinaceli made a report to the king on the state in which he had left matters, he discussed the causes and the solutions and some people convinced the king that the second rebellion had been provoked by the severity of the duke of Alba'.[81] Philip could no longer afford to finance a policy of repression. In his Council of State the majority now favoured an end to the violence in the Netherlands. As we have seen, his ambassador Francés de Álava wrote from France advising against the further use of force. From his position in Italy as viceroy of Naples, Cardinal Granvelle also urged the king to change his approach. In his correspondence with others the cardinal did not mince his words; Spain's policy was a disaster. 'If they do not win the goodwill of their vassals, even sending 20,000 Spaniards will not achieve anything.' The Spaniards despise the Netherlanders and are therefore hated: 'the hatred that the country has for those who now rule, is greater than you could possibly imagine'. As for Alba, for whom he had nothing but praise as a person, 'under his rule the states of the Netherlands have been ruined'. In short, he reflected in July 1574, the king's advisers had not the slightest idea of the affairs of the Netherlands: 'they do not understand them and will not understand in very many years'.[82] The cardinal was no less frank in his letters to the king. 'For the last ten years,' he told Philip in 1576, 'I have always written that the policy adopted was wholly mistaken.'[83]

The debate on the Netherlands in 1574 among those who governed Spain, was one of the most momentous ever to occur in the history of an imperial nation. Philip well remembered the debates in 1550 over America, when his father had taken the unprecedented step of suspending the conquests there. Now, a quarter of a century later, his own measures were being scrutinised. An important part in the debate was played by Spaniards who had served in the Netherlands and could advise on the basis of their own experience. A signifi-cant role, as we have seen, was assigned to Benito Arias Montano, whose letters significantly helped to change Philip's attitude to Alba. Subsequently, the king asked him to stay on in the Netherlands and advise Luis de Reque-sens, who consulted closely with him. In his letters Montano condemned certain Spanish attitudes and defended the views of the Netherlanders. 'When a whole people clamours that there is oppression,' he wrote to Philip, 'it is certain that it is so.'[84] But the humanist had many other battles to fight before he left Flanders in April 1575. The inquisitor general and bishop of Cuenca, Gaspar de Quiroga,[85] who adhered to a hard line on Flanders, tried to have him recalled in 1574 'because of the harm he might do there if he shows his true colours'. Another significant adviser of the king was the Valencian humanist Fadrique Furió Ceriol, who had spent over sixteen years in the Netherlands. In 1573, encouraged by the king's new policy, Furió wrote his important *Remedies*, a programme for full-scale change in the north. In 1574 the king sent him back to the Netherlands to reconsider options in the light of the policy pursued by Requesens. In the summer of 1575 Furió recom-mended that the only way to split the southern provinces from Orange was to restore their old privileges in full. The withdrawal of the Spanish troops from the Netherlands early in 1577 – a concession favoured by Furió, who accompanied the army to Milan – did not unfortunately bring a solution to the problem any nearer, however.

One of the king's key advisers in Madrid was Joachim Hopperus, informal spokesman for the States of the Netherlands, who had been resident at the Spanish court since 1565. Like Granvelle, he tended to support a tough pro-Spanish line and was in favour of the king's decision in April 1565 to prosecute heresy. But he was also openly opposed to Alba's intervention. From as early as 1566 he tried without success to interest Philip in an alternative policy.[86] Despite obstacles placed in his way by others in Madrid, he managed to play an important role in the formulation of policy.

The debates over the Netherlands held in Spain in 1574 were frank and open. In a remarkable session of the council at Aranjuez on 28 January 1574, the duke of Medinaceli and Diego de Covarrubias attacked the Tenth Penny. Dr Andrés Ponce de León astonishingly claimed that the Flemish had a right to their liberties as much as the Aragonese had a right to theirs.[87] Philip was left little option. In March he sent letters to Requesens, authorising him to abolish the Council of Troubles and the Tenth Penny and issue a general pardon. The grand commander was already convinced of the need for an about-face. Alba, he said, had arrived in a peaceful Netherlands, but had left the country in ruins. The only firm solution – it was perhaps the first time the idea was suggested; over twenty years before Philip adopted it – was for the king's eldest daughter, the Infanta Isabella, to be made ruler of an independent Netherlands, with a son of the emperor as her husband.

The concessions decreed by Requesens failed to achieve their desired effect. The pardon was considered inadequate. The States General met on 7 June and repeated its demands, of which the most fundamental had always been that the Spanish troops be withdrawn. By now the troops had begun a series of mutinies which ended by paralysing the whole Spanish war effort.[88] In May 1574 the soldiers at Antwerp mutinied for their pay. In November those in Holland mutinied, deserted, and left the province to the enemy. For a helpless and despairing Requesens it was 'the most terrible time in the world'.[89] The king was equally depressed but still accepted, as he affirmed in December 1574, 'that it is not possible to make any progress in Flanders through a policy of war'.[90] He set up a special committee of four to meet urgently and reconsider policy, in the light of written papers presented by all shades of opinion.[91] Members were specially chosen because the king trusted them to be impartial. It met seven times between 14 and 30 December. Its principal business was to decide whether the demands of the States General could be accepted, as Requesens was suggesting and as the memoranda of Hopperus advised. The king was giving his full support to Hopperus, which seemed to augur a foregone conclusion. But the committee also had instructions to consult with Alba, though without letting Hopperus know that they were doing so.

The duke used the opportunity to fight as well as he could. The struggle was not easy because in effect the duke had to face up to the king. The discussion papers presented by Hopperus and others were unmercifully critical of Alba's policy. The very title chosen for one of the papers – 'The causes and origin of the troubles that arose between 1568 and 1573' – aimed to identify all the problems exclusively with the duke's period as governor. Alba remained immovable and impenitent. At every point he disagreed with Hopperus's proposals. When Hopperus suggested accepting the scheme from Brussels that a prince of the blood be sent to govern them, Alba dismissed the idea as a 'pretext offered by the States in order to achieve their ends', and consequently opposed sending Don Juan of Austria to the Netherlands. On another point, when it was proposed that a new 'council for Flanders' should be set up in Madrid to liaise with Brussels he warned that 'the idea should be looked at with caution, since Hopperus misunderstands it'. Alba resolutely refused to admit that any change had been made by him in the government of the Netherlands: 'let them put down in writing how the government was altered, and what privileges were taken away, they won't be able to do so because these are all pretexts to cover up what they want and to raise complaints when there is no reason for any'.[92] The junta was under heavy pressure from both the king and Requesens, and at the end of its sessions very reluctantly arrived at the conclusions that were expected of it. This was, they said, because of 'the need over there for a rapid solution', and not because they were convinced by Hopperus, whom they tartly criticised.

In the end, therefore, Alba found there was a gulf between him and the four members of the committee. They advised 'that we should restore the privileges' of the Netherlanders; Alba said 'not yet'. They advised 'that the Council of Troubles be abolished'; he insisted 'that it be retained'. All along the line, on nearly every recommendation, Alba was firm: insisting that concessions might possibly be made, but 'not now', and only 'later on'. On only one point did he agree. They said that the Tenth Penny be dropped; he agreed readily to this: 'let it be done, and at once'. It was a long struggle. At the end of January 1575 he used his position as a member of the Council of State to present a memorandum in which he expressed outright opposition to the proposals of the committee. He also took the opportunity to blame Ruy Gómez for having in the past dipped his hand into the affairs of the Netherlands. 'The case of the count of Hornes,' he wrote, 'was not how Hopperus explains it, rather it was Ruy Gómez who convinced Hornes' that decisions would be made in his favour, 'and since matters turned out the opposite way his indignation grew and he did the worst that he could.'[93]

The failure to find a speedy solution disposed Requesens in September 1574 to recommend a further resort to military force. But he quickly realised that this, too, was impracticable. In January 1575 he summarised the situation. 'I shall say only that matters here are in such extreme straits and so impossible to remedy that we shall have to agree to all they want, as long as religion is left entire, and it must be done so rapidly that there will be no time for consultation. I agree with the opinion of Hopperus, that Your Majesty send these people a personage of the blood, remove the foreigners, and restore the old form of government.'[94] In short, capitulation. At this stage the mediation of the emperor Maximilian II was sought. With his help, talks between the parties began at Breda in March 1575. Requesens set up a parallel committee at Antwerp.

When the negotiations with the States General began in 1575, from being a marginal figure at the Spanish court Joachim Hopperus was suddenly propelled centre-stage with a key role to play. The negotiators at Breda dealt directly with him. Philip turned to him for advice, carefully read all his memoranda, and adopted Hopperus's ideas as his own. Even finance was affected. One of the king's main bankers, the house of Fugger, 'will not make a move [Philip reported with chagrin] without the opinion of Hopperus'. All the ministers were by-passed in favour of Hopperus. 'Everything has to go through his hands', some of them complained. Philip's special committee of four, set up to deal with the problem, grumbled strongly but recognised that 'it is necessity' which forced acceptance of the new conditions.[95] In a note to Hopperus in April 1576 the king wrote: 'I am very pleased that you agree with the decision I have taken . . . I am so satisfied with all you say that I have decided to keep you at my side for this period.' He fully accepted Hopperus's proposal that a general pardon, with no exceptions whatever, be issued. Unfortunately, not much time remained. Hopperus's good services were terminated by his death in December 1576. After him, there was nobody in the councils of Spain (except, of course, Alba) who had any practical experience of the situation in the Netherlands. Cardinal Granvelle commented at the end of 1577 that those who were now making the decisions 'know no more about the Netherlands than I do about Turkey'.[96]

The whole apparatus of repression was undone in the course of the year 1576. A royal decree of 2 May abolished the Council of Troubles, and the Tenth Penny was suppressed by a decree of 15 July. At the end of the year a political compromise (known as the Pacification of Ghent) was agreed between all parties in the Netherlands and accepted formally early in 1577 by the new governor, Don Juan of Austria. The king's remarkable ability to change both policy and advisers when the need arose demonstrates that he did not have a closed mind and was capable of accepting realities. But there was no clear solution in sight. 'The affairs of Flanders,' Philip complained, 'keep me so busy and preoccupied that they don't leave me time to attend as I should to other matters.'

Throughout this period Alba continued to take an active, but increasingly ineffective, part in the councils of state. By right he could assist at meetings of the Council of State, and did so. In that council, whose membership the king did not modify, his views might sometimes prevail. But something was changing, as a friend of the family observed. 'He goes every day,' he commented, 'to the Council of State, but in spite of everything there is a strange brusqueness in some people. I don't know what it can mean.'[97]

Throughout 1576, when Hopperus' influence was high, Alba did not fail to make his voice heard: he had audiences with the king over Flanders, and also sent him memoranda. He also accompanied Philip to the celebrated meeting with King Sebastian of Portugal. Son of Philip's sister Juana, Sebastian was aged only three when in 1557 he had succeeded to the throne of Portugal. As he grew up his penchant for war-games turned into an obsession over pursuing the crusade against Islam. He disappeared for three months into North Africa in 1574 on a reconnaissance visit. Philip was working hard to secure peace with the Turks and saw no purpose in military adventures. He tried to dissuade Sebastian from his plans to invade Africa, and eventually agreed to meet him to talk about the matter. Talks were arranged to be held near the frontier of Spain and Portugal, at the monastery of Guadalupe in Extremadura. Alba was asked to be in attendance. The journey, in the winter of mid-December, did not agree with the duke's health. He was taken ill at Talavera on his way to Guadalupe. On one night 'it was so cold that he could not sleep well'. Three days later, reported his nephew Hernando, 'he dined last night at ten with a good appetite', on an invalid's diet of melon taken with water, some stewed quince and a stewed pear, as well as a small pie.[98] The two kings arrived at Guadalupe in the third week of the month and had their first meeting on 22 December 1576. Philip tried in vain to reason with his wayward nephew. Sebastian, however, was interested only in concrete offers of help for his plans to invade Africa. At a moment when Philip was working to bring about a truce with the Turks in the Mediterranean, it made little sense to open up a new war in the south. The meeting achieved little, for Sebastian did not promise to call off his plans and Philip offered only token military help.

When Alba returned to affairs of state in Madrid he made one last attempt to stop what he considered to be a policy of disaster in northern Europe. At a special meeting of the council held on a Sunday, in February 1577,[99] he, Don Antonio de Toledo and Quiroga were rock-solid in rejecting the terms of the Pacification of Ghent. It was a feeble gesture of protest. The king's commitment to a peaceful solution in the north effectively removed the duke from any positive part in decision making. Alba continued to be consulted, but his advice was seldom taken. The Venetian ambassador went so far as to express the opinion in 1577 that 'the duke of Alba has no influence and one could even say that he is finished; few people pay any attention to him'.[100] The duke continued to perform his duties and to take part in council meetings. He also clung firmly to his views about the need for a strong hand in the north. As it happened, his position was reinforced by events in 1577, which took a sudden turn for the worse when Don Juan had once more to resort to military force and the Estates General decided to seek the collaboration of the prince of Orange. The chaos in the Netherlands appeared worse than ever, exacerbated by Don Juan's death during 1578, aged only thirty-one. The king immediately appointed as governor Don Juan's deputy, the prince of Parma, Alessandro Farnese. He gave Farnese his full support for the change to a moderate policy. The long-term objectives were less clear. All that the councillors in Madrid knew was that 'the whole world did not contain enough silver to make it possible to solve the affairs of Flanders through the use of force'.[101]

At the end of 1578 Alba had a frank exchange of views with the Imperial ambassador, Hans Khevenhüller, who was serving a second term in Madrid. The king had just appointed Farnese, but there were still doubts in the government about accepting the terms of the Pacification of Ghent. Khevenhüller wanted to know in what way his master, the emperor, could help put into practice the religious clauses of the Pacification, and felt that a talk with Alba would be useful. Six years before in Brussels the duke had not hesitated to explain to Khevenhüller the policies he was following. The interview between them in Madrid lasted nearly two hours. Alba had lost none of his old fire. He attacked the clauses of the Pacification which offered the Netherlanders a free choice in religion. 'I ask you,' he told the ambassador, 'where you have seen a people being permitted to choose in matters of religion, something that not even the king or the pope can do except through a General Council.' He was quite right: nowhere in Europe had any state gone so far as to permit freedom of belief to subjects. The most that had been done, for example, was to permit a limited freedom to certain nobility and the regions they controlled.[102] Alba also insisted that armed force was still the only effective solution in the Netherlands. 'I know very well,' he informed the ambassador, 'that there is nothing His Majesty desires more than peace, and would to God his enemies did not know this also and that the king had more of a penchant for war, for then they would fear him more and the king would have more peace and more favourable results in Flanders.'[103] He added, in his typically exaggerated way of emphasising points: 'if he were only to do this, old as I am I would willingly cut off a leg for it'. Once again, Alba's views were not out of line. His two successors as commander in the Netherlands had begun their job with high hopes and intentions, but both had ended up with exactly the same conclusion as Alba: that no concessions should be made to freedom of belief.

Though he was on the retreat, there was every possibility that Alba might find himself justified by changes in events in the Netherlands. He had been removed, but no adequate policy had been set up to replace his. He was not yet a spent force. The duke's position in 1578, however, was suddenly undermined dramatically by an affair for which he was in large measure to blame. It concerned the marriage of his son Fadrique.

6   The Last Campaign, 1578–1582

It truly pains me to shed blood and earn a name for cruelty that this nation has through no fault of mine given me.

To Philip II, Cascaes (Portugal), August 1580

Alba's disgrace came about solely because of the problem of Don Fadrique. The matter of Fadrique's exile had still not been satisfactorily resolved at the time of his return to Spain in March 1574. No sooner had Alba and his son arrived in the country than an official document was handed to Fadrique informing him that he was still subject to the decree of 1567. Alba was understandably upset, since he had assumed that by his service in Flanders his son and heir had redeemed himself. Moreover, although the king and his officials did not know it, the cards in that affair had now been played well beyond any possibility of returning to the position prevailing in 1567. That fact would soon emerge. When Fadrique received the notice Alba wrote immediately to Antonio de Toledo, asking him to tell the king that 'Don Fadrique and I are vassals and servants so obedient that not only will he comply with what has been ordered but I too will comply with the exile and imprisonment and I shall go with him.'[1] The final angry phrase revealed the Alba of old, irascible and impatient with everybody, even with the king. This time, however, there would be no satisfaction for the duke. He was already being pushed out of politics by the change of policy over Flanders. He now became involved in a storm over Fadrique's marriage.

When Fadrique had arrived in Flanders six years previously in 1568, Alba decided to try and save his son – and by extension the whole family – from the marriage to Magdalena de Guzmán. He had opened negotiations with his cousin García de Toledo, marquis of Villafranca and viceroy of Sicily. The viceroy was at the very heart of the Alba connexions in Italy: his sister Leonor had married the grand duke of Tuscany, Cosimo I de' Medici, and he himself was married to a Colonna, daughter of the duke of Paliano. Alba's proposal, for a marriage between Fadrique and the marquis's daughter María de Toledo y Colonna, would place Fadrique in the mainstream of Toledo power. This was a highly irregular step, for the marriage with Magdalena was still in force and under scrutiny, and Fadrique was still serving the judicial punishment meted out for that affair. Anxious to find a way out for his son, Alba interviewed María de Toledo and explained the family's wishes that she should marry her cousin Fadrique as soon as possible. In dynastic marriages of this sort, the issue of consanguinity was always overlooked. Alba's own wife María Enríquez was his first cousin. In any case, Alba told María de Toledo, there was no problem because he had special permission from the king for Fadrique to marry. Oblivious to the possible consequences, the grandees of the Toledo family went ahead and drew up the clauses for a marriage settlement, which was agreed at Pisa in February 1570 and finalised at Brussels on 5 May 1571.[2] Only those who were party to the arrangement knew of it. Certainly, Alba knew exactly what the move meant, but seemed to be confident that he had pre-empted the situation, and that his son was now firmly protected against the scandal that had led to his punishment in 1567.

In 1574, however, the sudden reversion to his punishment took Fadrique by surprise and threw him into deep despair. His anxiety was made worse by a severe attack of gout and by indications of syphilis, evidently contracted in Flanders where both father and son had apparently frequented prostitutes. (According to a report by a Spanish official, Fadrique had gone 'frequently to Antwerp to resort to lascivious vices, to which he used to invite his father and whom he also took with him'.[3]) When his father hinted that his son's pains might be from syphilis rather than from gout, Fadrique replied: 'You are mistaken to conclude that because the pestilence has returned it is because I was ill treated by the ladies of Flanders.' From the town of Agudo, where he was held in confinement, he wrote to his father in the autumn of 1575, saying that he was bedridden with gout in all parts of his body: 'there is no part of my body which is not in pain'. He asked the duke to make no further attempts to help him over his case, which he regarded as hopeless. 'I see no better solution than to forget about it and distance myself from anything that reminds me of it. I was thinking only that in the New Year I could beg the king to give me permission to go and cure myself somewhere where there is a doctor and medicine and where the air does not do me harm, and if His Majesty were unwilling to do this at least he could order my head cut off, for honestly I don't know if there is a death in this world as bad as the life I am leading in this place.'[4]

Events in the affair of Don Fadrique continued to drag on for a couple of years without resolution. Philip's rigidity over questions of marriage among the aristocracy was not new. In January 1577, for example, the duke of Feria got into serious trouble over a similar issue.[5] On that occasion Alba was consulted and advised the crown not to interfere but to leave the matter to be settled in the courts. His advice was not heeded, and Feria was placed under strict house arrest. It was now Alba's turn to come under pressure. One day in Madrid that summer the duke, the prior Don Antonio de Toledo and Don Fadrique went to see the king. They wished to plead with him about the matter of Fadrique's marriage. They were received in the king's study but Alba made the mistake of closing the door behind him. Philip normally insisted on leaving the doors open. 'Is this a threat?' he objected. 'Are you going to attack me?' He went into another room and would not speak to them.[6] A few months later, in 1578 the young count of Fuentes, brother of the duchess, was thrown into prison because of a public brawl.[7] It was not a good year for the Alba family.

During 1578 the matter of the marriage moved towards a dramatic climax. For motives that remain unclear, Magdalena de Guzmán, still in her convent at Toledo, and certainly encouraged by her family, now chose to write to the king asking for justice in her twelve-year-old plea against Don Fadrique. It is possible that the renewal of the problem may have been due to interference from the king's secretary Antonio Pérez and his close friend the princess of Éboli.[8] Philip referred the matter to a special committee presided over by the recently appointed president of the Council of Castile, Antonio Mauriño de Pazos, who had been the Inquisitor of Toledo.[9] In June 1578 Pazos informed the king that the vows exchanged between Fadrique and Magdalena constituted marriage, but only under the rules that had been in force before the Council of Trent. Since 1565, when the Church in Spain had made such vows invalid, the rules for marriage had changed. It would be unwise, he said, for the king to order Fadrique to comply with those vows, and the matter should be investigated by the theologians. The king's own view was that the change in Church rules did not affect the obligation: 'both in conscience and as a gentleman Don Fadrique had the duty to marry her'.[10] The issue was not simply a matter of the king's preferences. Relationships among the higher aristocracy were always delicate, and nowhere more than in questions of marriage. The king played an essential role as arbiter between the great families. But he deferred to the views of the experts.

In the first week of September 1578 Alba was unable to attend a meeting of the Council of State to discuss the deteriorating situation in the Netherlands. 'Zayas came to see me,' he excused himself to the king, 'and told me that Your Majesty ordered me to go to the council to see the despatches from the lord Don Juan, but I am so incapacitated in both feet and my right arm and hand that I find it wholly impossible to use them, and because of this I told him that unless I were carried in this bed it was impossible for me to come.'[11] He may have had other reasons for staying away from court. In those very days he was planning to get round the Magdalena problem by completing his long-planned *fait accompli.* He intended to make sure that the secret marriage with María de Toledo, already in effect through the marriage agreement, should be made rock solid with a ceremony *de presente.* This would eliminate any danger that the old marriage with Magdalena be declared valid. On 2 October Fadrique secretly left his place of arrest at Tordesillas, without asking for the king's permission, and went to Madrid. There in front of a small number of witnesses got together by Alba because their presence was necessary to make the marriage legal, he was married by a priest to María. He then returned to Tordesillas.

Though the ceremony was celebrated in secret, rumours were quickly flying around the court and tempers were hot. The princess of Éboli appears to have been the first to report the rumour to president Pazos. The duke waited nervously for the king's reaction. He tried to carry on with his duties as normal, but both his health and the tension aroused by the presumed marriage made his position difficult. A few days later, however, he was fit enough to go to the palace, where he embarrassed the king's secretary by taking him aside and complaining about his treatment. Mateo Vázquez's report to the king merits quoting in detail for the light it throws on the duke's humours:

> The duke cornered me at the entrance to the gallery, sat down and began to complain that in business relating to his job his own junior officials were used by Your Majesty to tell him your wishes. He then passed to the question of his son (which was clearly why he wished to speak to me) and I don't know how to express to Your Majesty how injured and insistent he presented himself, demanding justice, saying that he could not go on, and that he had to speak to Your Majesty, and that he would leave here, and mentioned going to live in another country. In short so great was the anger and nervousness that made him talk this way that neither heaven nor earth could restrain him. I tried to soothe him the best that I could, saying that Your Majesty was attending to the matter, but I could not get away from him.[12]

When, in mid-October, Philip heard the rumour about the marriage he at first refused to believe that the duke could have been responsible for such an act. Pazos received orders from the king to have a formal talk with Alba, who duly went to the president's house on the night of 19 October. 'I repeated to him,' Pazos reported next morning to Philip, 'word for word what Your Majesty ordered me. He became disturbed when he heard what I said and asked me to repeat the words two or three times.' Alba could not believe the message. 'What did His Majesty mean or what could be understood from those words "I shall not fail to carry out the justice required in such a case"?' he asked. Pazos replied that he did not know what the words implied; he had only repeated what the king had told him. Alba realised that it was a grave matter if he had to receive a threat from the king himself, and decided to lay all his cards on the table. He said quietly, 'His Majesty knows that Don Fadrique has married.' Pazos replied that he did not believe the king was aware of it. Alba said, 'Well, the fact is that he has married Doña María de Toledo, and with the approval and permission of His Majesty.' He went on to explain that 'the marriage was carried out first by proxy from Flanders, and afterwards Don Fadrique agreed to it and ratified it with his direct word, in the presence of a priest'. It was Pazos's turn to be shocked. 'I told him,' he informed Philip, 'that it seemed to me a most serious matter and I did not know what good would come of it.' Alba could not get over the very clear threat in the message from Pazos. He complained to the king's secretary, Mateo Vázquez. 'This morning after I said my mass,' Vázquez wrote to the king, 'I listened to the duke, who said how he regretted the threatening terms in which the president had spoken to him. He has owned up to nothing about the marriage, but I suspect that it is done.'[13]

With Alba's clear admission to Pazos, there could no longer be any doubt of the marriage. But the duke, who had managed to convince himself that everything was in order, now had the difficult task of trying to convince others. At the end of November he visited Pazos. 'Late tonight,' the president reported to the king, 'I received a visit from the duke of Alba, who was so full of complaints that I really needed tender ears to be able to listen to them.' Alba pleaded with the president: 'For the last six years I have been begging Don Fadrique to get married, I have even fallen to my knees at his feet to ask him.' So if he is married now, he told Pazos, what is the problem? 'I replied that if he had married six years ago it would not have been any problem, but if he had just got married then it was very much a problem.' Pazos went on to ask Alba further questions. But the duke was evasive on every point. Instead, he started to get angry. 'What does His Majesty want of us?' he burst out. 'Does he want to cut off our heads? He might just as well do so and get rid of us. We shall go off to another country and kingdom. I have placed my life at risk so many times in the service of His Majesty and did not expect such an affront. Go on, cut off our heads!' Pazos tried to soothe him: 'this is not a matter for cutting off heads'. By now Alba was in full stride: 'What His Majesty is doing is much worse than cutting them off, for that is over in a moment, while the other matter has been going on for twelve years and is still not over!'

In a sense, Alba was justified to feel aggrieved that the matter had dragged on for so long. But he was helpless in the face of the mood at court. When Philip received confirmation from Pazos that a marriage had taken place, on 12 December he ordered Fadrique's arrest.[14] Pazos and his committee of five persons (among them the king's confessor Chaves) on the 14th decreed further steps in the case. Both Alba and his son were banned from court: Fadrique was to be imprisoned in the castle at La Mota, and his father was exiled to the town of Uceda and forbidden to leave it. The three grandees who had assisted at the marriage – the prior Don Antonio de Toledo, the prior Don Hernando, and the marquis of Velada[15] – were placed under house arrest.[16] Alba's secretary Albornoz and Fadrique's secretary Esteban de Ibarra were also arrested and interrogated; the latter was subjected to torture.

The royal secretary Martín de Gaztelu brought notice of the sentence to the duke at his residence in Madrid, on the night of Saturday 10 January 1579. Alba was severely ill from gout, and received the secretary in a wheelchair. (Gaztelu later commented that the chair may have been there only for dramatic effect.) He listened to the sentence in silence, displayed a look of indignation, and then shrugged his shoulders resignedly. He was given four days to leave the capital, but very typically – a sign of his anger – decided to leave at once. They packed all night, 'and in this way at dawn husband and wife left in a carriage on their way to eat at Barajas'. Both emerged from the house with defiant, smiling faces; but no sooner had they entered the carriage than they dropped the mask and showed 'very great sadness'.[17] Uceda was a quiet little town thirty miles to the northeast of Madrid. Alba and his wife were lodged in the castle, which belonged to the see of Toledo.

Foreign dignitaries, including the king of France and the pope, pleaded in his favour, but the king, displaying his well-known stubbornness, refused to relent. For him it was a matter of disobedience that brought its own consequences. A close colleague of Alba, Spain's ambassador in London, Bernardino de Mendoza, wrote to Zayas with the comment that 'in this world, where the sons usually suffer for the fathers' sins, he has been an exception and is assailed by all sorts of troubles through his son'.[18] The duke, of course, preserved his dignity and courtesy. On 23 March he wrote a personal letter to the king from Uceda, begging pardon for having offended him in any way. Alba continued to be consulted occasionally by the court. His advice was indispensable, for example, in the proposed reform of protocol procedures that was being mooted in those months. But for all practical purposes the Alba party had been shattered, its power wholly marginalised. For the next two years the duke had to wait silently in the wings while the king came forward to occupy centre stage in some of the most dramatic episodes of the reign.

The arrest of the duke coincided with other major changes that were destined to have a profound impact on politics at court. In March 1578 Don Juan of

Austria's secretary Juan de Escobedo was murdered in Madrid while riding at night through a street near the royal palace. Rumour quickly pointed to Philip II's secretary Antonio Pérez as the author of the crime. There were also voices hinting that the king himself was implicated. The affair, which has never been adequately resolved,[19] became for several months the main topic of gossip at court and inevitably overshadowed the much smaller matter of Fadrique's marriage. It polarised antagonisms among the political elite, particularly the existing differences between Philip's secretaries Mateo Vázquez and Antonio Pérez. Vázquez complained to the king that his life was threatened by both Pérez and the princess of Eboli. Indeed, as suspicion of La Eboli's role in the Escobedo affair grew, president Pazos said to the king that 'we suspect that she is the leaven of all this'.[20] As fragments of information filtered through, the king seems to have become convinced that the killing of Escobedo was merely a detail in a turbid matter involving his secretary and Anna de Mendoza. Events moved to their climax on the night of 28 July 1579. Antonio Pérez, unsuspecting, had been working on papers with the king until ten at night. 'Your business,' the king commented to the secretary, 'will be dealt with before I leave.'[21] When Pérez returned home, at eleven, he was detained and placed under house arrest. Moments later the captain of the royal guard detained the princess and conducted her to prison in a castle at Pinto.

The arrests broke up what remained of the power grouping at court centred round the prince of Eboli and his wife, Alba's main rivals. The fall of the princess, in particular, brought about intense satisfaction among Alba's friends. But the days of the Toledo clan were also drawing to an end. In the early summer of 1578 the prior Don Antonio died of illness, removing from the inner councils of the king the member of the Toledo family who had most faithfully served the monarchy during the ups and downs of the duke's career. Another leading member of the Toledo family, the duke of Sessa, also died in the course of the year. The king was inevitably affected by these changes in the web of court politics. Unable to rely any longer on Antonio Pérez or on the duke of Alba, he was forced to look outside the peninsula for an administrator to take over the direction of affairs. In March 1579 he wrote to Cardinal Granvelle, then serving in Rome, and summoned him to Madrid. Granvelle coincidentally arrived in Madrid on 28 July, a few hours before the arrest of Pérez and the princess. He visited the king at the Escorial five days later, kissed hands and received his instructions.

The virtual settlement of the conflict in the southern Netherlands enabled the Spanish government to pay more attention to the urgent matter that most pressed: the question of the Portuguese succession. Philip had a direct interest in Portugal. His mother was Portuguese and his sister Juana had married into the Portuguese royal family, giving birth to the ill-fated Sebastian. When the latter became king of Portugal Philip began to take an interest in the career of his unpredictable nephew. As we have seen, the two kings met at the monastery of Guadalupe in Extremadura at Christmas 1576 to discuss matters of common interest. Philip unbent to the extent of offering some support. 'I decided to offer him fifty galleys and five thousand Spanish troops', for which he would have to pay.[22] He also insisted that, because of the obvious risks, Sebastian must not participate personally in the campaign. The Spaniards would be among those returning to Italy from Flanders. On his return to Madrid Philip told ambassador Hans Khevenhüller that Sebastian 'has good intentions but little maturity'. 'I have pressed him by word and by letter,' he said, 'but to no avail.' Once back in Lisbon, Sebastian felt that he had omitted something in his talks at Guadalupe. He had been enormously impressed by the presence at his deliberations of the most famous general in Europe, Alba. He had gained nothing from the king of Spain save empty promises that were unlikely to be fulfilled. But what if he could persuade Alba to lead his proposed army? When he returned to Lisbon he wrote to Philip asking for the duke's services. Philip passed the request on to Alba, instructing him to do his utmost to persuade Sebastian of the imprudence of his expedition.[23]

In spite of Spanish efforts, the expedition to Morocco took place.[24] King Sebastian made every attempt to turn it into what he had always dreamed of: a European crusade against the Muslims. Over eight hundred vessels left the mouth of the Tagus, carrying a force of twenty-five thousand men drawn mainly from Portugal but also with units from Castile, Germany and Italy. On 4 August 1578 the impressive army, containing the flower of the nobility of Portugal with the young 25-year-old king at their head, was destroyed by Berber forces at the battle of al-Qasr al-Kabir. Over 10,000 men were taken prisoner and Sebastian was killed. The news reached Madrid on 12 August. The king had only just left the city for San Lorenzo, and was in the Escorial when messengers brought him the news on the 13th. He was visibly shaken, and immediately withdrew.[25] He spent the next few hours walking around the patio garden, alone.[26] Sebastian's death opened up the formidable question of the Portuguese succession, and Philip had to proceed very carefully in examining the options available to him.

The death of his nephew Sebastian coincided with a number of other important deaths in the king's family. On 22 September the same year his nephew the archduke Wenzel, son of the empress María, died in Madrid at the age of seventeen. Barely a month later, it was the turn of the little Infante Fernando, who had raised great hopes as heir to the throne but who died on 18 October.

Don Juan of Austria had died just a fortnight before in the Netherlands. The loss of two nephews, one son, and a brother in the space of three months, was shattering. The king took what little comfort he could by immersing himself in the question of Portugal. The day after receiving the news of al-Qasr al-Kabir he went to Madrid and issued orders to the marquis of Santa Cruz to take the Andalusian galleys to protect the Portuguese forts on the African coast. He also sent Cristóbal de Moura, a Portuguese and one of his most trusted advisers, to Portugal to sound out the situation. Moura, aged forty in 1578, had come to Spain in 1554 in the train of the princess Juana. Like several other Portuguese (among them Ruy Gómez) who sought their fortune at the court of Spain, Moura won the king's favour. This was thanks largely to the patronage of Juana. He proved exceptionally useful in missions involving his native land, and had helped to arrange the meeting with Sebastian at Guadalupe. At the same time, Philip despatched letters of sympathy to the chief authorities in Portugal, a country that was now defenceless and leaderless and where the most urgent issue was the succession.[27]

The nearest male heir was the late king's great-uncle, the 67-year-old Cardinal Henry. He was proclaimed king at the end of August. Henry was deaf, half-blind, toothless, senile and racked by tuberculosis. He was, reported Moura, half-dead with fright at being nominated king.[28] The best legal right to the throne after him was held by Philip, through his mother the Empress Isabella. There were Portuguese claimants to the throne, notably the cardinal's nephew Antonio, prior of Crato, and a niece who was married to the duke of Braganza.[29] Philip was determined to win over public opinion to his side, and was obliged to court the support both of the Portuguese and of Europe. He firmly hoped to secure the throne without the expense and blood of a fight. But he also accepted that even strong claims needed the firm consent of the political elite. Three approaches were made. First, leading jurists from all over Europe were employed to write in support of his cause, so as to convince not only the Portuguese but other European powers. Second, his representatives in Portugal, most notably his ambassador Juan de Silva, his representative the duke of Osuna, and his special envoy Moura, attempted to win over individuals as well as cities. Finally, selective bribes were used. Moura orchestrated a brilliant campaign to win support for his master. He talked to nobles and clergy, collected information on Portuguese defences, and distributed money liberally.

Philip was leaving little to chance. Already by the end of January 1579 he was informing Moura of 'how we are, secretly and discreetly, taking the necessary measures for all eventualities'. 'You may be sure,' he wrote, 'that although I hope that none of this will be necessary, on my side nothing is being overlooked.'[30] Moura agreed on the need for military preparations. 'I have great hopes,' he wrote to the king, 'that though the swords are ready there will be no need to draw them.'[31] Philip supervised plans for a possible military and naval intervention. In the spring and summer of 1579 the galleys of Spain were assembled. In early July, Cardinal Granvelle arrived from Italy at Rosas, with twenty-four galleys under the command of Admiral Doria, and a force of Spanish tercios, veterans of the war in the Low Countries, who were sent on to Cartagena. The joint naval force for the Portuguese campaign, totalling some sixty galleys, was assembled off the coast of Andalusia under the command of the marquis of Santa Cruz. Ships from Italy brought with them detachments of Italian and German soldiers. Intensive recruitment of Spanish troops took place in Andalusia and the provinces neighbouring Portugal. The cavalry troops were in October put under the command of the Flanders veteran Sancho Dávila. Santa Cruz was to sail for Lisbon immediately on hearing of the death of cardinal Henry. The duke of Medina Sidonia, seconded by other nobles whose estates bordered Portugal, was to help raise troops for a land invasion. The mobilisation was in theory secret, but Philip made sure that the Portuguese knew of it. 'Even if it doesn't come to a use of force,' he informed Moura in April, 'it would be all the more helpful to press ahead with negotiations while keeping up the threat of arms.'[32] He added that when the Portuguese ambassador came to him to complain about the mobilisation, 'I replied that the preparations and military exercises on the frontier were not being done by my order.'[33]

Then in March 1579 Philip convened the Castilian Cortes. In May the whole history of the Portuguese succession was presented to the assembled deputies, who responded with enthusiasm. Further sporadic sessions of the Cortes were held over several months and the assembly did not dissolve till 1582. On the eve of the Portuguese campaign, pressure on other fronts also eased up. In the Netherlands the new commander Alessandro Farnese was to prove himself one of the most brilliant generals of the age. Aged thirty-three when appointed, the son of Margaret of Parma (and consequently nephew of Philip) had been educated in part at the court of Spain. He was able to profit from the growing political split, based on religion, in the Netherlands. Early in 1579 a group of northern provinces, led by Holland and Zealand, formed themselves into a Calvinist-led Union of Utrecht. At the same time some of the southern provinces, led by Catholics, formed a Union of Arras. In May this Union, consisting now of six provinces,[34] signed a treaty accepting the authority of Spain. The accord guaranteed all their privileges, but reaffirmed the exclusive position of the Catholic religion. Parma backed up this success by capturing the important stronghold of Maastricht in June. 'Good news has now come from Flanders', Philip wrote cheerfully to Moura in June, asking him to spread the information in

Portugal.[35] It seemed as though what had been lost during the years of Alba and Don Fadrique might now be recovered. The return of the provinces to Spanish obedience would confirm him in Portuguese eyes as a successful, but also liberal and magnanimous, monarch.

There was also good news from the Mediterranean. Peace negotiations were in progress which led, in March 1580, to a renewal of the truce between Spain and the Ottoman empire. The king was free to devote himself exclusively to Portugal. He instructed Osuna and Moura to tell the Portuguese they should not fear any threat to their liberties, and that the union of the crowns in one person did not imply any union of the realms. 'Uniting some realms with others does not follow from having the same ruler, since though Aragon and Castile have a single ruler they are not united, but as separate as they were when they had different rulers.'[36] Even his more unpopular actions in Flanders could be disavowed. Alba, responsible for the repression there, was in disgrace. His name did not feature among the roll-call of nobles who were asked in July 1579 to raise men for the Portugal campaign.[37] In that month only two military commanders had been appointed: the marquis of Santa Cruz, who was in charge of the fleet, and the duke of Medina-Sidonia, who was in charge of forces on the Portuguese frontier.

When Cardinal Granvelle arrived in August at San Lorenzo, Portugal was one of the first matters to be placed in his hands. All through the year Cardinal Henry lingered on the point of death, but stubbornly refused to designate a successor. The succession was nonetheless largely resolved in favour of Philip II, who had won (or bought) the clear support of the majority of clergy and nobles in the Cortes held at Almeirim in January 1580. But the situation was no longer simple. Antonio of Crato had active support among very many Portuguese, who hoped for help from abroad, particularly from France. The longer the delay, the greater the risk of foreign intervention. During the weeks of autumn 1579 the court was busy with activity resulting from the detention of Antonio Pérez and La Eboli. It was a wet December, with continuous rain. This may have helped Philip decide, for once, to spend Christmas in the royal Alcázar in Madrid. He busied himself with his papers, primarily with Flanders but also with ordering the transfer of La Eboli from her prison at Pinto to the more spacious fortress at Santorcaz. 'He is as shut up as if he were in a monastery,' an observer said of the king, 'only the chamberlains and gentlemen of the household see him'.[38]

Philip was also waiting for the news, expected at any moment, of the death of Cardinal Henry who died at last on 31 January 1580. 'Nothing else can be attended to until the matter of Portugal is settled', the king observed.[39] Although he had made a great effort to bring together the men, supplies and arms needed for an invasion, he now opposed any hasty military move. 'I think that everything humanly possible must be done so that a resort to arms is not necessary', he warned Moura on 6 February.[40] By contrast his advisers, headed by Granvelle, felt that invasion was unavoidable. They also urged him to bring Alba out of retirement and put him at the head of the troops. As the months passed and it became clear that a commander for the Portuguese campaign had to be appointed, Philip was faced with the embarrassing prospect of having to choose Alba. In October 1579 Pazos had already sent a recommendation on behalf of his committee to the king that Alba should be pardoned, but Philip refused to budge, citing unexplained reasons of his own. He could not hold out for long. His councillors were unanimous that only Alba had the required reputation and prestige. It was the simple truth, for at that moment there were no Spanish commanders available with the necessary experience. On 15 February 1580 Pazos informed Philip that 'the council believes that no other person we know is more fitting and suitable than the duke'. 'We are aware,' he added, 'that there is great discontent among all the soldiers because they believe the duke will not be chosen to lead them.'[41] The special committee for Portugal[42] sent its secretary Gabriel de Zayas to inform Philip that their unanimous choice was the same. The king still refused to give way. He wrote to Moura the next day that 'last night Zayas told me that everybody is of the opinion that I must appoint the duke of Alba'. Moura offered no comfort. He wrote stressing that the 'man from Uceda' was the most likely to terrify the opposition in Portugal.[43]

Browbeaten by his advisers, Philip finally recalled the old duke, now aged seventy-three and (in his own words) 'frail and finished',[44] to active service. Alba had already been warned to expect the appointment, and in mid-February was sending, in his typical manner, brisk orders to the royal secretary. 'They've told me that His Majesty is sending 4,000 Spaniards of those who served in Flanders, and 4,000 new Italians. I would like the Spaniards to be here, but instead of the Italians who have to come, 5,000 more Germans. For the love of God don't let His Majesty bring more Italians, they're money thrown away. Instead, 5,000 more Germans.'[45] After nearly seven years of absence from the war front, his old enthusiasm flamed again. Castile would win back its pride, relying on the 'old Spanish soldiers'; 'just with them alone,' he told the king, 'I would dare the conquest'.[46] Meanwhile he anxiously awaited the king's letter, which was brought to Uceda by special messenger at 10p.m. on the cold, wet night of 22 February. He insisted on sending a written acceptance back with the same messenger. He was grateful 'to be back in the good graces of Your Majesty, which is what I most desired'.[47] Excited by the call of duty, he made preparations to leave immediately, that same night. The duchess would have to go home first, to Alba de Tormes, but he would head directly for Extremadura, passing through Madrid and Talavera. The king brushed aside Alba's request to come and pay his respects, and instructed him to proceed within three days to Llerena, where the army was assembling. It was not the moment, judged Philip, to waste time on courtesies.

Some felt that one way to avoid a military operation was, as suggested by both the pope and the five regents who had run Portugal in the interim since cardinal Henry's death, for Philip to submit his claim to arbitration. The king was willing to talk to the regents. On 1 March 1580 he had the Cortes of Castile swear to Prince Diego as heir, in a little ceremony in the chapel of the royal palace in Madrid. The royal family left the court on 5 March and made their way to the monastery of Guadalupe, where they spent Holy Week and Easter. Philip met the regents later that month. He refused arbitration, for this would have been to admit the possibility of a doubt over his rights. In any case, prior Antonio was also unlikely to accept any decision based on arbitration. In these circumstances the preparations for an armed strike went ahead. As was to be expected, the duke of Alba advised him not to dither with negotiations with the Portuguese or their Cortes. He suggested that since the kingdom was his, he should simply send troops in and seize it. Everybody in Portugal should be allowed up to 8 June to submit, after that they should be treated as rebels.[48] It was a typical soldier's perspective.

From the end of March the duke was in Llerena, where he remained throughout the spring, organising the movement of soldiers and of provisions. He was back in the saddle, this time without the obstacles he had faced in the Netherlands. It seemed, on the face of it, a straightforward military operation, and his letters oozed confidence. In May the court transferred itself to Mérida. Alba, who had left Llerena two days before, arrived there on 12 May. The king was despatching letters with secretary Gabriel de Zayas, and saw him arriving. He immediately sent his aide Sebastián de Santoyo to tell the duke to come to him. When Alba strode in, the king refused to let him kneel down. 'He raised him up, embraced him, and with great contentment asked him how he was, and other things.'[49] During the next three days the two men were locked in discussion, morning and afternoon. The affable reunion between the two gives the lie to the commonly repeated story that the king refused to see Alba. On 15 May Alba left for Badajoz. The king and queen left three days later. As a gesture to the duke, Philip that week ordered Don Fadrique to be freed from confinement and given permission to live with his new wife, but to be confined to the town of Alba de Tormes.[50]

On 12 June Philip issued the orders appointing Alba as captain-general of the invading army. The opening sentence of the orders reflected the king's decisive stance. The original draft had read: 'Whereas I am the direct and rightful successor of the realms of Portugal, they belong to and devolve on me.' Philip struck out the limp phrase after the comma, and wrote in: 'I have determined to take possession of them'.[51] Strangely, for a nation weary of war abroad, most Castilians warmed to the idea of a conquest at home. An imperialist dream began to take shape. Among the few dissonant voices was the influential religious reformer Teresa of Avila. She commented that 'if this matter is pursued through war, I fear great harm'. A leading Jesuit lamented that Christians should be fighting Christians: 'This realm [Castile] is ailing and has little wish to see any growth in His Majesty's power.'[52]

On 13 June the king and queen, flanked by Alba and members of the royal family, reviewed the forces, numbering some 47,000,[53] on an open plain at Cantillana, before the camp near Badajoz. A shelter protected the royal group from the burning sun. Alba, who had been ill in bed the day before, was in good spirits, dressed elegantly in his family colours of white and blue.[54] The file-past, which went on all day, left admiring observers almost speechless. 'It is something to see, even as I am writing this', wrote one.[55] The Portuguese, he felt, were crazy even to think of resisting. 'It was a fine sight,' commented a seasoned soldier, 'a great many men, all in good order.'[56] Half the army consisted of Spanish soldiers and veterans from Flanders (among them Sancho Dávila). The other half were German and Italian mercenaries.[57] The land force was to be given naval support by a fleet under the marquis of Santa Cruz. This sailed from Cadiz on 8 July, with orders to make its way up the Atlantic coast.

Alba was fully occupied preparing his men. 'At this moment, which must be about midnight,' he informed the king on 17 June, 'the men have mounted and will leave at once, for everything is ready.' On 18 June the frontier fort of Elvas surrendered without a fight. On the 27th the army, after another march-past before Philip and his generals at Cantillana, crossed the frontier in force. It was the formal date for the beginning of the invasion. Don Antonio had been proclaimed king by dissident Portuguese, but there was little effective resistance to the Spanish. Meanwhile an army raised by the Spanish nobles whose lands bordered Portugal, protected the rear of the royal forces. In a letter to the pope in July, the king claimed (with justification) that he had sent the troops in because of the threat of intervention by foreign powers. They were there 'not to wage war against that realm but to save it from oppression and restore it to peace and tranquillity'.[58] In practice, plunder, outrages and brutality occurred throughout the process of occupation. 'We are beginning to feel pity for all the harm that is being done to these poor people', an officer wrote.[59] The operation was somewhat more difficult than Alba had expected. To the often insupportable heat of the summer were added the problems of primitive roads, poor supplies, and a hostile population. 'Yesterday was a day of unbearable heat,' he wrote to Philip early in July, 'the roads are bad, the going is long and we have many carriages broken.'

Setúbal, besieged by land and sea, capitulated on 18 July. The fleet under Santa Cruz sailed in two days later and gave support to the land forces.[60] In Lisbon there was stiff street-by-street resistance, but the city eventually surrendered in the last week of August. Don Antonio fled. He took refuge in the north and was eventually rescued by an English ship. 'Here, Sir, you can stop thinking about war', Alba wrote to the king on 28 August.[61] From that date all his letters were despatched from Lisbon. Coimbra surrendered on 8 September as the forces moved north. Philip was lost for words to express his gratitude. 'I am well aware how much is due to your care and experience and to the zeal and concern that you have had and have towards me, and would like to express to you here the thanks that with such good cause I owe you for all this', he wrote to the duke.[62] His enthusiasm was so great that he had no compunction in proposing to the overworked duke yet another military expedition, this time to Ireland, in pursuit of what the pope had mentioned 'several times with great insistence, the conquest of England'.[63] We may imagine what the duke, who had never in his life supported proposals for invading England, thought of the suggestion.

On 12 September the absent Philip was proclaimed king in the Portuguese capital. The campaign had been completed, Alba wrote proudly to him, 'two days short of two months, for this army set out on 27 June and at midday on 25 August Your Majesty was master of all.'[64] The biggest problem during these weeks was not military, for there was little effective resistance, but political. Alba soon found that when the generals finish their work, the politicians take over. Philip, the politician *par excellence*, had always been reluctant to use force over Portugal, and had never ceased to press Alba to direct a campaign that would do minimum damage. Like any military man, however, the duke saw that war can never avoid damage. A month into the invasion, he protested that the policy could not be implemented. 'Bearing in mind Your Majesty's wish,' he wrote from Setúbal on the day it capitulated, 'that no action be taken about which the Portuguese with or without reason might complain, I attempt at all times to achieve what is impossible.' The ironical consequence of the royal order was that the duke seemed to be carrying out more hangings among his own soldiers than among the Portuguese. 'It is normal in a campaign,' he informed the king, 'for soldiers to lose control but it has irritated me greatly, and we have hanged and are hanging so many that I think we shall run out of nooses.'[65] Even more troublesome than the order to respect the local population, was the king's insistence that Lisbon should not be stormed. Fortunately for Alba the capital opportunely surrendered, though it was still necessary to use force to eliminate the substantial resistance from Don Antonio's supporters.

The army was not permitted to enter the historic city, but remained camped outside. By way of compensation the disappointed soldiers were allowed to plunder in the outskirts of the capital. The affected districts were 'sacked and robbed brutally for three whole days', according to the Imperial ambassador, who saw the results with his own eyes; 'the looting was very extensive, principally in the properties of the merchants'.[66] Alba also tried to maintain a rigid curfew of troops within their camp. It did not work. 'I have the whole camp closed,' he informed the king, 'both day and night so that the soldiers cannot get out, but all the precautions I have taken, all the soldiers I have hanged, all the heads I have cut off, all those I have sent to the galleys to control them, have not been enough, for what we have is a general mutiny that is driving us crazy since we don't know how to deal with it. In all the time that I have dealt with soldiers, I have never found myself in the state that I am with these.'[67]

The problem of discipline was a major preoccupation for Philip II. One of the Spanish administrators accompanying the duke told his government that Alba seemed to have lost control of his troops in a way that would not have happened previously. Observing 'the total lack of order among the troops of this army, robbing and looting without concern for friends or foes,' he commented that 'it is true that the duke does what he can and what is feasible in a man of his age, but his instructions are carried out so badly that instead of obtaining a solution we are the first to suffer disorder; the duke gives orders but they are not carried out.'[68] A few months later a military official made a similar comment. Antonio of Crato had slipped out of their hands, he said, and the duke was to blame: 'I have already written to you many times that the duke is very old.'[69] Was it a sign of his years that Alba himself felt he had lost control? 'There are so many disorders,' he wrote helplessly to Philip II, 'that they drive me out of my mind and I never thought I would see what I now see here.' He put the blame exclusively on his own officers for not controlling their men: 'the disobedience and disrespect is very great and it is all the fault of the officers'.[70]

Alba was also faced with the problem of having to live down his own reputation. While grateful to have his only experienced commander at the head of his troops, Philip was – as his directives to Alba indicate – nervous about employing in Portugal a general who had become notorious throughout Europe for his ruthlessness. The eyes of the world were concentrated on the manner in which he carried out the operation. Alba inevitably had doubts of his own. 'Your Majesty ordered me,' he wrote to the king on the first day of August, just after capturing the fortress of Cascaes, which had resisted him and was therefore guilty of rebellion, 'to set an example by cutting off the heads of those caught with weapons in their hands fighting against Your Majesty.' Should the order be carried out literally? 'Although I received this order from Your Majesty, it truly pains me to shed the blood of gentlemen and earn a name for cruelty that this nation has through no fault of mine given me.'[71] As had happened in the case of the Netherlands, the court did not feel it could make decisions that should be made by the military commander. Alba was therefore forced to decide for himself. His reasoning, as he explained to the king, was that it was impossible to pardon everybody, but it was also unacceptable to punish the soldiers and let their officers off. So his decision, carried out promptly, was to execute the garrison commander and some of his men.

During the weeks of campaigning, Philip remained behind in Badajoz. An epidemic of influenza was raging through most of the peninsula in the summer of 1580. The outbreak ravaged Madrid, where 'there are so many dead that no one takes note of them, and the deaths continue'.[72] Cardinal Granvelle fell gravely ill, and many members of the administration died. The court in Extremadura did not escape. Philip, Prince Diego and the Infanta Catalina were all laid low, but recovered. Queen Anna was not so fortunate and died of the epidemic in October. The loss marked the king profoundly. Yet another epidemic, moreover, threatened from Portugal. An infection that was reported to be the plague broke out in Setúbal in October and spread rapidly through the area, fading away only in the spring of 1581. It was obvious that the king could not be expected to go to Lisbon while the outbreak lasted, so the political settlement of the kingdom was carried out from the north, where Philip had held the first Cortes of his reign.

Alba, meanwhile, had to cope with the pacification of Portugal, and found the task neither easy nor to his liking. He had to deal with the restless soldiers of the conquering army, the remnants of Portuguese opposition in Lisbon and the provinces, and the endless number of citizens who wished to present their respects and make sure that their position under the new regime would be secure. One of his staff commented in September that 'I think I can say that since I have known him I have never seen him work so much, for from the time he gets up, which is very early, until now which is just after midnight, he does not stop working'. The same secretary felt that the duke's chief cross was less his ill health than the people he had to deal with: 'these Portuguese are the death of him, they are the most trying and exasperating people in the world'.[73]

Events in Portugal had to await the end of a short period of court mourning for the death of the queen. The king inevitably had to resume his duties as soon as possible, though in practice he remained in mourning for Anna for the rest of his life. In the last eighteen years of his reign he habitually wore black, save on special festive occasions. On 4 December he left

Badajoz for the frontier, and was officially received at Elvas by Portuguese representatives. From here he issued summons to the Cortes of Portugal to assemble in April at Tomar, selected because of the epidemic in Lisbon. The Cortes of Tomar, which met in April 1581, was a historic occasion, attended by 178 deputies representing ninety-two cities and towns with a vote. They confirmed the union of the whole peninsula under one crown. The Cortes swore fealty to the king and recognised Prince Diego as his successor. In return, Philip confirmed all the privileges and the independence of Portugal, on terms similar to those that had united the other realms of the peninsula with Castile over a century before. The Portuguese overseas possessions fell in line with events at home and accepted Philip. Only in the Atlantic islands of the Azores, where prior Antonio held out with the help of a French force, was there resistance. In July 1582 a fleet was sent out under the command of Santa Cruz, and inflicted a bloody defeat on the French ships off the island of Terceira. A further engagement took place in the summer of 1583, confirming Spain's control over the islands.

In view of the fact that the majority of the nobles and towns came to accept him voluntarily as king, Philip and his supporters developed an argument that the army had been employed simply to give backing to the faithful kingdom of Portugal. The Portuguese had been and were loyal subjects, according to the official view; only a tiny minority led by the bastard Antonio had attempted resistance. The argument was by and large correct. Its corollary was, however, problematic: since the Portuguese were loyal, no conquest had been necessary and therefore no conquest had in fact occurred. When Alba heard that this was to be the official line, he could not control his irritation. 'I find it very unhelpful,' he wrote to the king's secretary Zayas, 'to throw doubt on the conquest.' It was an outright lie to claim that there had been no resistance to the army. 'Did Elvas surrender before it saw His Majesty's army? Did a single one of the other towns that surrendered do so without weapons in their hands? . . . What name can you give to this except "conquest"?'[74] Other contemporaries were able to adopt a more objective view of the process. A noble who some time later became viceroy of Portugal, perhaps gave the best summary: 'the method by which this crown became united to Castile was through inheritance, conquest and purchase'.[75]

The differences of opinion between the duke and the king were many and profound, as they had been throughout the forty years that they had worked together. Philip appointed an official to enquire into excesses committed by the soldiers during the occupation. Alba pointedly refused to collaborate with him. The king gave in, but complained that 'the duke's arrogance is on a par with his loyalty'.[76] Partisans of the duke have persistently accused the king of being ungrateful for his services in Portugal, but the claim has no substance to it. The king was indeed grateful. The problem was that Spaniards at court who were ill-disposed towards the duke began to make capital out of the difficulties created by the occupation. The failure to capture Antonio of Crato and the soldiers' excesses around Lisbon provoked at court 'much attention to and criticism of the actions of the duke of Alba, while those who were rivals or jealous of him drove the point home to the king and exaggerated the duke's responsibility and negligence'. 'These and similar matters,' noted the Imperial ambassador, 'were spoken and complained about at court.'[77]

The king was left in the difficult position, once again, of having to choose between the duke and his critics. He also came into conflict with the duke's own wishes, for Alba felt he had done his job and wanted to go home, but Philip considered that the duke though old was still wholly indispensable. Ailing and anxious to return to his wife, from December 1580 Alba tried to resign his command, but Philip would not hear of it, since there was no one adequate to replace him. 'Everyone is saying "What is the duke doing here?" "What is his role, since the king is now in the kingdom?"' Alba complained to Zayas that month. 'I am here without anything to do', he insisted in February. The king in return protested from Tomar, where he was preparing to meet the Cortes: 'when you say that you are not needed there I do not agree, for you are much needed'. He went on to thank him profusely for his services, but offered little hope of letting him go home. 'I cannot for the moment tell you how much longer you will have to be there because it is something I do not know and depends on the way the Cortes go.'[78] The hapless duchess, who knew that her husband was unwell and kept in regular touch with him through couriers, was angry with despair. In March 1581 she protested to Zayas that 'His Majesty should be happy to know that he has displayed to the world all the cruelty he uses to us in keeping him in that place. I could become truly angry about this, but I shall end here.'[79] The aged duke was no less angry and despairing that he could not see his invalid wife. He wrote openly to Zayas, in words that sum up all the suffering of his life, that 'in no other matter have I given so much proof of my obedience and the desire I have to serve His Majesty than in this, for I have not got into a litter and gone to visit my wife'.

The duke was, beyond all doubt, seriously ailing. His health had deteriorated considerably since he returned from Flanders, and during the exile at Uceda he got steadily worse. In November 1579 he had written confidentially to Mateo Vázquez from Uceda that 'since winter began I have had a recurrence of the illness in my chest, the doctors have ordered me to speak as little as possible'. It was not an empty complaint. He begged the royal secretary: 'You will do me a favour in not speaking about my illness because I have kept it a secret from the duchess, I do not want her to know.'[80] He was perceptibly ill throughout the Portuguese campaign but could expect little sympathy from others since hundreds were dying of the flu epidemic in Spain and in Lisbon the plague had struck. In mid-August he was ill and constantly attended by his physician, who put him on a diet of 'flesh of young chicken with oil and vinegar, three figs, and three mouthfuls of cooked lamb', according to his son Hernando, who was at his side during these difficult weeks.[81] Shortly after he arrived in Lisbon he was laid low with the infection that had been sweeping the Iberian peninsula all summer. His long-serving and faithful secretary Albornoz died of it in Lisbon in October 1580. In addition to flu the duke's gout was playing up: 'it affects the entire right side from the shoulder to his toe, and he has very great trouble in signing letters'. Alba also feared being caught by the plague epidemic. Towards the end of the year he complained to Zayas that 'these three or four days I have been unable to walk on one leg so that I have gone back to bed and I passed last night in very great pain'.[82] In the few months of life that remained the pain never left him.

The king visited him during his illness and listened to his last words of advice.[83] The duke's confessor, Fray Luis de Granada, who was present at the meeting and wrote an account of it to the duchess, recorded what passed between Philip and his principal commanding officer.[84] Alba reaffirmed to Philip that he had always served his king faithfully:

> Three things I must say to Your Majesty, the first is that there was no interest of yours that I did not put before mine; the second is that I took greater care to watch over your financial affairs than mine; the third is that I never proposed to you a man for a post who was not the most suitable that I knew.

He died on 12 December 1582 in Lisbon. The previous day he had received a visit from the Imperial ambassador Hans Khevenhüller who left a record of the meeting. The ambassador found him 'so infirm and feeble that he had to be breast-fed by a woman as though he were a baby, and turning to me he said, "What I did as an infant I now do as an old man"'. He retained his good humour to the end. 'During his illness he always displayed high spirits which mocked the world and death itself', reported Khevenhüller. The duke's passing, and the break-up of the Eboli grouping with the arrest of Pérez and the princess in 1579, marked the end of an era. For nearly thirty years the Alba-Eboli polarisation had dominated politics at the court of Philip II. The king had had to manoeuvre his way carefully between the clashes of interest, but did not emerge unscathed. 'The king's government,' fumed a pro-Eboli grandee, the Admiral of Castile,[85] early in 1578, 'is not a government of justice but of tyranny and vengeance. Everything is in the hands of lowly and vindictive people, many of whose fathers were Comuneros.'[86] Family hatreds and rivalry of this type would continue to affect government. But from the end of 1582 the greatest of the protagonists, whose name had made Spanish power known and feared throughout the continent, was no longer in the fray.

Hernando de Toledo was at his father's deathbed, and took charge of the transport of the body back to Alba de Tormes.

7 Servant of the Crown

Obedience in everything, I don't know what more one could ask for.

To Cardinal Espinosa, April 1569[1]

Castile in its great age of empire produced few military commanders of distinction. The best known military figure of all had been the Great Captain, who antedated the period of dynastic expansion and overseas settlement.[2] But in the generations that followed most prominent generals were foreigners, such as Farnese and Ambrogio Spinola. Thus Alba stands out in Castilian history as virtually unique. When Philip II's ministers demanded that he lead the Portuguese campaign it was because there was no other commander available. He was the only one, and indispensable. Curiously, however, during his time Alba had been absent from nearly all the famous events associated with the use of military power. He was not in Spain during the revolt of the Comuneros (1520) or the revolt of the Granada Moriscos (1569), or present either at the battle of St Quentin (1557) or the battle of Lepanto (1571). At the time of St Quentin he was not at Egmont's side in the field but with the king in Brussels, helping with administration and logistics. Apart from a small part in the African ventures and a significant role at Mühlberg, his military experience was gained principally in Italy, where he earned his enduring reputation for severity.

He never took part in a full-scale battle. Mühlberg and Jemmingen were his most notable successes but they were routs rather than engagements contested in the open field. Famous military men are usually thought to be those who win battles, but Alba does not belong in that category. Far more than merely a general, he was also an active creator of Spanish military power. For over forty years he led the campaigns of the crown in the peninsula and in Europe, administered the army's supplies, coordinated military and naval movements, organised payments and liaised with the soldiers. His family alliances in Italy were almost as powerful as those of the crown itself, and helped to consolidate Castilian authority there. Wherever he went, his commanding presence evoked respect and fear. But none of his efforts was directed to his personal betterment, indeed his expenses in the royal service helped to create a debt that his family was still struggling with a hundred years later. On his sickbed in Portugal he claimed quite truthfully that he had spent all he had in the royal service.

Brought up by his grandfather as a soldier, his whole life was ruled by the notion of service. His first loyalty, carried out conscientiously and often against his own interests, was to his king. Charles V put his confidence in the young duke very early on, and Alba responded with an absolute and firm loyalty. When, at Innsbruck, in 1552 the emperor was pursued through the snow by Maurice of Saxony, Alba was the first Castilian noble to take ship from Spain to go and help him in Austria. His professional dedication and fierce loyalty were part of his unbendingly conservative outlook. His decision at Valladolid in 1548 to obey Charles by journeying to northern Europe with the prince, though he had just received news of the death of his eldest son, both startled and impressed those who were with him. Above all, his loyalty to the emperor was personal. It managed to coexist side by side with the many serious issues over which he greatly differed from the emperor. (Since Alba tended to differ from the views of most people, that is not surprising.) The differences were usually kept in check. The startling and unacceptable image of an Alba who regularly hurled abuse and insults at the emperor comes fom an over-dramatised reading of the documents.[3] Brantôme, for instance, observed that the duke served Charles 'with pure and true affection,' and that in later years 'he never spoke of the emperor without a tear rising to his eye'. Was this emotion affected in part by the fact that his duties in Flanders had made it impossible for him to be present at Charles' deathbed?

By contrast, Brantôme felt, he served Philip II 'almost as if under duress'.[4] He obeyed all the directives of Philip II, but did not always agree with them and frequently argued against them in the hope that the king would change his mind. The evidence of twenty-five years of uneasy relationship between the king and his general serves adequately as proof of Brantôme's claim. Alba complied with Philip's orders out of a sense of duty, but seems to have believed – and through his condescending manner undoubtedly gave Philip the impression – that his own views were more correct than those of the king. Time and again, on matters relating to great issues such as the affairs of the Netherlands or the preparations for Lepanto, his views were directly opposed to those of the king. When it came to the crunch, however, Philip knew he could rely on Alba to obey. His disillusion was all the greater when he discovered that on the issue of Fadrique's marriage the duke had deliberately schemed to disobey him. That affair perhaps demonstrates that over and above his loyalty to the crown, Alba nurtured an even more profound loyalty:

to his family and lineage. The two were, of course, entirely compatible, and on occasion dedication to the family might have to take second place to the call of duty, with the result that he was unable to be present at the deaths of his grandfather and eldest son. At all events, Alba clung on grimly to his lineage. Wherever possible, he travelled with his sons and relations. They played as direct a role as he did, and – as we have seen from the case of Don Fadrique in the Netherlands – they may even have had a more decisive influence. He was also devoted to his wife, though it was rumoured that he sought other women in the many long years that he was away from her side.

A tall, stern and honourable aristocrat, he was Castilian from the roots of his hair to the tips of his boots. An unswerving conservative, he disliked novelty and clung to tradition. He detested, for example, the innovation of horse-carriages, which had come to Castile from the Netherlands at the beginning of the century. During most of his life he refused to use them, preferring to ride on horseback; only in his last years did he consent to ride in one.[5] In the same way, he disliked other foreign innovations. As the obedient servant of his master he brought the Burgundian court ceremony with him in 1548, but made it clear that he was completely opposed to it. He was not alone in this: throughout the century Castilians continued to petition the crown that the Burgundian ceremony be removed. The Cortes of Valladolid in 1558 asked the king to change it for 'the usages and customs of Castile', and made a similar request in 1580. Alba might disagree with the crown's policies and even advise strongly against them, but he never refused to carry them out. If it came to a clash between the crown and his conscience, the crown had to win. He took the view that authority must always be respected, and established rules maintained. This made him support a notion of power that was little short of dictatorial, as we can see in every public stance of his from the 1538 Cortes onwards.

Catholic and cultured, he tended to look down on the citizens of the empire who were not as he was. Throughout his life he allowed himself the liberty of making disparaging remarks about anyone who was not Castilian. His favourite targets were the French, the Italians and the English, but he also made remarks about the Germans, the Portuguese, the Dutch and indeed any other nation which happened not to share the Spanish point of view. His personal demeanour to these, indeed to everyone, was of a studied courtesy and respect; his social manners were impeccable. But he completely failed to understand that there were other people in the universe beside Spaniards. When he was trying to persuade the king in 1570 not to enter into an alliance with the papacy and Venice, he remarked that 'one should note that ancient complaint of Italy, with which they take children to baptism, men to their wedding and old men to their burial, namely the theme of throwing Your

Majesty out of Italy'.[6] Though he relied on Italians as soldiers, he periodically made critical remarks about them. His two visits to England gave him no enthusiasm for the English either. Though he saw the need for a political alliance with England and strongly opposed both the excommunication of Queen Elizabeth and subsequent plans to invade the country, he confessed in 1573 to having a 'personal dislike' of the English.[7] He went so far as to blame his antipathy to the duke of Feria on the bad influence of the duke's English wife, Lady Jane Dormer.

It is too easy, and certainly misleading, to judge the duke by his language. He never attempted to control his tongue, and his intemperate outbursts remain preserved for posterity in the many letters he dictated to his secretaries. The heated words may have appeared exaggerated or irrational, but they invariably reflected his real feelings. If he was angry he had to say that he was 'mad with rage' and not simply 'angry'. 'So great is the rage that seizes me when I come to the subject of my business, that it drives me mad', he wrote to a correspondent in Spain in 1571, emphasising his dissatisfaction that action on his behalf was slow.[8] If he threatened, as in the case of the town of Alkmaar, that every man, woman and child would be put to the sword, it was not an empty phrase: his intentions were real and could not be doubted. He did not mince his words, and always spoke what came into his mind. Khevenhüller, who had an immense respect for him, nevertheless admitted frankly that Alba was 'a backbiter who belittled the value of others and slighted many and despised other nations'.[9] 'He ruled', the ambassador stated, 'with far more pride and haughtiness than necessary.' It was an inborn arrogance which made him think that others would calmly accept his outbursts. Those who knew him intimately, such as Philip II, did not always take his arrogance seriously but neither did they tolerate it easily.

Unfortunately, the ill humour was a life-long obstacle to good relations with all his senior colleagues. When he encountered resistance among ministers in Brussels to his proposals for the Tenth Penny, he immediately gave vent to one of his explosions. 'I told them,' he informed Antonio de Toledo, 'that just as His Majesty had sent me here to cut off the heads of the disobedient so I would cut off the heads of those who stood in my way in this matter, and if there was no other solution I would break the dykes and flood everything, because His Majesty preferred a country drowned and destroyed to one that was preserved rich but disobedient.'[10] The words were wildly exaggerated, above all because they attributed to the king an attitude that Philip had never entertained or expressed. But the duke was also reflecting an authentic attitude entertained by many Spaniards in the Netherlands.

He was first and foremost a soldier, and resented the politicians, of whatever tendency. As Khevenhüller observed, 'he was much better in war than in

peace'.[11] In the talks at Bayonne in 1565 he had no patience with the policies
of the French royal family and the political leaders. By contrast, when he was
together with old veterans such as Montluc he felt he could speak directly and
frankly. The army of Castile was his life. His frequent impatience with Spanish
troops should not be seen as contempt for them, however.[12] He continued all
his life (like other commanders, such as Requesens) to believe that Castilians
were the key to military success. But he was also aware of the difficulty in
training and maintaining adequate soldiers, and raw Castilian recruits (such
as those brought to Flanders by Medinaceli) always received sharp criticism
from him. By contrast he had complete faith in the veteran tercios. He felt
most sure of himself as a commander when he was among the men with
whom he had served in Italy, in Provence, in Germany and in the Netherlands. Like all good professional officers, he attempted to preserve the confidence of his men and the policy often worked. Most of them loved and
respected the duke. Those who supported recalling him to take command of
the campaign in Portugal, affirmed that the soldiers themselves wanted him as
general. Brantôme recalled how on learning of Alba's death a soldier said to
him, 'Ah Sir, the good father of his soldiers has died!'[13] When the confidence
of his men collapsed, during the mutinies in the Netherlands, Alba experienced some of the most painful moments of his life. He tried to treat his
soldiers as gentlemen, as he felt that a proper army should consist of
gentlemen. The early tercios were drawn from recruits of good social standing,
and Alba sought to maintain this standard. 'In our nation,' he wrote to the
king in 1561, 'there is nothing more important than to have gentlemen and
people of standing in the infantry and not leave it wholly in the hands of
peasants and common people.'[14] Towards the end of the century, however, the
rising demand for soldiers drew in a wider range of social classes, and fewer
recruits to the tercios were of noble origin.

When he knew that he would be called to lead the Portuguese campaign,
he informed the king's secretary that it was essential to use the veterans of
Flanders:

> Since they have to be Spaniards who have served in Flanders (as is desir-
> able) it is essential that no change be effected in how they are, but the units
> should come with the captains and men they have, for even if they have
> only twenty or even fifteen men in each unit they can be augmented here
> with recruits and can all together be counted as seasoned units, and so Your
> Majesty will have your veteran Spanish militia, and just with them alone I
> would dare to carry out the conquest.[15]

But his confidence was not limited only to Castilians. Time and again he
showed that he prized German soldiers highly. When Germans served under

the Spanish flag, as they did in Italy and Africa, Alba was normally given command over them, because of his direct experience with them on the campaigns of the emperor, and his acquaintance with a few words of their language. He was often scathing in his criticism, but in practice he put his trust in them time and again. 'The Germans are good enough and will do well', he reassured the emperor in 1555, when he was recruiting for the army of Flanders.

Though Spain's best-known commander of the Golden Age, his military achievement was not primarily on the field, and the subsequent successes of the duke of Parma in the Netherlands easily overshadow his. Though nephew to the king of Spain, Parma was an Italian and as a result was resented by Castilians in his own day and subsequently downplayed by their historians. Alba by contrast was retained at centre-stage, a position he holds in the classic biography of Philip II by Cabrera de Córdoba. The image of Alba as a winner of victories has been in some measure promoted by admirers concerned to vindicate his personal triumphs and the achievements of Spanish power. Their accounts present the duke as a masterly field commander, moving detachments of men like pieces of chess, with an unerring eye. The picture is misleading, for Alba was not an enthusiast for battles.

When he was at the height of his career, a Venetian ambassador passed a judgment on his capacity that bears careful consideration. 'The duke of Alba,' Michele Suriano reported in 1559 from Madrid, 'has seen and directed many wars, and from the experience gained he can analyse them better than anyone else I know at this court. However, he has two weaknesses. One is, that he spends too long in his preparations. The other is, that his caution in campaigns verges on timidity.'[16] We have seen from Alba's work in Navarre, Perpignan, Milan, Naples and the Netherlands that he was an excellent organiser of supplies and recruitment. In all cases the preparations were necessary because nobody else was capable of carrying them out. It is doubtful whether Alba took 'too long' in them, for without good administration no war could be fought. The accusation of 'timidity' would seem to be more sustainable, for the ambassador was referring to Alba's Fabian[17] tactics against the duke of Guise just two years before. Alba was similarly criticised in 1567 and 1568 for refusing to engage his troops during his campaigns against the forces of the prince of Orange. It was, however, a strategy at which he had arrived on the basis of mature experience. By avoiding battle he not only saved the lives of his men but also forced Orange to spend his meagre resources and eventually withdraw. (He was not the first commander to profit from avoiding an engagement.) By the time he became a significant general in the 1540s, he was adept at conducting sieges, skirmishing and evasion tactics rather than field battles. Virtually all his activity in Italy was concerned with sieges, and his campaigns in Germany (Metz) and in the Netherlands followed the same pattern. When in the field in Germany he was seldom in sole command, and tactical decisions were usually made in conjunction with other officers. He was not for example in sole command at Mühlberg, the victory generally attributed to him in some accounts.

Alba came to represent for contemporaries as well as for future generations the unacceptable face of Spanish imperialism. They quite reasonably saw personified in him every aspect of Spanish chauvinism: arrogance, aggression, complicity in assassination, unmerciful brutality in war. Both Elizabeth of England and William of Orange identified him as the arch-devil of Spanish evil. In effect, everything they insinuated about him had a measure of truth. But they were also guilty of precisely the same faults as he was. Both sides, for example, believed in the policy of political assassination. Alba began the train of events that ended with the murder of William of Orange in 1584. The idea of killing the prince had its origins in the sentence of death passed on him by the Council of Troubles,[18] which gave legal justification to the scheme. Albornoz had a plan which Philip approved at the time. Later the idea was put to Luis de Requesens, was actively pursued by Juan de Escobedo in 1577 and subsequently by Bernardino de Mendoza in 1579. In his turn the prince of Orange also (in 1573) paid an assassin to murder the duke, albeit the attempt misfired.[19] By contrast the duke never approved the Ridolfi plan to assassinate Elizabeth of England, because he distrusted both the motives and means of the Italian adventurer.

It is not easy to decide whether Alba overstepped the norms practised in his age. Within the limits of his responsibility, he felt that he had observed the rules. During his campaigns in Italy he ordered the execution of garrison troops who had resisted his forces. The action may have been permitted by prevailing conventions, but Alba himself recognised that it was an extreme step to which he resorted with the specific intention of deterring resistance. In one fortress in northern Italy in July 1555, he called on the French garrison to surrender with the guarantee of their lives. They refused to do so, but had to surrender anyway when the fortress fell. 'I have given orders,' he reported to the emperor, 'that all be hanged, that is around forty-five Italians and Gascons, so that the other fortresses take note of the example and don't hold up the army.'[20] The same policy of executing garrisons was followed by him in the Netherlands, and also in Portugal.

He sincerely believed in the need for ruthlessness. It may explain why on his deathbed he told Luis de Granada 'that his conscience did not trouble him over shedding a single drop of blood in all his life against the dictates of his conscience'. The affirmation very soon became widely known, and was treated with scepticism by many, including Brantôme, who claimed to have direct evidence that the duke expressed regret for his excesses in Flanders.

Brantôme may have been misled on this point. In so far as he felt he had acted correctly, the duke never regretted his actions. Khevenhüller reported on hearsay ('it is said') that 'one day at a public dinner [in Madrid] Alba boasted that during the six years he was governor in Flanders he had ordered to be executed 18,000 men, without counting those who died in the wars'.[21] If the duke said it, the wine must have loosened his tongue, for diligent research by historians disproves any such exaggerated figure. The phrase, in any case, appears to have been spoken in December 1578, when Alba was under severe stress as a result of the secret marriage of Don Fadrique, and spoke often and loudly of his services to the crown. The wars and the military excesses on both sides certainly produced a massive mortality that ruined a great part of the Netherlands countryside for many years, but though Alba was the chief person responsible for this he was by no means the only cause of the tragedy. In the Netherlands, as later in Portugal, many of the worst military excesses took place when he was not fully in control. Spanish captains who blamed 'the house of Alba' were pointing the finger not only at the duke but also at his sons Fadrique and Hernando.

With hindsight, it is difficult to reject entirely the conclusion that Fadrique was the cancer that weakened and then undermined the duke's life.[22] Everywhere he went, Fadrique provoked opposition among the Spaniards. In 1570 a Spaniard serving in the Netherlands sent a denunciation of alleged corruption by the marquis to Madrid. 'As soon as he arrived in those states he began to reveal the understanding he had with the Prior Don Hernando his brother and many others, disordering the lives of everyone there, both Spaniards and foreigners, and making many visits to Antwerp to indulge in lascivious vices and gaming.'[23] The accusation need not be believed, but very many other officials said much the same. In 1574 a despairing Requesens, who had taken over a ruined Netherlands from Alba, had no hesitation in pointing to the duke's family as a primary cause of the situation. His testimony, which coincides with other complaints, cannot be discounted and merits quotation. Fadrique, he testified in a confidential letter to the king, was probably the reason why a substantially tranquil situation changed into one of rebellion.

> The common opinion is that the cause was the arrival of don Fadrique de Toledo [in 1568] and the duke's wish to give him full authority, which he took over absolutely. I have been told that in many matters he failed to respect his father but the duke did not dare to contradict what he did even though he disapproved, and this was either through the excessive love that fathers have for their children, or for fear of alienating him into concluding the marriage that the duke so detests.

All the factors noted – Fadrique's conduct, his father's lenience, the shadow of the marriage – are amply confirmed by the facts available to us. Even if we accept that picture, of course, it is highly improbable that blame can be fixed solely on one person. But Requesens seems to have had little doubt in doing so.

> The opinion I have mentioned, that he was the cause of all the harm here and that he is the most malign person in the world, is so general that you will not find a single person, whether Spaniard or Netherlander, relative or servant of his father, who will not confirm it.[24]

Fadrique, the governor added, was not alone; Hernando had also played a part. 'Matters here were gravely affected by the differences between the two brothers, which gave rise to many factions among the army officers'. There was also the hint of corruption: 'the rumour is that women and money had a great part to play in that government'. The sum total of such accusations was that they reflected very seriously on Alba himself. Requesens could not avoid calling into question the duke's entire achievement. 'In affairs of war the duke knows much more than those who accuse him, but that does not dissuade them, and their main accusation is that he let his son do what he wanted.'

The duke's religious ideals were unswervingly Catholic, but though he repeatedly denounced 'heretics' he was not at first a zealot in religion. Throughout the 1540s and up to the peace of Cateau-Cambrésis he worked alongside men whose sympathies were clearly with the Reformation, such as Maurice of Saxony and William of Orange. In the political circumstances of that period, religion had not yet become a subversive force and it was possible for men on both sides of the Reformation split to live and work together. It is therefore difficult to give credence to the anecdote which claims that after the victory at Mühlberg the duke wished to destroy the tomb of the recently deceased Martin Luther at Wittenberg. The emperor, it is said, stopped him and said, 'I wage war not against the dead but against the living'.[25] Alba was able to work with Protestants, as the emperor did, so long as they remained faithful allies. In effect, there was no political reason why Catholics should have been trusted more than Protestants. In June 1559 Alba (motivated, certainly, by his distrust of all the French) actually advised Philip II not to ally with French Catholics against French Protestants. 'We have had long experience over many years', he wrote, 'of what fickle and bad friends the French are. Because of this my opinion is that in no way should Your Majesty decide to enter into any agreement with them.'[26]

Very soon, however, the era of religious conflicts broke out in Europe. The groups unsympathetic to Spain tended to ally themselves with rebels and with Protestants. For Alba there could be nothing worse than rebellion. From around 1560, over thirty years after the start of the Lutheran Reformation, the duke began to use the word 'heretics' in his correspondence.[27] In each case, the word tended to refer to rebellion rather than to difference of religion, and the specific reference was nearly always to the French Huguenot nobles. In the talks at Bayonne in 1565, his concern was for the rebels who were opposing the king of France; their ideology was a secondary consideration. On the eve of his departure for Flanders in 1566, as we have seen above, the duke affirmed to the French ambassador that 'in this question of Flanders the issue is not one of taking steps against their religion but simply against rebels'.[28] He had precisely the same message for the papal nuncio, who was trying to persuade Spain to join an alliance of Catholic states against Protestants. He brushed aside the idea, and explained that the planned military expedition to Flanders 'is for reasons of state and is directed against rebels'. It would be absurd to describe it as a campaign against heretics, Alba explained, since a good part of the troops on whom the king relied in Flanders were German Protestants, probably more heretical than the people against whom they would have to fight.[29] And when the duke began his first military campaigns in the spring of 1568 he referred to the forces of Louis of Nassau as 'rebels' and 'traitors'; the issue of religion was never mentioned.

Later that year, however, after his first months in Brussels, he became more directly aware of the danger posed by 'heresy'. The evidence suggested to him very plainly that dissidents, always supported by members of the nobility in the Netherlands, Germany and France, were plotting to subvert authority. It was not simply an issue of religion, but of religion and rebellion combined. He became irate that politicians in the Mediterranean continued to think only of the threat from the Turks, when there was a far larger threat looming in the north. The Church, he emphasised in 1570, must watch out: 'it is not the Turks that threaten it now, but heretics'.[30] His line on the issue became much harder. He was soon complaining that 'the bishops are not as efficient as I would like at a time when there is dire need for punishment; they think that preaching is enough, but I would also like punishment'.[31] And on his deathbed the affirmation was the same. He told Luis de Granada that 'all those executed in Flanders were executed as heretics and rebels'.[32]

Tragically, Alba was totally wrong on the matter of religion. He professed to believe that the enemy were heretics, and tried to convince the king that this was so. But during the years of his repression the threat of heresy was actually much smaller than that from rebellion. Netherlanders had lived for a generation with small heretical groups (as Philip knew from his own experience there), and the problem appeared to be controllable.[33] They were not so happy, on the other hand, with the presence of foreign troops, and it was Catholics who took the lead in opposing the duke's policies. A high proportion of the nobles and officials proceeded against in the first months of Alba's governorship were Catholics. They perhaps got off more lightly, suffering largely through exile and confiscation of property, whereas the death sentence was applied mainly to supporters of the Reformation who had taken part in the image-breaking. But Catholics continued to be the backbone of resistance and were the most prominent victims. Egmont, Hornes, Montigny and Vandenesse were Catholics. All the towns besieged and attacked by Alba's army were overwhelmingly Catholic. Alkmaar, which made itself famous for its resistance in 1573, was a Catholic town that a couple of years later still had only 176 Calvinists in a population of around five thousand. 'Professed Calvinists', it has been pointed out, 'formed only a small minority of the people in revolt against Spain throughout the sixteenth century.'[34] The duke's great achievement, in actual fact his great failure, was that by his repressive methods he impelled all Netherlanders, both Catholics and heretics, to unite in defence of the national cause. It was a situation that benefited the Calvinist minority. As some of the Catholic bishops of the Netherlands informed the king shortly after Alba's recall: 'It is necessary that the foreign troops be recalled; instead of saving the religious situation, they rather ruin it.'[35]

A lifetime of service devoted to the crown brought power and honours but also a great many debts. Throughout his career the duke was plagued by the problem of his expenses.[36] He was not alone: it was normal practice at that time for great nobles to meet costs out of their own income and be subsequently compensated by the crown. The interminable journeys, always accompanied by a retinue of relatives and servants, called for a substantial expenditure, which would have to be covered by international bankers. Alba's family was one of the richest in Spain: around 1600 its income was reckoned to be in excess of 200,000 ducats a year. This, however, may not have been enough to pay his costs. Apart from expenses in the royal service, the duke spent considerable sums in rebuilding and furnishing the palace at Alba and also that in Piedrahíta. Maintenance of the family personnel also consumed sums. But the duke's debts certainly contributed to future financial problems. At his death the money owed him by the crown was around 474,000 ducats.[37] Shortly after 1600 the house of Alba had to come to a legal agreement with its debtors, and agreed to set aside a minimum of 60,000 ducats a year to pay debts.

Already during his lifetime the duke had irreparably lost the good reputation that he might have deserved after his long years of service. A constant friend and ally, but also stern critic, was another of the great servants of Philip II, Cardinal Granvelle. Shortly after the duke had left the Netherlands, Granvelle gave his verdict. Alba was 'the most prudent prince that I know';

'but the truth is that the way in which he handled the matters of Flanders was as though he were quite a different man'. The duke was an 'expensive general, clean as a whistle in what touches his person but Flanders and His Majesty's finances have been ruined by the expense. The states of Flanders have been ruined under his government, to the extent that His Majesty is in danger of losing them.'[38]

Alba's successor in the Netherlands, Requesens, was no less damning. 'All I know,' he confided to his brother Juan de Zúñiga, Spain's ambassador in Rome, 'is that when he came to this post he found the disturbances in them settled and no territory lost, and everything so quiet and secure that he could wield the knife wherever he wished. And by the time he left all Holland and Zealand was in the power of the enemy, as well as a good part of Guelderland and Brabant, and all the opinion of these provinces, with the finances wholly ruined.'[39] It can be read as an attempt by Requesens to excuse his own failures, but all the evidence supports the accuracy of the judgment. The king, his principal ministers, and even ordinary Spaniards felt that Alba in the Netherlands had been a disaster. The duke had ample time to consider their verdict during the months in Uceda, when it seemed as though the whole world had fallen in on him. His conduct in the two months of the Portuguese campaign was patently an attempt to justify his methods, or at least to think out the rationale of his own conduct. But he was realistic enough to recognise that his reputation had now been decided, and that little could be done to alter it.

His conduct in the Netherlands determined the opinion of the Dutch, who saw him as the incarnation of evil in contrast to the heroic image they created for the saviour of the country, Prince William of Orange. The polarisation is probably best expressed in the pages of the classic work by Motley, where blood drips from the duke's hands but the children weep in the streets at the death of the prince. Motley's judgment is clearly partial, but he was in some measure right to claim that the documents supported him. 'The time is past,' he wrote a century and a half ago, 'when it could be said that the cruelty of Alba, or the enormities of his administration, have been exaggerated by party violence. Human invention is incapable of outstripping the truth upon this subject. To attempt the defence of either the man or his measures at the present day is to convict oneself of an amount of ignorance or of bigotry against which history and argument are alike powerless.'[40] Even so, the impact of the duke's government cannot be measured simply in terms of the thousand or more persons condemned by the Council of Troubles. Many thousands more died in battle, in repression, in violence, in exile, in resistance, in self-defence. It was an eighty-year-long effort to secure freedom against foreign occupation. Motley saw all this as a struggle between right and wrong: 'the country, paralyzed with fear, looked anxiously but supinely upon the scientific combat between the two great champions of Despotism and Protestantism'. The polarised images of the duke and the prince, however, were in no way an accurate picture of the conflict between Spain and the Netherlands. Just as there were many Spaniards – among them government officials and military men – who criticised the duke and his repressive methods as unnecessary and unjust and supported the cause of the Netherlanders, so there were many Netherlanders who retained a friendship and admiration for Spaniards even while opposing Spanish military policy. The Dutch cultivated a continuing interest in the culture of Spain, its imaginative literature as well as books on exploration, navigation, America and the Orient. In the sixteenth and seventeenth centuries, for example, Dutch private and public libraries stocked nearly six thousand editions of works in all languages dealing with Spain.[41]

Long after the duke had disappeared from the scene, polemicists in England referred to him as the archetype of evil. Few generals in history have received such unfavourable publicity as he did during his years in the Netherlands. It was the first great age of ideological propaganda and Imperial Spain was the first victim. Deft use of the printing press and the art of engraving in northern Europe helped to produce publications and pamphlets that familiarised the public with the misdeeds of Spanish policy. The Inquisition was among the first casualties: the *auto de fe* held in Valladolid in 1559 was depicted in imaginary form in various prints that offered direct proof of Spain's wish to suppress religious liberty. No less powerful was the pamphlet image of the execution of Egmont, Hornes and other nobles in Brussels in 1568, which circulated widely in the continent. The victims of repression were fortunate to have at their service a master of propaganda, the Flemish noble Philip Marnix de Sainte-Aldegonde, who was twenty-eight years old at the time of the execution of Egmont and decided to use his talents in the service of the prince of Orange. He composed a short song for the Orangist cause, extolling the prince and denouncing Spanish tyranny, which became known as the *Wilhelmuslied* and in the nineteenth century was adopted as the national hymn of the Dutch state. The executions and proceedings of the Council of Blood inevitably provoked a further torrent of propaganda. Two historical prints which appeared in 1569 helped to create the powerful image of Alba as a monster.[42] The duke was depicted as a sinister bearded figure seated on his throne of judgment (the 'throne of Alba', as the text of the prints described it), dispensing cruel sentences against a defenceless people. Subsequent pamphlets elaborated on the theme. From 1571 there were further satires issued against Alba, this time on the theme of his notorious statue. The European public was left in no doubt about the character and deeds of Philip's commander in the Netherlands.

Though many art historians have attempted to interpret specific paintings of the period as in some way a reflection of the situation in the Netherlands, there is manifestly no evidence to support their view. The most relevant case is that of Pieter Bruegel the Elder's famous canvas of *The Triumph of Death* (1562, now in the Prado). It is a horrifying vision of apocalyptic cataclysm and cruelty, but it was painted long before Alba arrived in Brussels and was therefore unrelated to the events of the Spanish occupation. Bruegel died in September 1569. One of his last works, the *Massacre of the Innocents* (1566, now in Vienna), was finished just before the duke's arrival and had no connexion whatsoever with the duke. This has not prevented ingenious art critics from identifying the presence of the duke in the painting,[43] or interpreting the painting as a valiant protest against Spanish massacres or as an expression of the artist's support for Calvinism.[44] By contrast, there is an uncanny coincidence in the fact that Bruegel's sinister masterpiece *The Magpie* was completed in the year after Alba's arrival in the Netherlands. The painting may have had no political intention, but appears all the same to be a perfect parable of the tragedy that was about to engulf the people of the Netherlands.

In Castile many generations later a fiercely traditionalist current, coinciding with the emergence of a xenophobic tendency during the nineteenth century, set out to rescue Alba's damaged reputation through the remarkably simple method of refusing to accept historical facts or enter into detail about any part of his career. The traditionalist writers attempted to create a myth about Alba by ignoring available documentation and inventing a wholly fictional image of a Castilian war hero who bravely defended Europe against Muslims, enemies and heretics. This was the duke's second death. Alba became a tool of Castilian polemics, a response to the 'Black Legend' created round him, instead of a historical figure. Apart from a hagiographical outline of his life published in Latin by the Jesuit Ossorio in the generation after his demise, his fellow countrymen virtually forgot about his existence. The many pages devoted to him by the early seventeenth-century writer Cabrera de Córdoba became lost in the sheer volume of the pages dealing with the author's main theme, King Philip II. It was left to Khevenhüller, the Austrian who knew and respected Alba, to comment sadly that 'many more people remember him outside Spain than inside it'.[45] Not until 1983 was a reliable life of the duke published, not by a Spaniard but by an American.

In the last analysis, Alba was the paradigm of a professional army man, whose principal pride was that his father and grandfather had led his nation to glory. He was at his most confident when out in the field, in direct contact with the soldiers under his command. He felt that he was as they were, and that he knew how to deal with them. It was consequently one of his most bitter disappointments that he appeared to have let his men down in Flanders, and for that he blamed the bureaucrats who were meant to be supplying the money, rather than the men rebelling for their wages. He was at his most unsure when pushed into the world of politics and political decisions. Even as he began to put into effect the repression in the Netherlands, he expressed his dismay to Antonio de Toledo. From his desk he wrote: 'I know very well that for some people what I am doing now is a good life, turning over papers and looking into people's lives and into criminal cases, and I assure you they would change their job for mine if they could; but the truth is that I would be happy to change my lot in order not to be dealing with these matters.'[46] His proper arena, he always felt, was war and not politics. He detested and even despised politicians, whether they were in Spain, in Italy or in the Netherlands. But he knew he had to keep an eye on them, for they were capable of anything; hence the intriguing instructions from Albornoz in Brussels to the family agent, Dr Milio, in Madrid: 'Don't forget to inform me in detail of all the childish matters that go on there, who is closest to those in the treasury, who is most in touch with the cardinal, who eats with him, and other matters of that sort, who looks after the affairs of the Council of State, and a hundred thousand other foolishnesses which fill paper and give them satisfaction here.'[47]

Only a soldier, Alba insisted, knew how to make the relevant decisions and arrive at appropriate solutions. Was there a rebellion in Peru? Send in an army and subdue it. Were there rebellious nobles in France? Cut off their heads. This type of solution seemed to work superbly in the Netherlands, where the opportune execution of nobles in 1568 resulted in four years of tranquillity. That, for him, was success. By contrast, he felt, politicians messed everything up. He strongly opposed the Holy League of 1570, judging it to be a conspiracy against Spain by France and Venice and warning the king not to join it. What, he asked, was the sense of a military league directed against the Turks where all the decisions were being made not by soldiers but by diplomats and cardinals? 'On this matter anyone who is not a soldier would have not the slightest idea what to do.'[48]

Nearly half a century before, his good friend the poet Garcilaso de la Vega had foretold a great and famous future for him:

> They will speak of you throughout the world,
> time will pass and what till now was never seen
> will never find an equal
> in the future.[49]

The years passed and they brought honour and fame, but at the same time they brought a doubtful eminence. Brantôme, who knew him in his mature years, described him in his last days as still full of energy, 'neither more nor less than a fine, grand, old tree, still putting out small, green branches to show that it had been in former times the pride of a great forest'.[50] But it was the Netherlands that fixed him for all time in the memory of Europeans. Their vision of him was the result of the five years that he spent there. Few judgments are more equitable than that of his friend and ally, but also one of his firmest critics, Cardinal Granvelle. Recently created chief minister of the crown, he was working at the time in the royal palace in Madrid. When he received news of the duke's death he commented sadly, 'He was a great man, but I wish that he had never seen the Netherlands!'[51] The epitaph that Alba might have desired for himself was penned in a melancholy letter to Cardinal Espinosa in the spring of 1572, when the 'order' that he had imposed on the Netherlands was about to split apart into a chaos of revolution and war: 'When I am under the earth it will be with the comfort of knowing that I never defaulted from my duties as a born gentleman, and that I rendered to my kings the greatest and most outstanding services that any vassal or soldier of my time has given.'[52]

Appendix: The Toledo Family

The Toledo clan was vast. It had the custom of choosing the same forenames, with the result that only the most dedicated expert can make out its various members. Genealogical studies seldom help, since they tend to classify titles rather than descendants. The following list identifies those who occur in this book, but my dates may sometimes be unreliable.

Fadrique, second duke, grandee of Castile and the king's High Chamberlain, knight of the Golden Fleece 1519, councillor of State 1526, d. 18/10/1531. He had five sons (in order of birth, García, Pedro, Diego, Juan, and Fernando) and one daughter (Leonor). Diego became Prior of San Juan. Juan (d.1557) became Archbishop of Santiago, and cardinal. Fernando became Grand Commander of Alcántara. Leonor m. (1505) the third Count of Alba de Liste.

García, Fadrique's heir, had two sons and four daughters. His sons were Fernando, the third duke; and Bernardino (d.1535). Because of his early death at Djerba (1510) he did not inherit the ducal title, which passed to Fernando.

Pedro, second son of Fadrique, b. in Alba 1480, d. in Florence 21/02/1553. First wife was Juana Pimentel Osorio, second marquesa of Villafranca (from whom Pedro received the title), daughter of first marquis of Villafranca, m. Pedro in 1503, d. in Naples 1539. Second wife (1552) was (after many years of living together) Vincenza Spinello, widow. His youngest daughter was Leonor de Toledo, b. 1522 and d. 18/12/1562, who marr on 29/03/1539 Cosimo I de' Medici, later Grand Duke of Florence. From this marriage most of European royalty eventually descended.

Leonor's brother García de Toledo, became the fourth marquis of Villafranca and in 1573 the first duke of Ferrandina and prince of Montalbán (titles of Naples, purchased 1569), m. (1552) Vittoria Colonna y Aragón. Became viceroy of Catalonia and of Sicily (1565–1568). He was general of the galleys of Sicily (1535), and Captain General of the Sea 1564. He d. in Naples 31/05/1578.

Fernando, third duke, had three legitimate sons, plus a natural son Hernando, and two daughters. The sons were García, b. 21/07/1530, d. 1548;

Fadrique, b. 21/11/1537, who inherited the title; and Diego, b. 6/11/1542, who died at Alba 11/07/1583. Diego m. Brianda de Beaumont.

Fadrique, fourth duke, married three times but was childless. His first wife was Guiomar de Aragón, daughter of the dukes of Segorbe, whom he married on 31/05/1551. His second wife was María Pimentel, daughter of the count of Benavente, whom he married on 10/01/1562. His third wife was María de Toledo, whom he married on 5/05/1571. He was suceeded as duke by the son of his brother Diego.

Antonio, fifth duke, son of Diego, was born at Lerín, Navarre, in November 1568.

Another line of the Toledo family was formed by Fernando de Toledo y Herrera, first count of Oropesa (1475), second grandson of an Álvarez de Toledo, m. María Carrillo, daughter of first count of Alba. Francisco de Toledo the viceroy of Peru was third son of the third count of Oropesa. Among the other important nobles belonging to the Toledo family, one should single out the marquis of Velada: Gómez Dávila y Toledo, second marquis, who m. Ana Álvarez de Toledo y Colonna, daughter of García de Toledo, marquis of Villafranca and viceroy of Sicily.

Abbreviations

AA	Archivo de la Casa de Alba
AGS:E	Archivo General de Simancas, section Estado
AGS:E/K	Archivo General de Simancas, section Estado, serie K
BL Add.	British Library, London, manuscript room, Additional MS
BN	Biblioteca Nacional, Madrid, manuscript room
BP	Biblioteca del Palacio Real, Madrid
BZ	Biblioteca Zábalburu, Madrid, manuscript collection
CODOIN	*Colección de Documentos Inéditos para la Historia de España*
CSPS	*Calendar of State Papers, Spain*
CSPV	*Calendar of State Papers, Venice*
Discurso	*Discurso del Duque de Berwick y de Alba*, Madrid 1919
Docs. escog.	*Documentos escogidos de la Casa de Alba*, ed. Duquesa de Berwick y de Alba. Madrid 1891
EA	*Epistolario del III duque de Alba, Don Fernando Álvarez de Toledo.* 3 vols. Madrid 1952
Favre	Collection Favre, Bibliothèque Publique et Universitaire, Geneva
HHSA	Haus-, Hof-, und Staatsarchiv, Vienna
Homenaje	*Homenaje al Gran Duque de Alba*, Salamanca 1983
IVDJ	Instituto de Valencia de Don Juan, Madrid
leg.	legajo

Notes

1   Family Beginnings, 1507–1533

1 *Crónica de Don Álvaro de Luna*, ed. J. de Mata Carriazo, Madrid 1940, p. 249.
2 *Crónica de Don Álvaro de Luna*, p. 268.
3 Some of the family links of the Toledo family, too complex to explain here, are touched on in the Appendix.
4 Hernando Sánchez 2001, p. 205.
5 J. B. Vilar and R. Lourido, *Relaciones entre España y el Magreb, siglos XVII y XVIII*, Madrid 1994, p. 47.
6 A biography of Ferdinand was composed in Latin in the seventeenth century by a Jesuit, Ossorio, but although it appears to have used documentation, its intention was solely hagiographic, and unfortunately there are many basic errors of fact. The duke of Alba commissioned a translation into Spanish which was published in 1945, retaining all the errors.
7 Pedro de Mexía, *Historia del emperador Carlos V*, Madrid 1945, chap. IV p. 147.
8 Gachard 1874, p. 27.
9 Catherine was one of the daughters of Isabella and Ferdinand.
10 Santa Cruz, vol. I, p. 265.
11 Santa Cruz, vol. I, p. 515. Santa Cruz's information on aspects of the English visits is erroneous, and it is essential to refer to Gachard 1874, pp. 27, 32.
12 Vives to Erasmus, Bruges, 1 April 1522, *Epistolario*, ed. J. Jiménez Delgado, Madrid 1978, p. 239.
13 Cf. Hernando Sánchez 1994, pp. 54–64, the best presentation of this subject. For an excellent survey of another noble family see Helen Nader, *The Mendoza Family in the Spanish Renaissance*, New Brunswick 1979.
14 Santa Cruz, vol. II, p. 81.
15 Bustos Tovar, in *Homenaje al gran Duque de Alba*, p. 57.
16 I have followed the details given by an officer who fought in the battle: García Cerezeda, vol. I, 113.
17 The action of the three Castilians is verified by Eloy Benito Ruano in 'Los aprehensores de Francisco I de Francia en Pavia', *Hispania*, vol. XVIII, 1958, p. 547.
18 There are many books on this famous episode. Vicente de Cadenas y Vicent, *El Saco de Roma de 1527*, Madrid 1974, contains good contemporary documentation.
19 Garcilaso, *Egloga II*, lines 1433–42.
20 Garcilaso, *Egloga II*, lines 1702–28.

2   *The Emperor's General, 1534–1556*

1 EA, vol. I, p. 431.
2 Santa Cruz, vol. III, pp. 255–61.
3 Carande, III, pp. 175–6.
4 Figures for both ships and men are based on Martin García Cerezeda, vol. II, p. 21.
5 Tracy, pp. 155–6.
6 Solnon, p. 55.
7 García Cerezeda, vol. II, p. 51.
8 Strictly speaking, Naples recognised Ferdinand and then Charles as rulers, but the kingdom was not a dependency of either Aragon or Castile. In practice, Spaniards began to increase their role in Neapolitan affairs.
9 Pedro de Toledo acquired the title through his marriage in 1503 to the marquesa of Villafranca.
10 Garcilaso, *Elegia I*, 'Al duque d'Alva en la muerte de Don Bernardino de Toledo'.
11 Hernando Sánchez 2001, p. 116.
12 Hernando Sánchez 2001, pp. 398–404.
13 Cited in Tracy, p. 161.
14 García Cerezeda, vol. II, pp. 173–4.
15 Cited in Tracy, p. 163.
16 Sandoval, p. 76.
17 Santa Cruz, vol. IV, p. 57.
18 Brantôme, p. 26.
19 To Cobos, 23 Jan. 1540, EA, vol. I, p. 2.
20 Cited in Tracy, p. 168.
21 Carande, vol. III, p. 218.
22 Ossorio, p. 50.
23 Cf. Tracy, p. 174.
24 There are several accounts of the disaster; I follow the documents cited in Carande, vol. III, pp. 219–23.
25 Merriman, vol. III, p. 339.
26 The letters of Alba from Navarre, preserved in the archive of Simancas, are quoted without further reference from the text edited by Ascensión de la Plaza, and published as 'Cartas del Duque de Alba a Carlos V', in *Cuadernos de Investigación Histórica* (see the Short Bibliography).
27 Khevenhüller, p. 262.
28 I quote from the version offered in *Corpus documental de Carlos V*, 5 vols. Salamanca 1975, vol. II (1539–48), p. 109.
29 Alba to Charles V, Barcelona, 6 May 1543, EA, vol. I, p. 25.
30 To Cobos, Alba de Tormes, 19 July 1543, EA, vol. I, p. 42.
31 Zúñiga to Charles, 8 June, 1543, AGS:E leg. 60 f. 201.
32 Alba to Charles, 29 July 1543, CSPS, vol. VI, no. ii, p. 449.
33 J. M. March, *Niñez y Juventud de Felipe II*. 2 vols. Madrid 1941, vol. II, pp. 71–2.
34 AGS:E leg. 64¹ f. 82.
35 Juan Cristóbal Calvete de Estrella, *Rebelión de Pizarro en el Perú y vida de D. Pedro Gasca*. 2 vols. Madrid 1889, vol. I, p. 98.
36 This man was the priest Pedro de la Gasca, whose fortunes may be followed in the pages of W. H. Prescott's classic *History of the Conquest of Peru, with a preliminary view of the civilization of the Incas*. London 1886 (reissued 2002).

37 Keniston, p.270. Keniston explains the problems with this account, but on balance accepts it as authentic. I have retouched some phrases.

38 Vandenesse, in Gachard 1874, vol. II, p. 529.

39 The previous count, Charles d'Egmont, had died on Spanish soil after the retreat from Algiers, and was buried in Murcia.

40 Gachard 1875, p. 125.

41 The duchy of Saxony had in 1485 been divided between brothers of the same Wettin family into an 'electoral' and a 'ducal' territory. The conflicts of the Reformation era sharpened the differences between the two Saxonies.

42 I take the figures from the account in Tracy, p. 221.

43 The famous portrait by Titian, showing Charles on a horse at Mühlberg, was completely faithful to reality.

44 The Venetian ambassador says that an Italian noble, Hippolito da Porto, captured the duke.

45 Avila y Zúñiga, p. 28.

46 Gómara appears to be the main source for Merriman (vol. III, p. 258) claiming that 'it was largely with Spaniards that Charles won the battle of Mühlberg'.

47 Vicente de Cadenas y Vicent, *Dos años en la vida del emperador Carlos V (1546–1547)*, Madrid 1988, p. 148.

48 Brantôme, vol. I, p. 27. Alba's heraldic colours were white and blue.

49 Motley, p. 338.

50 J. M. Jover, *Carlos V y los españoles*, Madrid 1987, p. 307.

51 The various texts of the Instructions of 1548 are considered in Berthold Beinert, 'El Testamento Político de Carlos V de 1548', in *Carlos V*, pp. 401–38. No original of the Instructions exists; Beinert opts for the version in Sandoval as the most genuine.

52 A preliminary draft of Alba's instructions is in 'Ce qu'il semble se devra observer pour le commencement du service de son Alteze a la mode de Bourgoigne', in Favre, p. 59, ff. 341–60.

53 The immediate household of the prince after the introduction of the new ceremonial consisted of around two hundred persons (document dated to 1548 and cited in Christina Hofmann, *Das Spanische Hofzeremoniell von 1500 bis 1700*, Frankfurt 1985, p. 209), but this did not include soldiers, pages, and servants.

54 Calvete de Estrella, p. 3.

55 Calvete de Estrella, p. 5. There were also a number of other vessels for transporting servants and horses.

56 Cf. Kamen 1997, chap. 2.

57 Calvete de Estrella, p. 29.

58 What follows is drawn from Kamen 1997.

59 For the family links between the great nobles of the Netherlands, see the family trees in Parker, 1979, pp. 271–3.

60 Calvete de Estrella, p. 281.

61 Another source lists forty-four galleys. The naval commander Bernardino de Mendoza, brother to the scholar–diplomat Diego Hurtado de Mendoza, was no relation of the later ambassador of Philip to England.

62 This modifies the presentation in Lagomarsino, pp. 24–6, where Eraso is shown as joining Gómez in 1556. The correspondence of Gómez with Eraso in AGS:E leg. 89 shows that the two put their heads together long before.

63 Lagomarsino, pp. 24, 68.

64 Cf. Lagomarsino, p. 28; and Maltby's (1983) views.

65 Gómez to Eraso, Toro, 22 Sept. 1552, AGS:E leg. 89 f. 120.

66 Gómez to Eraso, Toro, 25 Nov. 1552, AGS:E leg. 89 f. 123.

67 The file on the Chancery is in AGS:E leg. 89 f. 139.

68 Gómez to Eraso, Madrid, 4 April 1552, AGS:E leg. 89 f. 129.

69 Ruy Gómez to Eraso, 19 May 1552, AGS:E leg. 89 f. 131. Maurice was killed in a campaign in Germany in 1553.

70 Tracy, p. 241.

71 Quoted in Karl Brandi, *The Emperor Charles V*, London 1939, p. 622.

72 11 Oct. 1553, Aranjuez, EA, vol. I, p. 57.

73 2 Nov. 1553, Alba de Tormes, EA, vol. I, p. 57.

74 The *rapprochement* between Philip and Ruy Gómez makes it all the more curious that a recent study (M. J. Rodríguez-Salgado, *The Changing Face of Empire. Charles V, Philip II and Habsburg Authority, 1551–1559*, Cambridge 1988, p. 15) should make the implausible claim that Alba 'changed his allegiance from Charles to Philip during the duke's stay at the Spanish court in 1553'. Alba quite simply did not change his allegiance, and did not stay at the Spanish court.

75 Feb. 1554, EA, vol. I, p. 62.

76 For more details on the English marriage, see Kamen 1997, chap. 3.

77 To Eraso, EA, vol. I, p. 64.

78 CSPV, VI, parts 1–3, nos 24, 32.

79 EA, vol. I, pp. 73, 78.

80 EA, vol. I, pp. 77, 320.

81 To Ruy Gómez, 28 Oct. 1555, Milan, in EA, vol. I, p. 322.

82 To Philip, 11 Jan. 1556, EA, vol. I, p. 353.

83 EA, vol. I, p. 114.

84 EA, vol. I, pp. 110, 118.

85 Quoted in Carlos Javier de Carlos Morales, 'El poder de los secretarios reales: Francisco de Eraso', in J. Martínez Millán, *La corte de Felipe II*, Madrid 1994, pp. 126–9.

86 *Discurso*, p. 69.

87 EA, vol. I, p. 216.

88 EA, vol. I, pp. 103, 277.

89 EA, vol. I, p. 272. I refer to this incident again in Chap.7, below.

90 EA, vol. I, p. 270.

91 To Antonio de Toledo, Milan, 3 Aug. 1555, AA, 65/112. Alba's letter gives 1,500 soldiers, whereas the text printed in EA gives, erroneously, 1,200.

92 To Fadrique, Milan, Dec. 1555, AA, 65/109.

93 EA, vol. I, pp. 344, 349.

94 EA, vol. I, p. 370.

95 EA, vol. I, pp. 390, 447. Alba's letter states that 3,000 tercios were lost at sea; this seems improbable. Since he also mentions they formed three companies, I have corrected the total to 1,000 men.

96 EA, vol. I, p. 363.

97 Quoted by Manuel Rivero Rodríguez, 'El servicio a dos cortes: Marco Antonio Colonna', in Martínez Millán, *La corte de Felipe II*, p. 321.

98 EA, vol. I, p. 431.

99 Interpreting Nostradamus's fancies is unprofitable but entertaining. The rebellion of Alba was presumably against the pope, and at the moment he wrote Nostradamus could not be sure whether in fact Guise would win the war and capture Alba.

100 EA, vol. I, p. 465.
101 Manuel Rivero, 'El service a dos cortes', p. 324.

3   The King's Counsellor, 1557–1566

 1 EA, vol. I, p. 471.
 2 At several points where I have been able to check the documents in the archive of Simancas, the over-dramatised picture given in M. J. Rodríguez-Salgado, *The Changing Face of Empire* (cited above in Chap. 2 n.74), of a bitter struggle between Charles V and Philip II, is not justified by the sources.
 3 Suriano to the doge, Brussels, 26 Feb. 1558, CSPV, vol. VI, parts 1–3, no. 1174.
 4 CSPV, vol. VI, parts 1–3, no. 1269.
 5 CSPV, vol. VII, nos. 22, 28.
 6 EA, vol. I, p. 502.
 7 Maltby, p. 151 ff.
 8 CSPV, vol. VII, no. 129.
 9 Report by L'Aubespine, 26 Sept. 1560, in Paris, p. 560.
10 CSPV, vol. VII, no. 198.
11 L'Aubespine, p. 560.
12 Lagomarsino, p. 30, states that 'Philip was fundamentally flexible at the start of his reign'.
13 Gonzalo Pérez to Granvelle, 16 April 1560, Toledo, BP MS.II/2291 f.103.
14 Lagomarsino, p. 28.
15 See also the sensible comments by Boyden, pp. 114–15.
16 Alba to king, 3 Aug. and 19 Sept. 1560, AGS:E leg. 139, ff.119, 123.
17 Braudel, vol. II, pp. 973–87.
18 CSPV, vol. VII, p. 213.
19 Thompson 1976, p. 16.
20 Gachard 1867, p. 76.
21 Cabié 1903, p. 78.
22 Cabié, p. 171.
23 To García de Toledo, 8 Aug. 1563, EA, vol. I, p. 554.
24 The king was in constant touch with Alba, as the correspondence in AGS:E leg. 143 shows.
25 Maltby, p. 123.
26 Alba to Pacheco, 13 Mar. 1564, EA, vol. I, p. 573.
27 Alba to king, 21 Oct. 1563, AGS:E leg. 143 f. 3.
28 Lagomarsino, p. 100.
29 Philip's draft notes and Pérez's draft and comments are in AGS:E leg. 527 f. 5.
30 Cabié, p.357.
31 Manrique de Lara to king, 18 May 1565, AGS:E leg. 145 f.196.
32 EA, vol. I, p. 582.
33 Alba and Manrique to Philip, 15 and 21 June 1565, AGS:E/K leg.1504 ff. 15, 17.
34 Alba and Manrique to king, 21 June 1565, AGS:E/K, leg. 1504 f. 21b.
35 Thompson 1910, p. 117.
36 What follows is drawn from Thompson 1910, pp. 277–8.
37 Alba and Juan Manrique to Philip II, Bayonne, 21 June 1565, AGS:E/K 1504/22.

38 AGS:E/K, leg. 1504 f.36.

39 EA, vol. I, p. 683.

40 Álava to Philip, 8 July 1565, AGS:E leg. 1504 f.50.

41 Hernando de Toledo to Alba, Santelmo, 30 Oct. 1565, AA, 53/100.

42 The background to this is superbly studied in Lagomarsino, pp. 136–47.

43 A full report on the verdicts, in HHSA, Spanien, Varia, karton 2, r, f.19.

44 Dr Juan Milio to duchess, 1566, AA, 44/40.

45 Cited Lagomarsino, p. 133.

46 AGS:E leg. 146, no. 77.

47 Lagomarsino, pp. 174–82.

48 Gachard 1848–79, vol. I, p. clxxvi.

49 For some Spanish views, see Kamen, 'Toleration', in Kamen 1993.

50 King to Francés de Álava, 27 Nov. 1567, in Pedro Rodríguez and Justina Rodríguez, *Don Francés de Alava y Beamonte. Correspondencia Inédita de Felipe II con su Embajador en París (1564–1570)*. San Sebastian 1991, doc. 70.

51 Fourquevaux to Charles IX, 5 May 1566, Douais, p. 86.

52 Del Canto to king, 4 July 1566, Brussels, AGS:E leg. 529 ff.61–2.

53 Luciano Serrano, *Correspondencia Diplomática entre España y la Santa Sede*. 4 vols. Madrid 1914, vol. II, p. xxxix.

54 Parker 1979, p. 78.

55 Gachard 1867, p. 264 n. 2.

56 He looked 'plus beau, plus frais et plus jeune' than ever: Douais, vol. III, p. 23. However, the next day he was unwell again.

57 Lagomarsino, pp. 254–8, gives the best summary of this meeting.

58 Cabrera, vol. I, p. 490.

59 Fourquevaux to Charles IX, 9 Dec. 1566, Douais, p. 150.

60 Gachard 1875, pp. 93, 99.

61 A discussion of these issues is offered in Léon van de Essen, 'Croissade contre les hérétiques ou guerre contre les rebelles?', *Revue d'histoire ecclésiastique* 51 (1956), pp. 42–78.

62 Lagomarsino, p. 270.

63 Lagomarsino, p. 262.

64 Khevenhüller, p. 71.

65 Lagomarsino, p. 284.

66 'Paresciendole que no se puede venir a matar 200,000 personas': Margaret to king, 18 Aug. 1566, AGS:E leg. 530.

67 Gachard 1867, p. 320.

68 Cabrera, vol. I, p. 525.

69 Mendoza was son of the third count of Coruña. His book was first published in Paris in 1591 and then in Madrid in 1592; it was translated into English in 1597. After his service under Alba, Mendoza was in 1577 appointed ambassador to England and then to France; his career in France is studied in the fine book by J. De Lamar Jensen, *Diplomacy and Dogmatism. Bernardino de Mendoza and the Catholic League*, Cambridge, Mass. 1964.

70 The best brief account of the Carranza case is by J. I. Tellechea, in *Historia de la Inquisición en España y América*, 2 vols. ed. J. Pérez Villanueva and B. Escandell Bonet, Madrid, 1984–93, vol. I, pp. 556–98.

71 EA, vol. I, p. 636.

4   *The Council of Troubles, 1567–1572*

1 The word-sketch is from Motley, p. 340, based on a later description by the Venetian ambassador. In 1566, in fact, the duke did not have a 'long silver beard', as we can see clearly from the portrait by Antonis Mor and the bust by Jonghelinck.

2 Dr Juan Milio to duchess, 8 Feb. 1566, AA, 44/39.

3 To García de Toledo, 29 Nov. 1566, EA, vol. I, p. 621.

4 Douais, vol. I, p. 225.

5 Cf. Lagomarsino, p. 263.

6 CODOIN, vol. L, pp. 288, 290.

7 A few details may be found in Angel Salcedo Ruiz, *Un bastardo insigne del Gran Duque de Alba*, Madrid 1903.

8 The best analysis of the Spanish forces at this time is in Parker 1972.

9 Julián Romero (1518–1577) began his career as a soldier in 1534 and served throughout Europe. He served in Flanders for the emperor, fought for the English against the Scots at the battle of Pinkie (1547), and later fought at St Quentin. He went on to fight against the Turks, then took part in the wars of the Netherlands. He was one of the principal commanders at Haarlem, and lost an eye in the assault. His regiment also took part in the mutiny of the Spanish Fury.

10 The best desription of the military routes of the Spanish armies is in Parker 1972, chaps. 2–3.

11 Khevenhüller, p. 71.

12 J.H.M. Salmon, *Society in Crisis. France in the Sixteenth Century*, London 1975, pp. 169–70.

13 'Diario del viaje del Duque de Alba de Italia a Bruselas', an account probably prepared by Francisco de Ibarra, in AA, 165/23.

14 Brantôme, vol. I, p. 29.

15 Baltasar de Vargas, *Breve Relación de la jornada que ha hecho el duque de Alba desde España hasta Flandes*. Antwerp 1568.

16 Kamen 1997, p. 126.

17 Eugenio Alberi, *Relazioni degli ambasciatori veneti al Senato*, Florence 1839–40, series I, vol. 5, p. 22.

18 Nicolas Castrillo, *El 'Reginaldo Montano': primer libro polémico contra la Inquisición Española*, Madrid 1991, p. 31.

19 F. E. Beemon, 'The myth of the Spanish Inquisition and the preconditions for the Dutch revolt', *Archiv für Reformationsgeschichte*, vol. 85, 1994, p. 255.

20 EA, vol. I, p. 665.

21 AA, 165/23.

22 Khevenhüller, p. 72. The reference to 'heretic' is reported differently by various historians; some suggest that Alba was calling Egmont a heretic. The phrase used is certainly ambiguous, but the interpretation given by Khevenhüller leaves no doubt that Alba was joking.

23 Margaret to Philip II, 12 July 1567, Gachard 1848–79, vol. I, p. 556.

24 CODOIN, vol. IV, p. 405.

25 King to Requesens, 22 Oct. 1567, Gachard 1848–79, vol. I, pp. 581–96.

26 Cabrera de Córdoba, vol. I, p. 529.

27 The cases recounted here are taken from Motley, pp. 346–7.

28 Gaspar de Robles, seigneur de Billy, a Walloon of Spanish origin.

29 Alba to king, 9 Sept. 1567, CODOIN, vol. IV, p. 416.
30 Hernando de Toledo, Alba's nephew, to duchess, Brussels, 22 Oct. 1567, AA, 52/101.
31 EA, vol. I, p. 670.
32 EA, vol. I, pp. 672–5.
33 Philip to Alba, 11 Oct. 1567, CODOIN, vol. LXXV, p. 15.
34 Philip to Alba, 16 Oct. 1567, AGS:E leg. 537 ff.3–6.
35 Douais, pp. 272, 282.
36 EA, vol. I, p. 697.
37 EA, vol. I, p. 711. The sentiment expressed by Alba was not original; it appears in statements made at this time by various French nobles, and the duke may have picked it up during conversations with them.
38 CODOIN, vol. LXXV, p. 20.
39 CODOIN, vol. XXXVII, pp. 42–70.
40 King to Alba, 19 Feb 1568, CODOIN, vol. XXXVII, p. 156.
41 Margaret to Philip II, 22 Nov. 1567, Gachard 1848–79, vol. I, p. 602.
42 EA, vol. II, p. 17.
43 'Defender of his country' echoes, of course, the romantic sketch of Orange in Motley, pp. 119–26, but there is no good reason for not using the phrase here.
44 Motley, pp. 153–63.
45 This agent was Jacques de Vandenesse, one of Philip II's gentlemen of the chamber, who was arrested shortly after.
46 Williams, p. 66.
47 Strada, vol. II, p. 633.
48 Reported by the abbé Morillon two days after the event, quoted in Motley, p. 390 n. 3. Brantôme's information also was that the duke had been deeply saddened: Brantôme, vol. I, p. 143.
49 EA, vol. II, p. 61.
50 Luis Venegas to king, Vienna 11 Oct. 1568, AGS:E leg. 665 f. 32.
51 AGS:E leg. 537 f. 26.
52 Strada, vol. II, p. 686.
53 King to Alba, Madrid, 18 July 1568, CODOIN, vol. XXXVII, p. 310.
54 Requesens to Philip II, 19 Sept. 1574, Nueva CODOIN, vol. V, pp. 224–35.
55 Motley, p. 398.
56 Alba to Council of State, in Gachard, p. 157.
57 Motley, p. 414.
58 Cf. the summary given in Parker 1979, p. 108. The original research on the subject was by A. L. E. Verheyden, *Le Conseil des Troubles. Liste des condamnés, 1567–1573*, Brussels 1961.
59 Alba to king, 18 Sept. 1567, CODOIN, vol. IV, p. 448.
60 To king, 13 April 1568, in *Discurso*, p. 122.
61 Motley, p. 359.
62 Alba to king, 2 Oct. 1567, CODOIN, vol. IV, p. 453.
63 Albornoz to Zayas, 3 Oct. 1567, CODOIN, vol. IV, p. 461.
64 Alba to king, Brussels, 6 Jan. 1568, Gachard 1848–79, vol. II, p. 3.
65 Alba to king, Brussels, 6 Jan. 1568, CODOIN, vol. XXXVII, p. 84.
66 Some of the measures are discussed in Parker 1979, pp. 113–14.
67 G. Moreau, 'Catalogue des livres brûlés à Tournai par ordre du duc d'Albe (16 juin 1569)', *Horae Tornacenses* (Doornik, 1971), pp. 194– 213.

68 Pedro Cornejo, *Sumario de las Guerras Civiles y causas de la Rebelión de Flandes*, León 1577, p. 114.

69 And that featured as the theme of the brilliant French film by Jacques Feyder, *La Kermesse héroïque* (1935).

70 *Discurso*, p. 122.

71 To king, 9 June 1568, CODOIN, vol. IV, p. 498.

72 EA, vol. II, pp. 135, 154.

73 These figures should, of course, be seen in perspective. The indigenous Inquisition of the Netherlands had, before the coming of the Spaniards, executed more people (mainly Anabaptists) than the duke of Alba ever did.

74 EA, vol. II, p. 599. In the Netherlands it was the papal Inquisition with which Alba worked, first introduced by Charles V. The Spaniards had no intention of bringing in their Inquisition.

75 King to Francés de Álava, 14 Oct. 1568, in Rodríguez and Rodríguez, doc. 126.

76 Philip to Alba, 18 Feb. 1569, CODOIN, vol. XXXVII, p. 552.

77 EA, vol. II, p. 185.

78 King to Chantonnay, 11 May 1566, CODOIN, vol. CI, p. 137.

79 King to Chantonnay, 20 May 1568, CODOIN, vol. CI, p. 422.

80 CODOIN, vol. XXXVII, p. 358.

81 CODOIN; vol. XXXVII, pp. 354, 573.

82 CODOIN, vol. XXXVIII, pp. 179, 186, 224.

83 Fadrique to Alba, Bois-le-Duc, 18 Aug. 1568, AA, 346/C-29.

84 *Discurso*, p. 168.

85 EA, vol. II, p. 218.

86 Cf. Parker 1979, p. 115.

87 Parker 1972, p. 140.

88 CODOIN, vol. XXXVIII, p. 187.

89 To Philip, 5 May 1570, EA, vol. II, p. 371.

90 To Espinosa, from Nijmegen, 12 Aug. 1570, EA, vol. II, p. 388.

91 This is the correct form of her name, and she always signed it this way. The Spanish form 'Ana' was not to my knowledge used by her. See her letters in HHSA, Spanien, Hofkorrespondenz, karton 2, mappe 12 pp. 1, 5.

92 To Zayas, 23 Jan. 1571, EA, vol. II, p. 501.

93 For Montigny, see Kamen 1997, pp. 128–30.

94 Motley, p. 445.

95 EA, vol. II, p. 404.

96 EA, vol. II, p. 548. Alba means that his long separation from his wife is as though he were on the other side of the Atlantic.

97 EA, vol. II, p. 382.

98 CSPV, vol. VIII, p. 296.

99 Alexandre Teulet, *Relations politiques de la France et de l'Espagne avec l'Ecosse au XVIe siècle*. 5 vols, Paris 1862, vol. V, p. 57.

100 In a letter to Zúñiga, from Brussels, 8 April 1571, EA, vol. II, p. 559; also the letters to Philip in EA, vol. II, pp. 660, 681.

101 Alba to king, Brussels, 7 May 1571, 'Your Majesty had no interest in this', Teulet, vol. V, p. 74.

102 'Lo que se platicó en Consejo', 7 July 1571, AGS:E leg. 823 ff. 150–8. The council did not *approve* the plot, but waited to be guided by the king. Merriman (vol. IV, p. 293) over-dramatises the incident.

103 Recently Geoffrey Parker has argued that Philip was committed, though the evidence he cites may in my opinion be interpreted differently: G. Parker, 'The place of Tudor England in the messianic vision of Philip II of Spain', *Transactions of the Royal Historical Society*, vol. XII (2002), pp. 189–205.

104 Cf. Manuel Rivero, 'Marcantonio Colonna', in J. Martínez Millán, ed., *La corte de Felipe II*, Madrid 1994, pp. 341, 348.

105 EA, vol. II, p. 448.

106 EA, vol. II, p. 821.

107 EA, vol. II, p. 594.

108 From Brussels, 7 June 1571, EA, vol. II, p. 629.

109 More to the point, Alençon was of dwarfish height, slightly hunchbacked, and his face was severely marked by smallpox.

110 Cited in Thompson 1910, p. 443 n. 2.

111 Diego de Zúñiga to king, Paris 22 Aug. 1572, AGS:E/K leg. 1529 f. 20.

112 Despatches of Zúñiga to king in AGS:E/K 1529 ff. 20, 21, 29.

113 Philip to Zúñiga, 18 Sept. 1572, AGS:E/K 1529 f. 53b.

114 Groen van Prinsterer, p. 125. A broad perspective on the massacres is given by N. M. Sutherland, *The Massacre of St. Bartholomew and the European Conflict 1559–1572* (London, 1973).

5 Revolt in the Netherlands, 1572–1578

1 Cf. Parker 1979, pp. 126–130; also H. van der Wee, 'The Economy as a Factor in the Beginning of the Revolt of the Netherlands', *Acta Historiae Neerlandicae* 5 (Leiden, 1971), pp. 52–67.

2 EA, vol. III, p. 37.

3 I quote the Paternoster of Ghent from Motley, p. 543.

4 EA, vol. III, p. 99.

5 EA, vol. III, p. 111.

6 Parker 1972, p. 27.

7 Thompson 1910, p. 447.

8 To Diego de Zúñiga, envoy in Paris, from Mons, 9 Sept. 1572, EA, vol. III, p. 204.

9 Quoted in *Discurso*, p. 128.

10 Genlis was executed in the fort at Antwerp on 17 Nov. 1573.

11 Quoted in J.-J. Altmeyer, *Une succursale du Tribunal de Sang*, Brussels 1853, p. 107.

12 Parker 1998, p. 127.

13 Motley, p. 493.

14 CODOIN, vol. LXXV, p. 110.

15 St Gouard to Charles IX, 31 May 1572, in Groen van Prinsterer, p. 122.

16 Khevenhüller, p. 91.

17 Morillon to Granvelle, 11 Aug. 1572, in Groen van Prinsterer, p. 114.

18 Motley, p. 497.

19 To Philip II from Nijmegen, 19 Nov. 1572, EA, vol. III, p. 248.

20 Zutphen, 11 Nov. 1572, CODOIN vol. LXXV, p. 116.

21 CODOIN, vol. XXXVI, pp. 119–30.

22 EA, vol. III, p. 251.

23 CODOIN vol. XXXVI, p. 73.

24 AA, 44/90, Dr Milio to Hernando de Toledo, 31 Dec. 1572.

25 Khevenhüller, p. 95.
26 From Nijmegen, 19 Dec. 1572, EA, vol. III, p. 261.
27 EA, vol. III, p. 275.
28 The best account of the siege is Motley, pp. 503–17.
29 CODOIN, vol. LXXV, pp. 163, 173, 180. Official Spanish historiography usually refused to recognise that anything had gone wrong at Haarlem. Cabrera de Córdoba limited himself to commenting that 'the siege of Haarlem was perhaps the most notable one of that time'.
30 Cited by the Marquis de Cerralbo, in *Hidalguía*, Jan.–Feb. 1955, no. 8.
31 Cited in Motley, p. 515, n. 8.
32 CODOIN, vol. LXXV, p. 135.
33 Gracián to Zayas, 25 July 1573, AGS:E leg. 155 f. 52.
34 Julián Romero to Zayas, Brussels, 24 June 1572, CODOIN, vol. LXXV, pp. 59, 62.
35 Secretary Prats to king, Nov. 1572, CODOIN, vol. LXXV, p. 129. The figures are not reliable; they are quoted here to show how even pro-Spanish administrators felt that Alba had failed.
36 Cf. Motley, p. 518.
37 Cited in Gachard 1875, p. 127.
38 Granvelle to Juan de Zúñiga, 8 Oct. 1573, BZ, 129 f. 148.
39 Requesens to Juan de Zúñiga, 29 July 1573, Favre, 30 f. 327.
40 To Philip, from Utrecht, 2 Aug. 1573, EA, vol. III, p. 485.
41 Parker 1972, p. 203.
42 To Juan de Ovando, cited by Eugenio de Bustos Tovar, in *Homenaje*, p. 66.
43 Morales Oliver, pp. 143–4.
44 Philip II to Alba, 24 Dec. 1569, AGS:E leg. 542 f. 4.
45 Morales Oliver, p. 174.
46 Strada, vol. II, p. 734.
47 James Tanis and Daniel Horst, *Images of Discord*, Grand Rapids 1993, pp. 29, 50, 86.
48 Motley, p. 420 n. 1.
49 Morales Oliver, p. 200.
50 Morales Oliver, pp. 200, 209–11.
51 Zayas to Montano, 17 July 1573, CODOIN, vol. XLI, p. 292.
52 Gracián to Zayas, 13 Aug. 1573, AGS:E leg. 155 f. 63.
53 Motley, pp. 459–461.
54 Álava to king, 1574, in AGS E:K 1535/109, printed in Rodríguez and Rodríguez, p. 50.
55 IVDJ, 76, f. 461, 'Presidente Juan de Ovando sobre el desempeño'.
56 CODOIN, vol. LXXV, pp. 190, 199, 236, from Alba to Zayas, in Feb., April and July of 1573.
57 Cited in *Discurso*, p. 119, without giving source or date.
58 Philip to Medinaceli, San Lorenzo, 25 July 1573, BL Add. 28357 f. 11.
59 *Discurso*, p. 65.
60 J. M. March, *Don Luis de Requeséns en el gobierno de Milán 1571–1573*, Madrid 1943, p. 315.
61 Favre, 30 ff. 30, 48.
62 EA, vol. III, p. 493.
63 Williams, p. 135.
64 To king, 23 Oct. 1573, EA, vol. III, p. 538.

65 Hernando to Alba, Barcelona, 24 Sept. 1573, AA, 52/255.

66 Requesens to Zúñiga, 18 Jan 1574, IVDJ, 67 no. 5.

67 Requesens to Pedro Manuel, 31 Dec. 1574, Favre, 30 f. 371.

68 Motley, p. 537.

69 EA, vol. III, p. 577.

70 AA, 131/118.

71 CSPV, vol. VII, no. 578.

72 Like General Macarthur at the time of the Korean War.

73 *Homenaje*, p. 61; *Docs. escog.*, pp. 118–19.

74 There is a good summary of this topic in *Discurso*, p. 32.

75 Cabrera de Córdoba, vol. II, pp. 125–6.

76 Boyden, p. 2.

77 Dr Milio to Albornoz, Madrid, 30 July 1573, AA, 44/103.

78 Dr Juan Milio to Albornoz, 14 Aug 1573, *Docs escog.*, p. 495.

79 AA, 52/255.

80 Hernando to duke, 16 May 1574, AA, 52/258.

81 Cabrera de Córdoba, vol. II, p. 639. The common practice amongst all Spanish officials, including Alba, was to distinguish between a 'first rebellion', namely the iconoclasm of 1566, and a 'second rebellion', which began with the Sea Beggars in 1572. The military events of 1568–1569 seem to have been considered an extension of the events of 1566, rather than a distinct rebellion.

82 Letters of Granvelle to Juan de Zúñiga, Philip's ambassador to Rome. The letters date from Oct. 1573 to Aug. 1574, BZ, 62 ff. 148–63.

83 Gachard 1848–79, vol. V, p. 69.

84 Montano to Zayas, Nov. 1573, cited B. Rekers, *Benito Arias Montano*, Leiden 1972, p. 31.

85 Marañón identifies Quiroga, with no secure basis, as the leader of the Eboli faction in Madrid.

86 See, for example, his 'Memorial touchant le redressement des affaires des Pays Bas': AGS:E leg. 531 ff. 54–5.

87 Gachard 1848–79, vol. III, p. 14.

88 Parker 1972, chap. 8.

89 Requesens to D. Pedro Manuel, 31 Dec. 1574, Favre, 30 f. 378.

90 'Lo que Su Magd manda que se platique', AGS:E leg. 568 f. 51.

91 The four were Quiroga, Luis Manrique, Chinchón, and Andrés Ponce de León.

92 'Lo que se platicó con Hopperus y con el duque d'Alva', AGS:E leg. 568 f. 47.

93 Memorial by Alba, 31 Jan. 1575, AGS:E leg. 568 f. 32.

94 Requesens to king, Antwerp, 9 Jan. 1575, AGS:E leg. 562 f. 4.

95 AGS:E leg. 568 f. 31.

96 Gossart, p. 247.

97 Dr Milio to Hernando de Toledo, 24 July 1574, AA, 44/116.

98 Dr Milio to duchess of Alba, from San Silvestre, 14 Dec. 1576; and Hernando de Toledo to duchess, 17 Dec. 1576, AA, 52/267, 53/107.

99 AGS:E/K, leg. 570 f. 1.

100 Cited by Gachard 1856, p. 187.

101 Gossart, p. 109.

102 This had happened in France, Poland and parts of central Europe.

103 Khevenhüller, p. 162

6   *The Last Campaign, 1578–1582*

1 Alba to Antonio de Toledo, Guadalajara, 21 Mar. 1574, AA, 131/116.
2 AA, 290/6 to 12.
3 *Docs escog.*, p. 90.
4 AA, 67/54.
5 Feria (Don Lorenzo de Figueroa, second duke of Feria since his father's death in 1572) was eldest son of the English Lady Jane Dormer. His case was a notable scandal. Having pledged himself to the daughter of the duke of Nájera, he then tried to pledge himself to three other aristocratic daughters: Favre, vol. 19 f. 83. The king ordered him to marry one of the latter, but he refused on the grounds that his honour was involved: BZ, 144 f. 130. The instructions for his house arrest are in BZ, 142 f. 1.
6 Cabrera de Córdoba, vol. II, p. 528; Ossorio, p. 466. Neither source cites the exact day and month of this incident.
7 Pedro de Solchaga to Juan de Zúñiga, 12 July 1578, Favre, 16 f. 45: 'el conde de Fuentes, hermano de la duquesa de Alva, han traydo preso a la fortaleza de Almonacir'.
8 Maltby, pp. 272–3, 278, sees the hand of Pérez in these manoeuvres.
9 Pazos, formerly inquisitor in Seville and Toledo, had just (in 1578) been appointed president of the royal council.
10 Note by king, 2 Aug 1578, CODOIN, vol. VII, p. 481.
11 Alba to king, 5 Sept. 1578, EA, vol. III, p. 641.
12 BZ, 144 f. 242. 'No supe con que escaparme del', Mateo Vázquez reported.
13 Vázquez to king, 30 Nov. 1578, El Pardo, BL Add. 28263 f. 206.
14 'Detenido por mandado de Su Mgd en la villa de Tordesillas', Pedro de Solchaga to Juan de Zúñiga, 12 Dec. 1578, Favre, vol. 16 f. 110.
15 For the family links of the marquis, see Appendix A.
16 Khevenhüller, p. 169.
17 CODOIN, vol. VIII, p. 497.
18 CSPS, II, 648.
19 Despite a superb (and probably definitive) examination of the evidence by Gregorio Marañón, *Antonio Pérez.* 2 vols. Madrid 1958. Since Marañón, no original research has been done on the case.
20 Cited in Marañón, vol. I, pp. 210–12.
21 Gaspar Muro, *Vida de la princesa de Éboli*, Madrid 1877, append. p. 53.
22 King to D. Juan, San Lorenzo, 1 July 1576, Favre, vol. 28 f. 17.
23 Khevenhüller, pp. 122, 130.
24 Carlos Selvagem, *Portugal militar*, Lisbon 1931, p. 337.
25 San Jerónimo, *Memorias*, CODOIN, vol. VII, p. 229.
26 Cabrera de Córdoba, vol. II, p. 484.
27 Sections of the text that follows are based on my *Philip of Spain*, chap. 6.
28 A. Danvila y Burguero, *Felipe II y la Sucesión de Portugal*, Madrid 1956, p. 23.
29 For the various claimants, Merriman, vol. IV, pp. 346–7.
30 Philip to Moura, 26 Jan. 1579: CODOIN, vol. VI, p. 78.
31 Moura to king, 7 Feb. 1579, CODOIN, vol. VI, p. 110.
32 Philip to Osuna and Moura, 14 April 1579, CODOIN, vol. VI, p. 350.
33 Philip to Moura, 5 June 1579, CODOIN, VI, 419.
34 Hainault, Artois, Walloon Flanders, Namur, Luxembourg and Limburg.
35 Philip to Moura, 4 June 1579, CODOIN, vol. VI, p. 416.
36 Philip to Osuna and Moura, 30 June 1579, CODOIN, vol. VI, pp. 519–20.

37 Philip's letter of summons was dated 12 July 1579: CODOIN, vol. VI, pp. 555–6.

38 Pedro de Solchaga to Juan de Zúñiga, 3 Jan. 1580, Favre, vol. 16 f. 120.

39 King to Juan de Zúñiga, 13 Feb 1580, Favre, 6 f. 44.

40 Danvila y Burguero, *La Sucesión* (cited n. 28), p. 232.

41 CODOIN, vol. VIII, p. 518.

42 Its members were the cardinal of Toledo, the marquis de Aguilar, Don Antonio de Padilla and Don Juan de Silva.

43 J. Suárez Inclán, *Guerra de anexión en Portugal*, 2 vols. Madrid 1897, vol. I, p. 96.

44 Alba to king, 9 Sept. 1580, CODOIN, vol. XXXII, p. 568.

45 Alba to king, Uceda, 20 Feb. 1580, CODOIN, vol. XXXII, p. 9.

46 Alba to king, 20 and 23 Feb. 1580, CODOIN, vol. XXXII, pp. 9, 18.

47 Alba to Zayas, 15 April 1580, CODOIN, vol. XXXII, p. 64.

48 Alba to king, 16 May 1580, CODOIN, vol. XXXII, p. 145.

49 HHSA, Spanien, Varia, karton 3, b, f. 59.

50 CODOIN, vol. VIII, p. 527.

51 CODOIN, vol. XXXII, p. 155.

52 St Teresa and the Jesuit Ribadeneira, quoted in Bouza, p. 96.

53 This is the figure for which the food suppliers catered. The actual size of the army varies in the accounts.

54 Cabrera de Córdoba, vol. II, p. 596. White seems to have been his preferred colour for formal military wear, if we are also to be guided by his practice at Mühlberg.

55 CODOIN, vol. VII, p. 295.

56 Jean Baptiste de Tassis to Juan de Zúñiga, Badajoz, 24 June 1589, Favre, vol. 21 f. 262.

57 Muster of April 1580, CODOIN, vol. XXXII, pp. 27–9.

58 King to marquis of Alcañizes, ambassador in Rome, Badajoz, 10 July 1580: Favre, vol. 29 f. 103.

59 Juan de Cardona to Juan de Zúñiga, Setubal, 2 Aug. 1580, Favre, vol. 21 f. 314.

60 This and other details of the Portuguese campaign can be found in the excellent journal by a German noble officer, the *Tagebuch des Erich Lassota von Steblau*, printed in J. García Mercadal, *Viajes de extranjeros por España y Portugal.* 2 vols. Madrid 1952, vol. I, pp. 1253–92.

61 Alba to king, 28 Aug. 1580, CODOIN, vol. XXXII, p. 482.

62 King to Alba, Badajoz, 29 Aug. 1580, BL Add. 28357 f. 356.

63 CODOIN, vol. XXXII, p. 507.

64 Alba to king, Lisbon, 30 Aug. 1580, CODOIN, vol. XXXII, p. 489.

65 Alba to Philip, Setúbal, 18 July 1580, CODOIN, vol. XXXII, p. 277.

66 Khevenhüller, p. 217.

67 CODOIN, vol. XXXII, p. 420.

68 Pedro Bermúdez to secretary Delgado, from Setúbal, 2 Aug. 1580, CODOIN, vol. XXXII, p. 353.

69 Esteban de Ibarra to Mateo Vázquez, Lisbon, 15 Mar. 1581, *Docs escog.*, p. 430.

70 Alba to king, Cascaes, 5 and 6 Aug. 1580, CODOIN, vol. XXXII, pp. 364, 369.

71 Alba to king, Cascaes, 1 Aug. 1580, CODOIN, vol. XXXII, p. 349.

72 President Pazos to Vázquez, 19 Sept. 1580, IVDJ, vol. 21 f. 803.

73 CODOIN, XXXIII, vol. 71, p. 108.

74 Alba to Zayas, 19 Jan. 1581, Lisbon, CODOIN, vol. XXXIII, p. 455.

75 Quoted in Fernando Bouza, vol. I, p. 222. This is the best study of the events leading up to the annexation of Portugal.

76 Ossorio, p. 518.
77 Khevenhüller, p. 218–19.
78 King to Alba, from Tomar, 10 and 30 April, 1581: BL Add. 28357 ff. 421, 426. Cf. the claim in Merriman, vol. IV, p. 397 that 'after the fighting had finished the king had no more use for him'.
79 *Discurso*, p. 98.
80 EA, vol. III, p. 649.
81 Hernando to duchess, 12 Aug. 1580, AA, 52/269.
82 CODOIN, vol. XXXIII, pp. 99, 387.
83 Cabrera de Córdoba, vol. II, p. 687.
84 'Copia de una carta que el Padre Luys de Granada escribió la Exma Duquesa de Alva en la muerte del Duque', BN MS.2058 f. 83.
85 Luis Enríquez de Cabrera y Mendoza, duke of Medina de Rioseco.
86 BN MS.2751 f. 227.

7   *Servant of the Crown*

1   EA, vol. II, p. 194
2   There is a recent researched biography of the Great Captain by Dr Ruiz-Domènec; see Bibliography.
3   The alleged abuse and insults are mentioned in Rodríguez-Salgado, pp. 13, 144, cited above in Chapter 2, n. 74.
4   Brantôme, p. 30.
5   Ossorio, p. 28.
6   EA, vol. II, p. 454.
7   EA, vol. I, p. xix.
8   EA, vol. II, p. 602.
9   Khevenhüller, p. 260.
10 Oct. 1570, EA, vol. II, p. 448.
11 Khevenhüller, p. 260.
12 Parker 1972, p. 30 n. 1, says that the duke's 'contempt for his men was unlimited'. In practice, it is unwise to accept the duke's intemperate criticisms at face value.
13 Brantôme, p. 31.
14 To king, 27 April 1561, EA, vol. I, p. 525. Another scholar has erroneously dated this letter to 1567.
15 CODOIN, vol. XXXII, p. 18.
16 Gachard 1856, p. 117.
17 As mentioned previously in this book, the word 'Fabian' derives from the military tactics of the Roman general Fabius Maximus, who was successful precisely because he wore down the enemy without engaging them in battle.
18 Cf Gossart, p. 132.
19 *Docs. escog.*, p. 393.
20 EA, vol. I, p. 272.
21 Khevenhüller, p. 169.
22 Maltby, p. 271, by contrast, considers that Fadrique cannot be blamed.
23 From a report by a Spanish official in Brussels, 1570, printed in *Docs escog.*, pp. 90–9.
24 Requesens to Philip II, 19 Sept. 1574, Nueva CODOIN, 6 vols. Madrid 1892–1894, vol. V, p. 230.

25 Quoted in *Homenaje*, p. 26.

26 EA, vol. I, p. 504.

27 In the EA, the word first occurs in 1562, in a quotation made by Alba from a French letter: EA, vol. I, p. 530.

28 Fourquevaux to Charles IX, 9 Dec. 1566, Douais, p. 150.

29 Gachard 1875, p. 95.

30 EA, vol. II, p. 448.

31 To Cardinal Pacheco, from Brussels, 21 May 1571, EA, vol. II, p. 599.

32 'Copia de una carta que el Padre Luys de Granada escribió la la Exma Duquesa de Alva en la muerte del Duque', BN MS.2058 f. 83.

33 The Netherlanders, in fact, 'controlled' their heresy with greater brutality than the Spaniards did theirs. On balance, though it is difficult to conclude whether heresy was a 'threat', its destabilising role cannot be doubted. Among the studies in English, see Phyllis Mack Crew, *Calvinist Preaching and Iconoclasm in the Netherlands 1544–1569* (Cambridge 1978), and A. C. Duke, *Reformation and Revolt in the Low Countries* (London 1990).

34 Parker 1979, p. 154.

35 Cited in Joseph Lecler, *Toleration and the Reformation*, 2 vols. London 1960, vol. II, p. 207.

36 There is a general perspective in A. M. Moral Roncal, 'Patrimonio y fortuna de un linaje: los Álvarez de Toledo', in *Los Álvarez de Toledo. Nobleza viva*, Valladolid 1998.

37 *Docs escog.*, p. 141.

38 Granvelle to Juan de Zúñiga, Naples, 11 Aug. 1574, BZ, leg. 62 f. 163.

39 Requesens to Zúñiga, 16 March 1574, IVDJ, envío 67 no. 11.

40 Motley, p. 542.

41 Jan Lechner, *Repertorio de obras de autores españoles en bibliotecas holandesas hasta comienzos del siglo XVIII*, Utrecht 2001, p. 309. I am grateful to Dr Lechner for making this very useful work available to me.

42 The prints are reproduced in James Tanis and Daniel Horst, *Images of Discord*, Grand Rapids 1993. See also H. F. K. Nierop, 'De troon van Alva. Over de interpretatie van de Nederlandse Opstand', *Bijdragen en Mededelingen betreffende de Geschiedenis der Nederlanden* 110 (1995), pp. 205–23.

43 The bearded figure allegedly representing the duke is in black, suggests one art critic, because the duke liked to dress in black (supposedly like Philip II) and because his heart was black. Thus, by extension, a military figure in black in the artist's *Conversion of St Paul* must represent the duke of Alba. At this date, in 1567, the duke did not have a long white beard.

44 In the 1570s the artist Martin van Cleve imitated Bruegel's painting and brought the theme up to date by making a specific reference to the massacres under Alba.

45 Khevenhüller, p. 262.

46 EA, vol. I, p. 678. This is a most difficult passage, because of the oblique reference to an unidentified person; I have given a free translation.

47 EA, vol. II, p. 629.

48 EA, vol. II, p. 448.

49 Garcilaso, *Elegia I*, line 304.

50 Brantôme, p. 31.

51 Gachard 1848–79, vol. I, p. lxxiv.

52 To Espinosa, 22 May 1572, EA, vol. III, p. 111.

Short Bibliography

The following is limited to principal items or to works cited frequently in the footnotes. A few works on specific themes are mentioned in their relevant place in the footnotes and do not appear in this listing.

The most comprehensive and scholarly life of the duke is that by William Maltby, now out of print but essential for serious students. Most recent books in Spanish about the duke and the Toledo family tend to be frankly hagiographic or devoted to little more than genealogy. The best detailed survey of the family and its political role can be found in Carlos Hernando's excellent study of Pedro de Toledo's viceroyalty of Naples. For the background to Alba's role under the emperor, the recent seminal work by James Tracy fills many gaps, though it says very little about the duke himself. The background under Philip II can be approached through the biographies of the king by Geoffrey Parker (1979 and later editions) and by Kamen (1997). A satisfactory history of the Spanish army in this period has yet to be written, but some attention to one of its pioneers can be found in the recent study of Gonzalo Fernández de Córdoba by J. E. Ruiz-Domènec, *El Gran Capitán* (Barcelona 2002). The best analysis of the military forces in the Alba period is by Jan Glete, *War and the State in Early Modern Europe. Spain, the Dutch Republic and Sweden as fiscal-military states, 1500–1660* (London 2002). No other Spanish commander of the sixteenth century has been studied in detail. It is therefore difficult to set Alba within the military context of his day, though the excellent study by Léon van der Essen, *Alexandre Farnèse, prince de Parme, gouverneur général des Pays Bas (1545–1592)* (5 vols. Brussels 1933), offers scope for comparison. Information about Alba's activities in Italy is patchy. The only context that has been thoroughly studied is the Netherlands, on which a large number of fine studies, mainly in Dutch, English and French, has been published. The classic work on the Netherlands revolt is by Motley, but it regrettably remains unknown to Spanish historians and readers. Motley's wildly prejudiced but nonetheless stimulating presentation was later superseded by the great work of Pieter Geyl. The superb scholarly researches of Geoffrey Parker (on Philip II's policies, the Spanish army and the Netherlands revolt) are essential reading, and also resume the work of other leading authorities on the subject. The unpublished thesis of Lagomarsino has been invaluable in supplying information about the prelude to the Netherlands campaign. The 1580 military campaign in Portugal, has never merited an adequate study, perhaps because no great events were experienced.

The greater part of the correspondence of the duke is accessible through the excellent volumes published by the Alba family, based principally on letters in the family archive but also providing references for papers in other places, notably the state archive at Simancas. I take this opportunity to thank the custodian of the Alba archive, Dr José Manuel Calderón, for his help and advice in consulting relevant papers in the archive of the Casa de Alba in the Palacio de Liria, Madrid. Since the duke corresponded with all the main personages of his day, there certainly remains considerable further documentation that would shed light on hitherto undocumented aspects of his career.

Avila y Zúñiga, Luis de, *Comentarios de la Guerra de Alemania hecha de Carlo V.* Antwerp 1549

Bouza Alvarez, Fernando, *Portugal en la monarquía hispánica (1580–1640).* Thesis of the Complutensian University 1987

Boyden, James M., *The Courtier and the King. Ruy Gómez de Silva, Philip II and the Court of Spain.* University of California Press 1995

Brantôme, Pierre de Bourdeille, abbé de, *Oeuvres complètes.* 2 vols. Paris 1898, vol.I

Braudel, Fernand, *The Mediterranean and the Mediterranean World in the Age of Philip II.* 2 vols. London 1973

Cabié, Edmond, *Ambassade en Espagne de Jean Ebrard, seigneur de Saint-Sulpice, de 1562 à 1565.* Albi 1903

Cabrera de Córdoba, Luis, *Filipe Segundo, rey de España.* 4 vols. Madrid 1876

Calvete de Estrella, Juan Cristóbal, *El Felicissimo Viaje del muy alto y muy poderoso Principe Don Phelippe.* Antwerp 1552

Carande, Ramón, *Carlos V y sus banqueros.* 3 vols. 2nd edn. Madrid 1965–1967

Douais, C., ed., *Dépêches de M. de Fourquevaux, ambassadeur du roi Charles IX en Espagne 1565–72.* 3 vols. Paris 1896–1904

Foronda y Aguilera, Manuel de, *Estancias y viajes del Emperador Carlos V.* Madrid 1914

Gachard, L. P., *Correspondance de Philippe II sur les affaires des Pays-Bas.* 6 vols. Brussels 1848–79

——, *Correspondance du duc d'Albe sur l'invasion du comte Louis de Nassau en Frise en 1568.* Brussels 1850

——, *Relations des Ambassadeurs vénitiens sur Charles-Quint et Philippe II.* Brussels 1856

——, *Don Carlos et Philippe II.* Paris 1867

——, *Collection des voyages des souverains des Pays-Bas, vol.II. Itinéraire de Charles-Quint. Journal des voyages de Charles-Quint, par Jean de Vandenesse.* Brussels 1874

——, *Les bibliothèques de Madrid et de l'Escurial.* Brussels 1875

García Cerezeda, Martín, *Tratado de las campañas de los ejércitos del emperador Carlos V desde 1521 hasta 1545.* 3 vols. Madrid 1873

Garcilaso de la Vega, *Obras completas.* ed. E. L. Rivers. Madrid 1968

Gossart, Ernest, *La domination espagnole dans les Pays-Bas à la fin du règne de Philippe II.* Brussels 1906

Groen van Prinsterer, G., ed., *Archives de la maison d'Orange-Nassau.* 1er série. Supplément. Leiden 1847

Hernando Sánchez, Carlos José, *Castilla y Nápoles en el siglo XVI. El virrey Pedro de Toledo.* Salamanca 1994

——, *El reino de Nápoles en el Imperio de Carlos V.* Madrid 2001

Homenaje al Gran Duque de Alba. Salamanca 1983

Janssens, Gustaaf, *Don Fernando Álvarez de Toledo, tercer duque de Alba, y los Países Bajos.* Brussels 1993

Kamen, Henry, *Crisis and Change in Early Modern Spain.* Aldershot 1993

——, *Philip of Spain.* New Haven and London 1997

——, *Empire: How Spain became a World Power 1492–1763.* New York 2003

Keniston, Hayward, *Francisco de los Cobos, Secretary of the Emperor Charles V.* Pittsburgh 1980

Khevenhüller, Hans, *Diario de Hans Khevenhuller, embajador imperial en la corte de Felipe II.* ed. Felix Labrador Arroyo, Madrid 2001

Lagomarsino, Paul David, 'Court factions and the Formulation of Spanish Policy towards the Netherlands (1559–67)', University of Cambridge unpublished Ph.D. thesis, 1973

Maltby, William S., *Alba: A Biography of Fernando Alvarez de Toledo, third duke of Alba, 1507–1582.* Berkeley, 1983

Merriman, R. B, *The Rise of the Spanish Empire in the Old World and in the New.* New York 1918, repr. 1962. Vol.III: *The Emperor.* Vol. IV: *Philip the Prudent*

Morales Oliver, Luis, *Arias Montano y la política de Felipe II en Flandes.* Madrid 1927

Motley, John Lothrop, *The Rise of the Dutch Republic.* London 1912 ed

Nueva Colección de Documentos inéditos para la Historia de España y de sus Indias, 6 vols. Madrid 1892–1894

Ossorio, Antonio, *Vida y hazañas de Don Fernando Alvarez de Toledo, duque de Alba.* ed. Madrid 1945

Paris, Louis, *Négociations, Lettres et Pièces relatives au règne de François II.* Paris 1841. (Collection des Documents Inédits sur l'Histoire de France, Ier série)

Parker, Geoffrey, *The Army of Flanders and the Spanish Road 1567–1659.* Cambridge 1972

——, *The Dutch Revolt*, Harmondsworth 1979

——, *The Grand Strategy of Philip II*, New Haven and London 1998

Paz y Espeso, Julián, *Arboles genealógicos de las Casas de Berwick, Alba y agregadas.* Madrid 1948

Plaza, Ascensión de la, 'Cartas del Duque de Alba a Carlos V', in *Cuadernos de Investigación Histórica*, separata no. 5 (1981), pp. 135–79

Rodríguez, Pedro and Justina Rodríguez, *Don Francés de Álava y Beamonte. Correspondencia inédita de Felipe II con su embajador en Paris.* San Sebastián 1991

Sandoval, fray Prudencio de, *Historia de la Vida y Hechos del Emperador Carlos V.* Vol. III. Biblioteca de Autores Españoles, vol. 82. Madrid 1956

Santa Cruz, Alonso de, *Crónica del Emperador Carlos V.* 5 vols. Madrid 1920–25

Solnon, Jean-François, *Quand la Franche-Comté était espagnole.* Paris 1983

Strada, Famiano, *Guerras de Flandes.* 7 vols. Antwerp 1748

Tanis, James and Horst, Daniel, *Images of Discord. A Graphic Interpretation of the Opening Decades of the Eighty Years' War.* Grand Rapids, Michigan, 1993

Thompson, I. A. A., *War and Government in Habsburg Spain 1560–1620.* London 1976

Thompson, James Westfall, *The Wars of Religion in France 1559–1576.* New York 1910

Tracy, James D., *Emperor Charles V, Impresario of War.* New York 2002

Verheyden, A. L. E., *Le Conseil des Troubles. Liste des condamnés, 1567–1573.* Brussels 1961, reprinted 1981

Williams, Roger, *The Works of Sir Roger Williams.* ed. John X. Evans, Oxford 1972

Index

Male members of the Álvarez de Toledo family are listed under the name Toledo; female members are listed by their first names. Countries to which reference is frequently made, such as 'France', 'Netherlands' and 'Spain', are not indexed.